# OF POLITICS
# AND ECONOMIC
# REALITY

# OF POLITICS AND ECONOMIC REALITY

*The Art of Winning Elections with Sound Economic Policies*

AMAR BHIDE

Basic Books, Inc., Publishers               New York

Library of Congress Cataloging in Publication Data

Bhide, Amar, 1955–
  Of politics and economic reality.

  Notes p. 229
  Includes index.
  1.  Economic policy—Political aspects.  I.  Title.
HD87.B48  1984      338.9      83–46094
ISBN 0–465–05184–7

TO

My Parents,

for their example of courage and enterprise

# CONTENTS

# PART II

## Escaping the Failure Zone:
## Setting Priorities for Cuts

# PREFACE

THE THESIS of this book grew out of my participation in a Harvard Business School research project which compared the performance of Western welfare states with that of certain Eastern "efficiency" states like Japan, Korea, Taiwan, Hong Kong, and Singapore. The comparison led Professor Bruce Scott, who initiated and conducted the research, to conclude that Western economies were in danger of being over-whelmed in international competition because of their commitment to welfare policies.

I was struck by a different paradox. It is often assumed that tough-minded (and not always democratic) Eastern regimes have squeezed their citizens to achieve high growth, while the freely elected governments of welfare states have been unable to impose the necessary economic discipline because of political reasons. In fact, I saw little evidence of great sacrifice in the East—living standards and incomes were growing rapidly, and expectations of the future were high. In welfare states like Sweden on the other hand, wages were in a slump, and people were pessimistic about being able to maintain their standards of living in the future. In trying to resolve this paradox, I hit upon the thesis of this book—that Western governments have not really been pandering to their electorates' short term needs and that politicians had failed to realize how sound economic policies can also be popular.

The generous and unstinting help of friends and family enabled me to turn this off-beat thesis into a book. The advice and moral support of David Chaffetz, Ken Pierce, and Roland Mann saw me through several frustrating drafts. Lynn Bendheim, Adam Meyerson, and Wolf Weinholt offered numerous constructive suggestions on structure and content. On many dreary production and research chores, I took undue advantage of the goodwill and patience of my parents, sister, and most of all, my wife, Geeta.

I would also like to express thanks to my former and present employers—Harvard Business School and McKinsey & Company. Working at HBS gave me a unique opportunity to meet a diverse set of individuals engaged in the study and practice of politics and economic policy, as well as the funds to travel extensively in Europe and Asia. My work at McKinsey has had less direct bearing on the content of this book and, indeed, the ideas expressed herein do not in any way reflect the views of that firm. Indirectly, however, working for influential public and private sector clients in the United States, Europe, Japan, and Hong Kong has given me practical insights into how economic policies really affect the behavior of individuals and corporations. Some colleagues, notably Bill Matassoni, have also been helpful in their individual capacities.

Finally, I am most grateful to my editor, Martin Kessler, who immeasurably improved the quality of this work by a skillful mix of encouragement and demanding standards.

# OF POLITICS

# AND ECONOMIC

# REALITY

# INTRODUCTION

POLITICS, we have been led to believe, is the archenemy of responsible economics. According to this view, our leaders don't lack for good economic advice; they just lack the will to make responsible but unpopular decisions. In principle they may agree on the need to control spending, balance budgets, promote free trade, and reform social security. But "political expediency" dictates that they fund pork-barrel projects, create tax loopholes, impose import quotas, and leave retirement benefits untouched. "There is, as it were," write Milton and Rose Friedman, "an invisible hand in politics that operates in precisely the opposite direction to Adam Smith's invisible hand."[1]

Presidential elections, observes *Fortune*, "have a way of putting economic policy through the wringer." For his 1972 reelection effort, the magazine notes, "an unpopular Richard Nixon suddenly shifted course, lifting the spending floodgates and slamming on wage and price controls." In 1976 Gerald Ford "opened up the pork barrel, funneling countless millions to districts in Florida and elsewhere." In 1980 Jimmy Carter supported the Chrysler bailout because "he was alarmed by the prospect of losing the blue-collar vote in the depressed industrial snowbelt."[2]

Nor is political "interference" with responsible decision making unique to U.S. politicians and institutions. According to the *Wall Street Journal*,[3] before the 1983 elections even the resolute Margaret Thatcher of the United Kingdom took several actions that flew in the face of her free market theory. The Thatcher government ordered the British Steel Corporation and the National Coal Board to keep economically unsound steel mines and coal pits open. The state-owned British Leyland Corporation was told to shelve plans to buy cheaper foreign-made parts, and local authorities were asked to accelerate the spending of their capital allocations. This was out of character for Thatcher, who is considered to be a relatively principled leader; other politicians are said to sacrifice good economic policy for short-term political gains even more freely.

Such politically motivated policies are often blamed for our ongoing economic problems. And indeed there is ample evidence that our economies are in serious trouble. The predictable growth and full employment of the 1950s and 1960s, interrupted only by brief and benign recessions, seem like a distant dream. The United States and countries such as West Germany, Sweden, Britain, and Italy appear trapped between a choice of double-digit inflation and double-digit unemployment. In just three years—1979 to 1982—we have seen in many Western countries swings from price instability reminiscent of the Weimar Republic and the bankruptcies that occurred in the Great Depression.

## Conflicting Evidence

If politics was really behind the policies that have brought us to the brink of an economic crisis, then we would indeed face the unpleasant choice of learning to live with a sputtering economy or reexamining the utility of our political arrangements. For is it not inevitable that in a free democracy public officials will play politics?

This book questions the conventional diagnosis that irresponsible economic policies are good politics. In fact, in recent years politicians have not been very successful in winning votes. Along with the economic crisis of the last decade, there has also been great political turmoil. Throughout the Western world, many powerful leaders and parties have been tossed out of power. Politicians have found that their policies have not only been economic failures, they have also alienated constituents.

For over forty years, from 1932, when Franklin D. Roosevelt defeated Herbert Hoover, to 1976, no incumbent president lost an election. Now two incumbents in a row, Gerald Ford and Jimmy Carter, have been rejected at the polls. Nor have there been secure havens in the Senate or the House. In 1980 many liberal Democrats—such as George McGovern, Gaylord Nelson, Birch Bayh, and Frank Church in the Senate and Al Ullman in the House—lost the favor of constituents they had represented for decades; two years later, in 1982, the tide turned equally dramatically and Republicans suffered a net loss of twenty-six seats in the House. Public officials have apparently not been successful at protecting their political flanks.

In Europe political instability and public disaffection are even more rife. Countries like Belgium and Denmark are ruled by squabbling coalitions that enjoy the barest of majorities in their parliaments. The Italian government usually falls at least once in slack years. Seemingly invincible and respected stalwarts like Valéry Giscard d'Estaing of France and Helmut Schmidt of Germany languish in involuntary retirement.

Incumbents have not lost to more popular challengers. Rather, the public is voting *against* officials they no longer have confidence in. Voters are increasingly dissatisfied with the choices they are faced with in elections. According to the Roper poll, surveys during the 1976 campaign showed that "more people feel that almost every candidate should *not* be President of the United States than feel he *should* be," and 43 percent of voters said they didn't care who won the election.[4] In June 1980 over 40 percent of those surveyed in a *New York Times*/CBS poll said they were dissatisfied with the choice between Ronald Reagan, Carter, and John Anderson;[5] and in the November election, nearly half the electorate didn't vote.

Political scientists have found an almost uninterrupted, long-term decline in public trust in political and governmental institutions. The percentage of the public that believes the government is "run for the benefit of all people" dropped from 64 percent in 1964 to 24 percent in 1978, while the percentage of those who think that the government is "pretty much run by a few big interests looking out for themselves" rose from 29 percent to 67 percent.[6] Between 1968 and 1978 the percentage of voters who agreed that "once elected, Congressmen lose touch with people pretty quickly" went up from 53 percent to 70 percent.[7] The authors of the *American National Election Studies Data Sourcebook* constructed a "trust in government" index from several such surveys and found that between 1964 and 1978, the percentage of voters who "trusted" government and politicians dropped from 61 percent to 19 percent, while the proportion of "cynics" rose from 19 percent to 52 percent.[8]

Voters have such little confidence in politicians' willingness to respond to their needs that they are turning increasingly to referenda and constitutional amendments to mandate the popular will. Proposition 13 in California and the proposed constitutional amendment to balance the budget are a reflection of the frustration at the grass-roots level with policies that public officials have legislated.

## Wanted: Better Politicians

The thesis of this book is that the economic crisis and the growing unpopularity of politicians have, at their root, a common cause—a failure by governments to adopt policies that are attractive to their constituents. What has gone wrong for a decade or more is that politicians seeking election (or reelection) have not rationally sought the largest possible share of the vote. Bad politics, in other words, has made for bad economics.

*6*

*Introduction*

Today good economic policies call for nose counting by coldly calculating politicians seeking votes. If only politicians would make decisions based on a disciplined calculation of how to attract the largest majority in the next election, we would be enjoying higher growth, lower unemployment, and stable prices.

The stagflation dragon will not be slain by more valiant knights from a new economic Camelot. Experts and their miracle cures—from the full-employment Keynesians to supply-side revolutionaries and the stern monetarists—have had their day in court and been found wanting. Experience has also shown that visionaries and statesmen like Lyndon Johnson, Charles de Gaulle, and Winston Churchill, who imposed their economic policies on a reluctant public, have in the end done more harm than good. Our best hope out of the current mess lies with a modern-day Dwight Eisenhower or a Konrad Adenauer: a pragmatic, if unglamorous, politician who understands and responds to his constituents' needs and is therefore good at winning votes.

Readers may be disconcerted by what appears to be an argument for more political selfishness. Yet the very basis of a competitive economy rests on the ability of its citizens to pursue their own desires in the marketplace. As Adam Smith wrote in the *Wealth of Nations:* "It is not from the benevolence of the butcher, the brewer or the baker that we expect our dinner, but from their regard to their own interest. We address ourselves, not to their humanity but to their self love, and never talk to them of our own necessities, but of their own advantages."[9]

Our economic system is said to work best when competing, profit-hungry businesses are responsive to their customers' choices and demands: when Apple and IBM compete to provide the most attractive personal computers, banks offer up savings schemes to meet the needs of their depositors, and publishers print books that readers will buy. Why shouldn't sound economic policy require that politicians respond to the desires of their voters?

7

## The Power of Ideology

More often than not, however, politicians have been unresponsive to their constituents and have ignored the majority interest. Some visionary leaders have been deliberately unresponsive—they have spurned voters to court posterity. Other
public officials who have tried to curry favor with voters have
failed to do so; instead of evaluating the political attractiveness
of their decisions in a reasonable, open-minded fashion, they
have adhered to rules that are obsolete or illogical. Statesmanship or ineptness have thwarted popular policies.

We will see many examples in this book of important decisions made because of a strong-minded president's or prime
minister's commitment to a principle—Lyndon Johnson's
Great Society legislation, Margaret Thatcher's monetarism,
Ronald Reagan's supply-side tax cuts and defense spending
hike, and François Mitterand's expansionary spending program. To these leaders it didn't really matter whether or not
the public wanted or favored their programs; if anything, popular opposition increases the strong-willed leader's commitment. Presidents and prime ministers who like to think of
themselves as statesmen believe that to be above politics is a
virtue. President Reagan insists that he has instructed his staff
never to consider the vote-getting potential of a decision, and
his advisers unanimously confirm it. As he said in an interview:

I guess I learned something when I was Governor of California for those eight
years. I made a decision then, and I have repeated it now, as a kind of
campaign promise to myself, that I did not want to hear any counsel on any
issue as to what might be the political ramification of it, or how it might affect
future elections or anything. And I made a promise that I would to the best
of my ability make any decision that had to be made on the basis of what I
honestly believed was right or wrong for the people. I found then, and it
continues now, that you sleep very well if you do that.[10]

Holding national office is regarded as a higher calling. A
businessman, peanut farmer, or actor may concentrate on
pleasing the public, but a president's loyalties are to his convic-

tions, to the truth. As Jimmy Carter insisted in the 1980 campaign: "I am not here to say that all my decisions have been right or popular. I know they certainly have not been easy ones. But I will say this. In the last three and a half years, we have been tested under fire. We have always done what is right and we have always told the truth."[11]

Senator Ernest Hollings, a 1984 Democratic presidential aspirant, says our trouble has been "ad hoc-ery. It's sort of 'seven o'clock news' and 'what's the issue?' and 'where are the people?' and 'get the pollster.' Shoot all the pollsters!" We should, says Mr. Hollings, "elect a couple of historians. You know what I mean? Get a feel of whence you're coming and where you're headed as the President."[12]

Leaders rationalize their inflexibility and unresponsiveness to public opinion because they believe voters are fickle and incapable of understanding or appreciating good economic policy; like children, they must be tricked or appeased, but their opinions or wants are of no lasting consequence. As de Gaulle said of the French: "they can't cope without the State, but they detest it. They don't behave like adults."[13]

## Political Fallacies: Precedent and Free Votes

Of course, even statesmen do recognize the need to win votes in order to implement their programs; other public officials consider winning elections to be an important end in itself. But vote-winning aspirations are often not translated into vote-winning policies because instead of making decisions logically and objectively, politicians tend to mechanically follow established rules. In the chapters that follow, we will see several such formulas that lead politicians down unpopular paths. They include:

"More spending equals more votes."
"Borrow, don't raise taxes on the rich and the powerful; future generations can worry about the debt."
"Pumping up the money supply helps win elections."

"Don't ever tamper with Social Security."
"All cuts in public services are unpopular."

Some of these rules lead to unpopular policies because they are out of date. In the next chapter, for example, we shall see that increasing spending was once a popular policy; then conditions that made spending growth popular changed but the formula did not. Politicians continue to believe that economically responsible expenditure cuts are politically dangerous and stick to the now-unpopular course of increasing spending.

Another problem that prevents politicians from responding properly to voter needs is their propensity to look only at the political benefits of their decisions and to ignore their political costs. Votes from expenditure projects, tariffs on imports, or the opportunistic expansion of money supply are, in essence, considered to be "free." Politicians expect their constituents to be wowed by the new school or handout and forget about their resentment of the higher taxes needed to pay for these goodies. They count on auto workers to cheer when quotas are imposed on Japanese imports without expecting to lose the votes of any other constituencies.

This free-vote mentality fits with the traditional political assumption that voters are gullible and their opinions can be easily manipulated. Politicians believe that what really matters in the political game is the symbol, the image of a dedicated public servant looking after the interests of his constituents. "In their minds," says Senator Barry Goldwater, "there is no difference between a candidate and a detergent. They are both products to be merchandised."[14] Like Proctor & Gamble, politicians rely heavily on television. As one expert writes:

The largest single chunk of campaign war chests always goes to television. And most of that amount always goes to 30- and 60-second spots because both politicians and broadcasters prefer it that way: brief, carefully sculpted political commercials (rather than five-minute or 30-minute broadcasts) which are over before a viewer can cross the room to turn them off.[15]

Now, it makes sense to sell such goods as soap, cereal, and toothpaste through apparently inane TV commercials because such products are a relatively cheap, low-risk purchase and it is difficult to differentiate them on the basis of their performance. But expensive stereo systems and automobiles cannot be sold like soap—the same consumers who appear to be so gullible about soap are, when it comes to automobiles or audio systems, quite discriminating and demand hard comparative information. Therefore, General Motors doesn't stress TV advertising—it spends less on TV commercials than P&G, General Foods, American Home Products, and Bristol Myers and relies instead on the personal pitch made by dealers and on printed advertisements with tables comparing the performance of competing models.

In choosing the soap model, politicians implicitly assume that voters are incapable of making hard comparisons and evaluations of performance. This is a serious mistake. It is true that most voters are not very knowledgeable about politics or economics. More than 70 percent of Americans, polls have found, agree that "sometimes politics and economics seem so complicated that a person like me can't really understand what is going on."[16] But most consumers don't understand how automobiles are made either; their ignorance doesn't free manufacturers from the task of producing attractive cars at competitive prices. Similarly, politicians cannot "take advantage" of the public's ignorance of fiscal or monetary policies, because even unsophisticated voters tend to be quite savvy about the state of their personal finances. All other things being equal (there being no Watergates or Falklands wars), they tend to vote their pocketbooks, even if they can't understand why things are going well or badly.

Consequently, there are no free votes. Spending projects, for example, *do* have political costs: the taxes needed to pay for the expenditures alienate voters even if they do not directly associate their higher taxes with the spending projects. A president or prime minister cannot always get reelected merely by increasing spending, just as a businessman cannot prosper merely by increasing sales. The leader has to be concerned about the tax burden and the businessman about the cost of the goods he sells. Sometimes the political costs associated with taxes are less than the benefits derived from spending projects, and the expenditures are thus net vote winners. Under other circumstances, if the political cost of taxation is higher, spending projects can lose net votes. In any event, there are no free votes from increasing spending, or from protecting declining industries, legislating tax loopholes, or playing games with money supply. Politicians who believe there are incur the wrath of even unsophisticated voters whose pocketbooks are hurt in the quest for free votes.

## What Lies Ahead

It is imperative to dispel the general misconception that good economics is bad politics as well as the individual myths about specific policies. Otherwise scholars and statesmen will continue a futile search for new panaceas like the gold standard or industrial policy, while politicians continue to avoid more reasonable and well-accepted prescriptions on the grounds that they are politically infeasible. The political assumptions that have dogged economic policy must be revamped if economic recovery is to be sustained in Western democracies. We need a fresh political look at economic reality.

The chapters that follow attempt to provide such an analysis of several important and specific issues of economic policy. For each issue I will describe the prevailing political beliefs, how these beliefs arose, and why they need to be reevaluated; what a cold-blooded, calculating politician would do about the issue at hand; and why the popular option is also economically beneficial. Following this approach, chapter 1 will look at the size of public expenditure—does it make political sense to continue to increase public spending? Chapter 2 examines taxation policy—what is the least unattractive method of accomplishing the inherently unpopular task of raising the revenues needed to finance public spending? Chapters 3 and 4 deal with the issue of some of the rules governments set: monetary rules

for the financial marketplace and international trade policies
—do easy money and tariffs win votes? Chapters 5 through 8
study various possible uses for spending public money such as
job creation programs, public services, defense, social welfare,
and capital investment—which of these programs are the most
popular and therefore deserve funding priority?

Some caveats about the approach and thesis of this book: I
am concerned only with economic issues—the assertion that
politicians do not efficiently follow their self-interest does not
apply to questions about foreign policy, law and order, or abor-
tion. But the restriction is not too limiting, since economics has
increasingly become the hub of politics. Nineteen seventy-six
was the first presidential election year since 1936 when the
American electorate was chiefly concerned about economic
problems and not about questions of war and peace.[17] Economics also dominated the 1980 election, in spite of Jimmy
Carter's attempt to capitalize on Ronald Reagan's alleged bel-
ligerence about the arms race. According to exit polls, two-
thirds of voters in the 1980 presidential election were most
influenced by economic issues.[18] The 1979 general election in
the U.K. revolved around tax cuts, and the issue in the 1983
election was unemployment. As a string of former prime ministers have found, the Irish problem, at least in the opinion of
the average man in the Dublin street, is high taxes and double-
digit inflation and not the difficulty of reunification with the
North.

Second, I do not claim that in a democracy competition
between aggressive, calculating, vote-seeking politicians
would lead to the best possible economic decisions. But there
is a wide range between the best possible policies and the
worst. There seems to be little evidence that democratic soci-
eties today are stumbling on the last steps of the pinnacle of
economic achievement. All this book intends to show is that
significant economic improvement—though perhaps way
below hypothetical perfection—would result from more self-
interested political choices.

Finally, I will not attempt quantitative proofs, because the

same political or economic facts are subject to numerous inter-
pretations—did Mr. Ford lose in 1976 because of the Nixon
pardon or the 1975 recession? Did Mr. Carter lose principally
because of inflation (as exit polls would suggest) or were voters
subconsciously thinking about Iran? My argument will rest
instead on common sense, examples, and inductive logic. International examples and comparisons are important to my
case for two reasons. First, because the leader of a single country makes only so many important national economic policy
decisions, examples have to be drawn from as many countries
as possible. Second, international examples will help eliminate
confusing institutional "noise." For instance, it has been argued that irresponsible fiscal policy in the United States is
primarily the result of the peculiar relationship between the
presidency and the Congress. This argument cannot be con-
clusively disproved, but it can be considerably weakened if the
fiscal trends evident in the U.S. can also be shown to exist in
two-party parliamentary Britain, Imperial presidential
France, or the inspired chaos of multiparty Italy.

## Conclusion

The cruel reality of economic crisis has been sustained by a
widespread myth—that politicians are too political. In fact,
however, politicians don't pursue their political interests effectively at all. Either they use their positions in office to pursue
ideological goals or, when they do try to court voters, they rely
on outdated precedent and free-vote logic. Their failure to
pursue popular policies has led to great public disaffection with
politicians as well as poor economic performance. For the situation to be turned around, conventional beliefs and assumptions must be revamped. If they are, and the politics of economic decisions is properly understood, then we could enjoy
policies that are both responsive and responsible.

# PART I

# The Failure Zone:
# Causes, Trade-Offs,
# and Dead Ends

# CHAPTER 1

# Spending: How Much?

THE SIZE AND GROWTH of public spending has become one of the most vexing problems of public policy. U.S. federal outlays now exceed $800 billion—more than four times their 1970 level. Public expenditures have grown even more rapidly in Europe, and in some countries they now account for over half of the national income. Many leaders believe that excessive spending leads to serious economic problems such as inflation and unemployment; but besides making speeches about the problem, they do little to curb the growth of expenditures. Actual cuts in programs, politicians believe, entail great risks: voters always want more spending; haven't the big spenders from the New Deal and thereafter always won big and the skinflints usually been turned out of office?

This conventional wisdom about the politics of spending is based on false logic and misleading precedent. More spending did win votes at the time of the New Deal, but it doesn't any longer. Total spending has now reached a level where further increases are politically dangerous and cuts may actually be popular. The change has not been adequately appreciated; the growth in outlays continues unabated because both conservatives who ideologically oppose heavy public spending and liberals who favor it still believe in the New Deal spending formula. Public officials, by failing to adapt to the new political need for fiscal discipline, have engendered great public frustration with their policies and put a heavy burden on the economy as well.

## Rhetoric and the Numbers

As U.S. spending grew rapidly in the last decade, U.S. presidents repeatedly stressed their determination to curb the growth of federal outlays. Their commitment was, however, primarily rhetorical: they liberally disbursed federal grants on the campaign trail, and they never did propose real spending cuts in the budgets they submitted to Congress because they feared the political backlash.

The speeches against spending start with Richard Nixon. Just three months into his first term, he announced that in order to follow policies of "fundamental economics," his administration would have to reduce "spending in fiscal 1970, significantly." He acknowledged that "the cuts will not be easy. Dealing with fundamentals never is."[1] U.S. spending was then under $200 billion; by the time Mr. Nixon bowed out, it had grown by more than a third.

It was then Gerald Ford's turn to urge Congress to set a spending limit of $300 billion for 1975. Naturally there would be "hard choices, but no Federal agency, including the Defense Department, would be untouchable." How could anyone "ask the American public to tighten their belts if Uncle Sam is unwilling to tighten his first?"[2]

When Jimmy Carter was inaugurated, the $300-billion limit was a memory. Jimmy Carter started his term taking on federal spending with the "zero-based budgeting" techniques he had mastered as Governor of Georgia and finished by declaring of his final budget: "The actions I have outlined involve costs, they involve pain."[3] Even so, federal spending grew from $400 billion in 1977 to $660 billion in 1980.

Ronald Reagan had long been a committed foe of public

spending. Campaigning for president when inflation was on every voter's mind, he said that it had "one cause and one cause alone—government. And therefore, less government is the only cure."[4] Two years later, when he was in the White House and the public was more anxious about unemployment, Mr. Reagan told Americans that the "root of the problem" was the "out-of-control government spending."[5]

Mr. Reagan's convictions led him to propose, two months after his inauguration, a package of budget cuts amounting to $41 billion, described by Professor Milton Friedman as the "first serious attempt in decades to construct a detailed and comprehensive program for reducing Federal spending."[6] Nevertheless, U.S. expenditures continued to rise. They touched $800 billion in just over two fiscal years of Ronald Reagan's term, and the percentage of national income taken by federal outlays reached its highest level ever.

These leaders' determination to curb spending growth apparently conflicted with their political duties. Presidential language on the election trail differs from the exhortations to Congress. In 1976 when President Ford was trying to tighten Uncle Sam's belt in Washington, he was distributing federal grants in the primaries. On the eve of the North Carolina primary, his opponent, Ronald Reagan, said: "If he comes here with the same list of goodies as he did in Florida, the band won't know whether to play 'Hail to the Chief' or 'Santa Claus Is Coming to Town.'"[7] President Carter didn't leave the White House during his renomination campaign, but emissaries used the power of federal grants (amounting to about $87 billion) to bring reluctant Democrats into line.

In the 1982 congressional elections the Reagan administration did not shrink, reported the *Washington Post*, from following "standard procedure for White House campaigning"[8] of announcements of bridges and housing projects. The paper described a typical campaign appearance Ronald Reagan made in New Jersey:

Catching Mrs. Fenwick [the Republican candidate for the Senate] by surprise, Ronald Reagan departed from his prepared text.

"Right now I'm going to make a little announcement here," he said. "In spite of all our cuttings, there are things that government has to do and should do. I am pleased to announce that the Department of Housing and Urban Development has advised me that they have agreed to approve Section 8 funding for 125 units of elderly housing at Park Place in Ewing, New Jersey." . . .

What the President did not mention was that his administration in the budget proposals it sent to Congress earlier this year proposed eliminating much of the Section 8 program for housing construction.[9]

The actual budgets that presidents have submitted to Congress have also been quite different from the hype about their austerity. Real cuts in programs have been avoided by administrations that feared they would lose votes. For example, Ronald Reagan introduced his first budget in 1981 with homilies about "standing up to the spending juggernaut."[10] Cabinet members admonished critics on the Hill that "everybody likes to be Santa Claus, Congressman, but these are not the times for that."[11] The numbers, however, told quite a different story. As President Reagan himself emphasized in his speech to Congress: "It is important to note we are only reducing the rate of increase in taxes and spending. We are not attempting to cut either spending or taxes to a level below which we presently have. . . .The $41.4 billion spending cut," he reassured legislators, "would still allow an increase of $40.8 billion over 1981 spending."[12]

The budget proposals lacked real bite because most administration officials believed it was politically dangerous to tamper with several large items of spending, such as the so-called safety-net programs and social security payments. The Office of Management and Budget (OMB) director David Stockman, who argued that the President could pull off cuts in these programs if he took his case to the public, was overruled. So, in spite of the initial alarums and exultations, there was no significant change in the size and growth of spending.

The Carter administration's budgets also displayed a similar dichotomy of language and numbers. Unwilling to risk cuts in sensitive but increasingly expensive social programs, Mr. Carter proposed in February 1980 a record $615 billion budget.

## Spending: How Much?

Although the President called his budget "prudent and re-sponsible,"[13] the financial markets did not share his opinion. Six weeks later, in order to stop the free fall of bond prices, the administration was forced to submit a revised budget with proposed reductions of more than $13 billion. Like the Reagan cuts of a year later, the Carter proposals were not real de-creases but rather slowdowns in the rate of increase. Milton Friedman compared them to "sending an infant to do an adult's job."[14] Carter aides, on the other hand, argued that they were already pushing the limits of political tolerance. Press Secretary Jody Powell said, "It's a pretty tough thing for a President to do anytime—election year or not."[15]

The Carter administration's assumptions were the same as the Reagan administration's: spending cuts mean lost votes, and what is good for the bond markets is not conducive to political longevity.

## Selective Evidence, False Logic

On the face of it, nearly fifty years of election results seem to support the conventional wisdom. Franklin Roosevelt, it is well remembered, gave federal spending its place in the sun and was reelected three times thereafter. The Democratic party that was identified with New Deal programs almost became the institutional ruling party in Congress. Outside the U.S. a similar pattern can be seen—the pro-spending Social Demo-crats in Sweden stayed in power for forty-four years, the Liber-als in Canada for sixteen years.

The evidence also suggests that politicians who "play straight" on the spending issue pay for their honesty. Barry Goldwater, for example, "defied tradition" in the 1964 presi-dential campaign: in Texas, he "shook supporters" by telling them that their state ought not to have received a multibillion-dollar defense contract; among Florida retirees "he attacked Social Security spending on health care for the aged," and, "in economically depressed West Virginia, he delivered a major attack on the Johnson Administration's 'war on poverty.' "[16] Senator Goldwater went on to be buried in a landslide.

But these are one-sided and somewhat dated examples. There is also a slew of more recent evidence that spending doesn't always pay and attacking it doesn't always hurt. Federal grants didn't get Gerald Ford and Jimmy Carter reelected or carry Millicent Fenwick into the Senate. President Reagan triumphed in 1980 in spite of his image as a fervent anti-spender. In traditionally liberal New York City, Mayor Ed Koch was reelected, virtually without opposition, after a term of preaching the virtues of austerity. California voters overwhelmingly passed Proposition 13 against the opposition of powerful special interests. Margaret Thatcher in the U.K. and Helmut Kohl in Germany have won sweeping victories, promising voters austerity where their opponents were offering large spending programs.

The formula "more spending equals more votes" is also, as I explained in the introduction, based on an illogical, free-vote assumption. It is true that average voters are always looking for more from their government—better roads and benefits, a stronger army, and more generous welfare programs; and expenditure projects are attractive enticements the politician can hold out to the public. But it is absurd to assume that such projects have no political costs: every cent of public expenditure has to be paid for through monies (either taxes or borrowings) raised from the public, which average voters don't like to pay. If spending had no political costs, fiscal conservatives would find it nearly impossible to dislodge free-spending governments, whereas in fact we see that in the past few years, many profligate politicians have been trounced by opponents who at least spoke the language of austerity.

## The Rational Spending Range

If there are no free votes to be gotten from spending, the crucial question is, at what level of expenditure are the political benefits likely to outweigh the costs? If voters knew their minds and could easily articulate their opinions about the costs and benefits of public spending, finding out the right level of spending would be easy—a politician would merely have to commission an opinion poll. But since people cannot easily articulate the link between the burden of taxation and the benefits of public spending, the level of spending at which a majority of voters will believe that they are getting good value for money needs to be intelligently estimated. Let us see how this might be done.

It is almost self-evident that the higher the total level of spending, the greater the number of voters who have to be taxed. A low level of spending can be financed by taxes raised from a few rich voters. As the total level of spending increases, however, it is impossible to collect all the required revenues only from the rich and it becomes necessary to tax the middle class as well. And at some very high level of spending, most voters—rich, middle class, and poor—have to bear a significant tax burden.

When total spending is low, all expenditure increases can be paid for out of the taxes of a few rich and are therefore highly popular with the rest of the public. Votes from new spending projects aren't free, but Harry Hopkins's famous dictum "tax and tax, spend and spend, elect and elect" is accurate as long as the expenditures are so low that the taxes needed to pay for them can be raised from the rich only.

At the other extreme, however, where the existing base of spending is so high that the majority of voters, including all the middle class and many poor, feel oppressed by their taxes, more spending will be highly unpopular. At that point voters will be at the end of their patience and convinced that they are taxed too heavily for whatever benefits they receive.

Public spending in this "failure-zone" range isn't a politically useful conduit for taking from the many to give to the few; typical failure-zone projects tax thousands of steelworkers in Ohio to pay for an irrigation scheme that benefits a few hundred rich California farmers. And when a government with failure-zone spending isn't playing Robin Hood in reverse, it takes on the role of a Big Brother who requires his wards to buy approved goods from the state store: "Thou shalt buy social security and the MX missile, not a new car or home."

Since voters don't like (even accidentally) to be robbed by a misguided Robin Hood or bullied by a Big Brother, failure-zone spending is obviously not rational. Politicians who gain office with a majority of their constituents suffering from high taxes can reap quick popularity by cutting spending out of the failure zone, just as businesses can immediately increase profits by shutting down excess capacity. Although some constituencies and groups are hurt by cuts (there are no free votes from cutbacks either!), spending reductions in the failure zone can deliver real tax relief to a much larger number of voters.

Spending in a middle range, where the middle class bears a moderate tax burden, makes the best political sense. Although complaints about excessive taxation can be avoided by very low spending, it is competitively dangerous. An airline that doesn't ante up to put enough planes on its routes may avoid empty seats, but risks getting muscled out by more aggressive rivals. Likewise politicians who restrict spending to a very low range encourage their opponents to court the electorate with proposals for attractive (if risky) new programs.

## The Historical Record

The somewhat theoretical sketch of the politics of spending just described explains the dramatic changes that have taken place in the real world during the last half century. Until the New Deal, spending was in a very low range, and the underlying sentiment for more projects was stronger than anti-tax feeling. Franklin Roosevelt hit upon this imbalance and gained great popularity by responding to the latent demand for more federal outlays. The New Deal policies were taken too far, however, and by the mid-seventies, public expenditure was pushed into a failure zone. It has stayed there since; although anger over taxes now outweighs demands for more spending, outdated New Deal political wisdom prevents politicians from responding to it.

By any measure, until 1932 government spent frugally and taxed sparingly. The highest annual expenditure in the U.S. until 1932 was just over $5 billion in 1919, which corresponded to a per-capita tax burden of $43. As the following table shows, a small minority of the population in the U.S. and elsewhere was paying taxes in that era.

| Country | Date | % of Population Paying Taxes |
|---------|------|------------------------------|
| Holland | 1902 | 7.0 |
| Italy | 1907 | 1.9 |
| Britain | 1907 | 9.4 |
| | 1931 | 12.0 |
| U.S. | 1863 | 0.67 (Civil War Income Tax) |
| | 1915 | 1.5 |
| | 1935 | 14.0 |

SOURCES: Compiled from Edwin R. A. Seligman, *The Income Tax* (New York: Macmillan, 1911) and Koussuth Kent Kennan, *Income Taxation: Methods and Results in Various Countries* (Milwaukee: Burdwick and Allen, 1910).

Expenditures were not low because of a lack of projects that could have benefited the public. Basic sanitary facilities in the rapidly growing industrial cities, to take just one example, were crying out for improvement. According to one contemporary description of Chicago:

One's nostrils are assailed at every point by the penetrating stench that pervades everything. Great volumes of smoke roll from the forest of chimneys at all hours of the day, and drift down over the helpless neighborhood like a deep black curtain that fain would hide the suffering and misery it aggravates. . . . long rows of some of the most unhealthy houses in this deadly neighborhood . . . have no connection with the sewers and under some of them, the accumulation of years of filth has gathered in a semi-liquid mass from two to three feet deep.[17]

Small wonder that, as one writer of the times observed, "the public demands grow steadily by the year. Better pavements, improved sewerage, more small parks, and manual training in schools are among the pressing needs of the hour, and a demand for other public expenditure is just beginning to be heard."[18]

Moreover, income was so distributed that the potential political costs of financing the expenditure were also low. In 1913 2 percent of the population earned 60 percent of the national income. If politicians had so chosen, therefore, a several-fold increase in federal expenditure (then around 3 percent of national income) could have been financed out of additional taxes levied on a small fraction of the electorate.

Yet the campaign for more public spending found it rough going. The rich feared that higher spending would be financed out of their pockets, and their influence was far out of proportion to their numbers. Reformers and populists were denounced as Communists, Socialists, or anarchists. The campaign "to keep expenses down and reduce the tax rate" never let up. Newspapers often carried headlines like "Retrenchment a Necessity."[19]

The common citizens who stood to benefit from higher spending lacked political clout, since popular democracy and universal suffrage had not quite been established. Women had just been given the vote, and literacy tests and property qualifications disenfranchised a sizable number of blacks and poor people. In Britain, the hereditary House of Lords had veto power over expenditure.

Deep-seated beliefs were also set against more spending and taxes. "We have been taught," one scholar complained, "to turn away from government. . . . We have been trying to reduce government to contemptible insignificance and, in many cases, have succeeded in reducing it to contemptible impotence. Lest men should do some wrong thing, we have made it impossible for them to do any good thing."[20]

Typical of the prevailing anti-spending ideology was President William McKinley's declaration in his inaugural speech:

Economy is demanded in every branch of the government at all times, but especially in periods, like the present, of depression in business and distress among the people. The severest economy must be observed in all public expenditures, and extravagance stopped wherever it is found, and prevented wherever in the future it may be developed.[21]

## A New Deal with Spending

Franklin D. Roosevelt defied conventional ideology and hit upon a popular spending strategy almost by accident. He hadn't calculated that he could put together a powerful coalition of workers, farmers, blacks, and the poor by increasing spending and "soaking the rich" to pay for it. In fact, he had run for president against Hoover on a traditional austerity platform, criticizing the incumbent for "a wildly extravagant budget" and promising to cut expenditure by a full 25 percent.[22]

In the first months of his administration, President Roosevelt did keep his word—from a total budget of approximately $3 billion, he slashed $400 million in veteran payments and $600 million in federal salaries. Luckily he changed course. The nation was saved from "the brink of revolution," writes Professor James Tobin, "less by the fact that Roosevelt had in the beginning any different economic views, than by the fact that Roosevelt was a flexible and pragmatic politician."[23]

The reversal was dramatic—in less than two years, Mr. Roosevelt doubled federal outlays. The conservative establishment was aghast. "The American government," wrote the *Wall Street Journal*, "has embarked upon a policy of spending; if the situation which impends so obviously that the sheer fear of it is acting as the one major restraint to a full-fledged recovery is to be averted . . . that policy must be reversed."[24] The *Baltimore Sun* declared that "the whole Federal machine has been tremendously expanded in all directions. All records for expenditures, size and cost of government have been eclipsed. There has never been anything like it in this or any other country. It is the most gigantic and expensive bureaucracy in the world."[25]

Acting on the assumption that "plain John Doe, citizen
. . . does not shoot Santa Claus because he does not yet realize
that this Santa Claus is a fiscal pickpocket,"[26] the Republicans
concentrated their 1936 election campaign on exposing the
potential consequences of the New Deal's extravagances. The
presidential contest virtually became a referendum on spending. A newspaperman assigned to "make a swing around the
Middle West to report on political conditions" found that: "By
far the most popular [issue] is the spending question. There is
more discussion of that I find than anything else so far as the
average mid-Westerner is concerned, be he city worker or
farmer, be he pro-New Deal or numbered among the opposition."[27]

Since total spending and taxes were still quite low (though
they had increased greatly), the Republican campaign didn't
sway the electorate. Contrary to hopeful conservative predictions that an economy wave would sweep over the next session of Congress, the Democrats and Roosevelt romped
home. Roosevelt's success changed political attitudes and
made a higher level of spending respectable. In the 1948
presidential election, for example, Democrat Harry Truman
naturally promised to continue the programs of the New
Deal, but even his Republican opponent Thomas Dewey
"heartily endorsed" several spending projects, which, "added
up, spelt a need for high tax revenues."[28] So similar were the
views of the two candidates that the *Wall Street Journal*
complained that "millions of voters" had been "disenfranchised," since "those who opposed huge spending and heavy
taxes . . . had no party to turn to. They could choose between
personalities, but could only vote 'Ja' on the continuation of
existing policies."[29]

In any event, spending continued to be popular. Liberal
parties like the Democrats in the United States, Labour in the
United Kingdom, and Social Democrats in many European
countries derived the most benefit and became, in Prime Minister Harold Wilson's term, the "natural parties of government." Even conservatives who were elected against this

trend went along with the irrepressible pressure for spending. President Eisenhower, although criticized by Democratic economists for following "orthodox fiscal policies,"[30] didn't reverse course—spending in his terms in office grew by 36 percent.

## The Rise of Spending Dogma

Economic growth protected the popularity of spending—the 47 percent increase in personal incomes during the Eisenhower administration, for example, erased the political costs of the 36 percent additional taxes needed to finance its expanding outlays. On the other hand, changes in income distribution were making it more difficult to minimize political costs of the increased spending by taxing only a few high-income earners. Decades of soaking the rich had diluted the concentration of incomes—the top 5 percent of the population saw their share of aggregate money income drop by nearly half between the Hoover and Eisenhower administrations.

By the mid to late sixties, expenditures in most countries had reached the limits of acceptability: the underlying anti-tax sentiment had begun to catch up with the desire for more spending. If politicians had been good at taking the pulse of their electorates, they would have fought their battles around the priorities for different spending projects instead of yielding to all demands and pushing the need for taxes to ever higher levels. Alas, politicians like Lyndon Johnson were not quite in touch with changing grass-roots sentiment and were still mesmerized by the success of the New Deal. The FDR experience had been distilled to a simple formula: More spending provides more benefits to the electorate and therefore more votes. In applying this formula, politicians became free-vote seekers rather than net-vote maximizers; the political costs of increasing expenditure simply weren't part of their equation.

Another legacy from the New Deal was Keynesian demand management. Simply stated, it was an attempt to moderate the ups and downs of the business cycle: if the economy stalled, it could be cranked back up by increasing demand through more public spending. And if the economy raced ahead too fast and was in danger of overheating, it could be cooled down by reducing public expenditure.

Demand management won great favor with politicians even though economists were less than unanimous in their approval. Politicians were intimidated by the claim of Keynesian economists that if it wasn't for demand management, the economy might slip back into another depression. The theory also provided politicians, at least during downturns, with a public interest cover for applying the free-vote spending formula— more was both politically rewarding and economically responsible.

During upturns, of course, the theory's prescription to cut spending was ignored. After all, who could tell if the economy was overheated or just naturally growing faster? Thus, after every business cycle, public spending would go up a notch during a business expansion because the robust economy could painlessly yield more taxes to spend, and up again during the following downturn to head off a depression. So attractive was this arrangement that President Nixon was moved to remark: "I am now a Keynesian."[31]

## The Failure-Zone Squeeze

Although by the end of the sixties there was little demand for a higher level of spending and taxes from a majority of the electorate, their own beliefs in free-vote politics and Keynesian economics led politicians to boost spending at record rates. Both conservatives and liberals, in the U.S. and elsewhere, fostered this growth—U.S. federal government expenditure more than tripled after 1969 under three avowedly fiscally conservative presidents. Olaf Palme, Socialist prime minister of Sweden, managed an expenditure increase from SKr 36.4 billion to SKr 89 billion between 1969 and 1976. Conservative Prime Minister Edward Heath of the United Kingdom started in 1970 with a total government expenditure of £18.9 billion; and when he relinquished office five years later, the expenditure had grown to £39 billion. His Labour party successors spent more in their last half year in office—1979—than the Heath government had spent in the entire year of 1974.

Public expenditure grew as a proportion of national incomes as well as in total size. The ratio of total public expenditure (federal, state, and local) to gross domestic product (gdp) rose in the U.S. from approximately 20 percent in the 1950s and 1960s to 33 percent by 1977. In Europe, between 1960 and 1980, the ratio of public expenditure rose from 32 percent to 44 percent in the U.K.; from 31 percent to 47 percent in Germany; from 25 percent to 47 percent in Denmark; and from 31 percent to 62 percent in Sweden.

The exact level at which spending enters the failure zone and voters become really unhappy with the level of taxes and spending cannot be precisely determined. Economic aggregates as such are politically unimportant—voters are far more concerned with the taxes they have to pay than with trends in the ratio of public spending to gdp. Nevertheless, by 1976 all of the middle class and most of the poor were paying substantial taxes, and there is little question that spending had fallen well within the failure zone. In that year there were 130 million taxpayers in the U.S. out of an adult population of 150 million people. (And since filing tax returns is mandatory and voting is not, 60 percent more adults paid taxes than cast votes in the 1976 elections.) Spending dogma had pulled people into the tax net at a dramatic rate—between 1935 and 1976 the number of tax returns filed grew eleven times faster than the adult population. And no surprise—the minimum income level for filing taxes had fallen in that period from over $23,000 to $2950 (1976 dollars, single-person require-ments). The failure zone threatened to take on a literal as-pect to the Internal Revenue Service (IRS) computer system, as it was swamped by a volume of data that no one had imag-ined it would ever have to handle. A similar pattern can be seen in Britain. In 1938–39 there were 4 million families pay-ing taxes. In 1976–77 almost all of the approximately 21 mil-lion families in the entire population were paying taxes.

The rates that the middle class and poor voters pay also point unambiguously to a failure-zone level of taxes and spending. Table 1.1 depicts estimates of the taxes paid in 1976 by produc-tion workers for various levels of income.

The table may appear to be tamer than the horror stories of

Table 1.1

*Income Tax and Employee's Social Security Contributions as Percentage of Gross Earnings (Average Production Worker, 1976)*

| Country | Income Level | | |
| | 1/2 Average | Average* | 2 × Average |
| --- | --- | --- | --- |
| | Percentage of Gross Earnings | | |
| Australia | 10.5 | 21.9 | 33.3 |
| Austria | 14.7 | 22.3 | 25.7 |
| Belgium | 15.8 | 24.7 | 34.9 |
| Canada | 13.0 | 21.0 | 30.0 |
| Denmark | 29.0 | 38.4 | 50.4 |
| Finland | 24.3 | 34.8 | 45.1 |
| France | 9.7 | 17.9 | 23.9 |
| Germany | 26.1 | 32.8 | 39.2 |
| Ireland | 24.1 | 29.6 | 36.9 |
| Italy | 10.9 | 14.5 | 19.9 |
| Japan | 10.3 | 13.3 | 18.9 |
| Netherlands | 27.2 | 35.4 | 38.1 |
| Norway | 23.5 | 32.4 | 46.7 |
| Sweden | 24.3 | 38.4 | 54.7 |
| Turkey | 28.2 | 34.2 | 41.3 |
| United Kingdom | 26.1 | 33.5 | 36.9 |
| United States | 19.0 | 25.0 | 29.0 |

SOURCE: Office for Economic Cooperation and Development, *The Tax Benefit Position of Selected Income Groups* in OECD Member Coun-tries (Paris, 1979).
*Production worker's income.

marginal tax rates of 98 percent under the former Labour government in the United Kingdom and 95 percent in Sweden. But the latter rates affect (if at all) less than a tenth of a percent of all voters, whereas incomes in this table constitute the electoral heartland. And in this politically crucial middle- and low-income group we find quiet but undeniable evidence of the failure zone—the average worker is being taxed at a rate between three and ten times the rate millionaires used to be taxed at; the bottom 10 percent of wage earners in Britain pay about 15 percent of their wages in tax; and the $3-an-hour workers in the U.S. give the government a fifth of their income.

## Popular Rejection of Failure-Zone Taxes

With spending inside the failure zone, the politics of public expenditure reversed itself: anti-tax sentiment became much stronger than pro-spending support. One of the first displays of the intensity of voters' resentment against their tax burden was provided in June 1979 when the people of California voted in Proposition 13, a proposal to cut property taxes, by a margin of 2 to 1. An ad hoc citizens' initiative prevailed over an awesome coalition consisting of Governor Jerry Brown, the California legislature, the *Los Angeles Times,* the Bank of America, the investment banks of Wall Street, and the state's public employee unions.

An intriguing aspect was the reaction of those voters who rented homes (over half the electorate) and therefore did not stand to benefit directly from the proposed $6 billion reduction in property taxes. The special-interest campaign against Proposition 13 not only had played on fears about cutbacks in vital public services but had also emphasized that other taxes might have to be raised to compensate for the tax cut and thus home renters would be worse off.

Nevertheless, a significant number of home renters voted for passage. Like home owners, they were upset about all failure-zone taxes, and since they weren't offered a choice, they took it out on property taxes, even at the risk of losing some public services. Not that Californians didn't like these services —opinion polls showed strong support for most individual items of spending—but with state and federal expenditures at failure-zone levels, the costs were no longer considered worth the collective benefits.

Proposition 13 spread like a brush fire. Five months later in the elections of November 1978, similar challenges to state taxes won overwhelming approval in twelve states. Then in 1980 failure-zone sentiment asserted itself in national politics and broke twenty-six years of Democratic control of the Senate. As Democratic Senator Hollings said, his party had "lost the faith of the American people. Every time a problem arose, we had but a single solution: spend more money."[32] Failure-zone anger also brought Ronald Reagan into the White House —half of all voters believed that he would cut spending, while only one in seven had that trust in Jimmy Carter.[33] A candidate whose views were once considered so extreme by members of his own party that he was thought to be "unelectable" won in a landslide.

As impressive as the Republican gains in the 1980 election was the ease with which the President and his party were able to push their program of expenditure cuts through Congress in 1981. The lobbies against the proposals were even stronger than the special interests who had opposed Proposition 13. For example, the food stamps cut was opposed by welfare, civil rights, and union groups and farmers; the federal highway construction program was defended by construction unions, mayors, and governors; Medicaid, by state governments, hospitals, and welfare constituents; trade adjustment assistance, by unions in the automobile, steel, and rubber industries; and Exim bank funding, by large exporters like Boeing.

That the cuts survived the lobbies, more or less intact, is in some part a tribute to the administration's superb legislative and public relations skills. But these skills would not, by themselves, have taken the program very far if politicians had not been convinced that there was "widespread public support for holding down government spending."[34] The President believed that "No one will want to stand up and oppose these cuts"[35] and in the Senate, Majority leader Howard Baker warned his colleagues that "if we don't pass this package, I think the country will rise up in a rage of indignation."[36] Democrats reluctantly agreed —as one senator said, "We all read the same election results."[37]

Failure-zone outcomes showed up in European politics as well. Since 1977 the pro-spending "natural parties of government" were thrown out of power or coalitions in Britain, West Germany, Belgium, Holland, Norway, Sweden, Denmark (which got its first conservative government in eighty-one years), and Luxembourg. Margaret Thatcher in particular can thank the failure zone for her victory in May 1979, since practically every personal factor was against her. She was a woman, and by 52 percent to 16 percent the electorate favored a male to a female prime minister. The incumbent, James Callaghan, smoked a pipe, projected a "Sunny Jim" image, and staked his claim to continue in office on the grounds that he could deal with the unions. Several opinion polls said he was preferred as prime minister to Margaret Thatcher by 47 percent to 35 percent.

The preference turned out to be irrelevant. Britain's prime minister is elected not directly by voters but by the members of Parliament of the winning party; and U.K. voters have traditionally been more influenced by expectations of a party's performance than by the personality of its leader. Besides, the issue in 1979 was not whether the prime minister could get on with the unions. Sixty percent of voters believed that Mrs. Thatcher's party was serious about cutting taxes, and their faith won Parliament for the Conservatives and prime ministership for the Iron Lady.

## The Hesitant New Princes

It is ironic that public officials who are usually accused of sway-
ing with every passing breeze have been so unresponsive to
the gale of voter anger over taxes. Resurgent conservatives are
extremely nervous about making the spending cuts that would
consolidate their recently acquired power. Although the political climate is as ripe for a radical change in spending policy as
it was in 1932, what we see are, at best, hesitant slowdowns in
the rate of spending increases.

Several beliefs cloud the conservatives' view of the changed
political realities and prevent them from considering serious
cuts. Foremost is the belief in a mutant version of the traditional free-vote spending formula. Although faith in the dictum that "more spending equals more votes" has been shaken
by recent election results, politicians are still intimidated by its
converse formulation that "less spending equals less votes."
Just as liberals once saw only political benefits in increasing
outlays, conservatives now see only the costs of reducing them.
Fiscal austerity is regarded as an act of statesmanship, of cajol-
ing or tricking a recalcitrant child into taking its medicine. The
advantages of spending cuts—lower taxes—are simply not
counted. Hence in the 1981 Reagan budget-cutting effort,
David Stockman was not allowed to touch sensitive social programs such as social security, Medicare, veterans' benefits, railroad retirement pensions, and welfare for the disabled— the
so-called safety net— which accounted for 36 percent of the
federal budget.

In addition to these political beliefs about social programs,
conservatives have a strong ideological commitment to increasing defense spending. Reagan's longstanding personal
faith in a leaner government conflicted with his other convic-
tion: "The No. 1 priority of the Federal government is national
security. Therefore defense cannot be looked at as part of a
budgetary solution. Defense must be looked at as to what
needs to be done to ensure our national security."[38] This con-

viction put another 25 percent of the budget outside the budget-cutting limits of the Office of Management and Budget
(OMB).

A third factor that reinforces the reluctance to propose serious cuts is faith in economic theories that suggest spending
cuts are unnecessary or unimportant. Mr. Reagan pinned his
hopes on what Vice President George Bush had once called
voodoo economics, or, to use its more respectable name, supply-side economics. Its thesis, as propounded by true believ-
ers like Jack Kemp and Arthur Laffer, was that the level of
public expenditure didn't matter. Don't bother with the budget, they said, just cut tax rates and watch the economy
zoom. (Professor Laffer thought that the timing of the $41
billion cut proposed in the 1981 budget was "just dumb." He
was "against the cuts in a down economy, the cuts in welfare
and in elderly programs. . . . when you reduce unemployment to 3.5%, then cut. Now people need it.")[39] As this theory fit with his determination to increase defense spending
and his reluctance to take on social programs of any signifi-
cance, the supply-siders found in their President a very
strong adherent.

These *beliefs,* rather than cold-blooded political calculation,
reduced the 1981 Reagan budget proposals to little more than
a symbol of the President's opposition to spending: Mr. Stockman was forced to look for budget cuts in only seventeen cents
of the federal spending dollar; 83 percent of the budget—that
is, Social Security, the safety net, defense spending, and debt
service—could not be touched. The best he could manage
under this constraint was a $41 billion decrease in the rate of
increase.

## Malleable Iron

Margaret Thatcher's is a similar record of lost opportunities to
stop the growth in spending. She started with the dice load-

ed in her favor. The Iron Lady had expressed her determination to make deep expenditure cuts during her campaign more strongly and specifically than Ronald Reagan had in his. She was head of both the executive branch and the legislature (in which she enjoyed a solid majority), and the opposition Labour party seemed bent on dismembering itself.

But Mrs. Thatcher's actions in office gave the lie to her words. The much-heralded attack on the excesses of social spending started with penny skirmishes in the first budget and then turned to disorderly retreat. Her chief ideological lieutenant, Sir Keith Joseph, who was appointed Industries Minister, spoke loudly against public spending but carried a small, pliable stick. For the armed forces, it was Christmas time. Three years into her term public expenditure had risen to 43 1/2 percent of gdp, up from the 40 1/2 percent in Labour's last year. The Prime Minister, reported *The Economist*, had given in to the view that "most of the key elements in public spending. . .should be protected against erosion by inflation."[40]

Margaret Thatcher cannot be accused of backing away from cuts because she lacked the stomach for inflicting pain. On the contrary, her faith in a painful cure prescribed by economic theorists diverted her government's attention from the politically rewarding course of giving the public tax and spending cuts.

The cure in question was monetarism, or the restricting of money supply to squeeze out inflation—a remedy that has traditionally been regarded with morbid fascination by conservatives. It appeals to Calvinist desire for a period of extreme self-denial to purge the system of the poisons that accumulate after years of excess and wanton revelry. If the patient has a fever, bleed him; if the economy is ill, tap out money supply, induce pain, and someday it will return to health.

True to her puritanical instincts, Mrs. Thatcher more than made up on the monetary front for her lack of resolve on spending. In the first three years of Thatcherism, real gross national product (GNP) fell by 7 percent and manufacturing output by 20 percent—declines steeper than had been experienced in the Depression. Unemployment crossed 3 million —its highest level since World War II.

If the object was to induce suffering, then the trade-off made by the Thatcher government—generous public spending and austere money supply—achieved its goal. But that choice was hardly good politics. If the government had concentrated on cutting expenditures, it would certainly have caused some pain to the erstwhile recipients, but since so many more voters could have been provided significant tax relief, it would have, overall, paid off politically, even in the short term. Margaret Thatcher managed instead to displease everyone with her focus on monetary policies.

Conservatives like Mrs. Thatcher don't appreciate why they have suddenly been so successful. Although their ideological positions on spending have only accidentally become congruent with popular sentiment, they are convinced the public has finally seen the light. They also take their recent success as a blanket endorsement of aggressive defense budgets, tight money, and the need to provide tax incentives for the rich— in fact, these issues now seem more important than cutting spending.

Such conservatives might consider Machiavelli's advice: "I will not fail to remind any prince who has acquired a new state by the aid of its inhabitants that he soundly consider what induced them to assist him—if the reason is not natural affection for him but rather dissatisfaction with the former government, he will find it extremely difficult to keep them friendly."[41] The British public did not vote for Margaret Thatcher because of nationalistic pride in providing the first modern laboratory for testing monetary theory, and Jimmy Carter probably did not become the first elected President since Hoover to lose a bid for a second term because voters were curious about the Laffer curve.

## The Reaction to Empty Rhetoric

Mrs. Thatcher's approval rating in the polls sank steadily as her economic policies took hold—in March 1982 a national opinion poll reported that the British public thought that she would go down as the worst prime minister in history.[42] Then the Falklands war broke out, and the same dogmatism that had made her economic policies unpopular proved to be a great political asset. Mrs. Thatcher's approval rating zoomed in the seventy-five days of the war from 25 percent to nearly 60 percent.[43] Before the first anniversary of the Falklands victory had passed, Margaret Thatcher called a snap election. The Conservatives were helped by a Labour party campaign described by the London *Times* as "the worst fought by any major party in modern times"[44] and by the emergence of the Liberal/Social Democrat Alliance, which split the opposition vote. The government retained its majority in Parliament, but with the lowest-ever share of the popular vote in British history.[45] Mrs. Thatcher won fewer votes in her victory than Conservative Prime Minister Sir Alec Douglas Hume had polled in his 1964 defeat.

But where liberals can get their act halfway in order and there aren't foreign policy crises to be heroic about, hesitant conservatives may not get second chances to get spending under control. Voters at large have little against food stamps, social security, or defense spending per se and mere talk about large cuts doesn't bring the tax cuts that might attract them to the rightist cause. In fact, since voters don't know that talk has not been accompanied by action, it gives austerity a bad name. The public takes the rhetoric of the anti-spending politicians at face value, observes the continuing slide in personal living standards, and decides, in the best democratic tradition (if the opposition is not in complete disarray), to "throw the rascals out." Conservatives are then free to conclude that voters are too cussed to accept responsible policies and liberals that more spending is still as politically attractive as it is ideologically desirable.

## Spending: How Much?

An example of the consequences of empty rightist rhetoric is seen in France. In 1976 President Giscard appointed Raymond Barre his prime minister, describing him as the best economist in France. Barre bided his time until the 1978 elections in which the government, in a surprising victory, increased its majority in the National Assembly. Its political base thus secured, the Giscard/Barre team announced a new policy of fiscal austerity and tough monetary and incomes policies.

Austerity talk brought the dutiful rebukes from the Socialists that it was "immoral," "bad for France, and unacceptable for the working class" but did nothing to slow the growth of taxes and spending. The monetary and incomes policies were more serious. A government official explained (off the record) that its objective was to bring the annual increase in consumer purchasing power down to zero. It could be kept there for three years, through the 1981 presidential elections, and M. Giscard would still win because the left was so fragmented. So the government could afford to wait until the late 1980s for its economic theories to show results.

Part of the plan worked—living standards did suffer—but the political scenario went askew. Their forbearance exceeded by failure-zone taxes, frozen wages, and the fear of unemployment, voters rejected the seemingly invulnerable Giscard in 1981 and put in the Socialists, who at least talked of better times (though the margin, reflecting the electorate's dissatisfaction with both the status quo and fear of the Socialists' unpredictable schemes, was very close). Thus "big spender" François Mitterand was able to defy the conservative trend and confirm for those who are eager for such reassurance the continuing validity of the New Deal spending formula.

Joe Clark of Canada provides another example. In June 1979 his Conservative party won office after sixteen years, promising voters a reduction in income tax and tax deductibility of interest payments on mortgages. The new government lasted six months. In his first budget Mr. Clark pared down his promise on mortgage deductions by a fifth, offered no tax cuts, and instead proposed increases in indirect taxes that would cost an average family more than $600 a year. Parliament rejected this budget, the government fell, and in the new election, which was held in February 1980, voters sent Mr. Clark back to where he had started from—Leader of Her Majesty's Loyal Opposition in Canada.

## Liberal Diehards

The gift that Rightist hesitation makes to Leftist reaction provides the liberals with an excuse to avoid questioning their beliefs and thus sustains politically unpopular spending increases. In his first year in office, President Mitterand of France boosted public spending by 28 percent; his standing in popularity polls fell and his party suffered unexpected reverses in several by-elections. But since the memory of their triumph over the conservative Giscard regime was still fresh in their minds, the Socialists saw no connection between their sudden decline in popularity and their spending policies.

Faith in the economic superiority of expansionary spending was also undimmed—when the government finally reined its spending spree (1983 expenditure growth was set at "only" 11 percent), it was due to a falling franc and high inflation—misfortunes brought about by callous foreigners. As the French prime minister complained: "If everyone had agreed on growth, we perhaps wouldn't be where we are today. But here was a leftist government surrounded by rightist governments which launched brutal and savage recessionary policies."[46]

Liberals have held to their spending faith for so long that questioning its reasonableness is well nigh impossible for the older politician. Mr. Palme of Sweden, for example, can hardly help his spending reflexes. He entered politics as a student in the early 1950s, joined the Cabinet in 1963, and became prime minister in 1969. In 1976 his Social Democratic party was thrown out of power after forty-four years because of public dissatisfaction over taxes. A conservative coalition governed for two terms thereafter and spent much of its energies bickering over nuclear power instead of implementing eagerly expected tax and spending cuts. In 1982 the Social Democrats were voted back into office. The new government immediately announced a plan "to get Swedish business back into action" by increasing government spending (and raising sales taxes). Asked why this policy would work when it had failed in France the previous year, Prime Minister Palme had a ready explanation:

Mitterand came to power after many years of bourgeois government, and he was forced to respond to his constituents, pent-up desire for consumer goods. So he stimulated demand and ran into trouble. Things are different here—we have had almost 15 years of Socialism and we have no great gaps between the working class and others. We have a far better chance to stimulate savings and investment which is what Western economies need.[47]*

## Opportunities in the Failure Zone

Thus a combination of ideology and outdated political beliefs induce public officials—both liberal and conservative—to continue with the now-unpopular course of increasing spending. Conservatives are deterred by the fear of cuts and distracted by other objectives such as increasing defense spending and changing tax and monetary policies. Most liberals have ideological faith in spending that causes them to ignore public anger about high taxes. The unfortunate voters, therefore,

*What Mitterand, Palme, and several other leaders refuse to appreciate is that under the fundamentally different conditions of the failure zone, the old rule of spending the economy out of a recession simply isn't politically sensible. In times past such countercyclical spending, like all other forms of public expenditure, was popular because it was financed out of the incomes of a few rich. Now that the revenue potential of the rich is exhausted, increased spending is politically unrewarding because it merely inefficiently and forcibly recycles income among the great mass of voters. Countercyclical spending, even in the midst of recessions, is no exception. Attempts such as Mr. Mitterand's to spend the economy out of a slump today inevitably end in political failure.

take out their frustration on whoever happens to be in power.

Although the intense dissatisfaction of voters represents a great threat to politicians afraid of change, it is a heaven-sent opportunity for those who aren't. As Machiavelli wrote:

Princes become great doubtless by overcoming obstacles that are set in their way. Therefore when Fortune wants to bestow greatness on a new prince she creates enemies and urges them on to attack him so that he may have cause to vanquish them . . . a wise prince will cunningly provoke opposition and then by routing it, increase his own stature.[48]

Whereas politicians of twenty years ago could hope for only modest advantages by changing the level of spending, politicians today can expect major payoffs if they can satisfy the electorate's hunger for real reductions in their tax burden. Consider the magnitude of the opportunity that Ronald Reagan had when he was elected: federal spending in 1980, the last year of Mr. Carter's term, was $580 billion, paid for by nearly 140 million taxpayers (out of a voting-age population of 162 million). If 1981 spending had been just 8 percent below 1980 spending, nearly 60 million voters could have been entirely freed from the burden of paying federal income taxes; and if spending had been cut by 13 percent, the IRS computer system could have erased over 74 million names from its memory.

Admittedly, an 8 or a 13 percent reduction is no easy task. It would require an abrupt change in five decades of spending policy and with real cuts, not decreases in the rate of increase. Some reductions in all programs, including the ones conventionally considered sacred, would be necessary, and real, universal cuts would cause such real, universal, and strongly resisted pain. On the other hand, the change would be less dramatic than the rate of increase of the New Deal. A public that has coped with the much greater deprivations of double-digit inflation and 20 percent interest rates, with unemployment and pay cuts, could live with a modestly lower level of state-provided benefits. And 74 million Americans (69 percent more than the 44 million who voted for Ronald Reagan in 1980) represent a potentially awesome political force for a 13 percent spending cut.

Harnessing this force would require a leader with good selling skills whom the public was willing to trust. The effectiveness of a campaign to reduce spending would also depend on astute political choices in spending priorities and taxation policy. Although cuts in all items of spending would be necessary —reductions are more likely to be unacceptable if some beneficiaries are exempted—the sacrifice would not have to be equal. As we will see in chapters 6 through 8, some types of spending make more political sense than others. Support for cuts would also depend upon who reaped the benefits of lower taxes, a subject we will deal with in the next chapter.

Ronald Reagan had the opportunity to reduce spending. Enjoying high public confidence as he started his term, he could have put the weight of his office behind a real $75 billion spending cut in February 1981. He could have been the first president in twenty years to move spending out of the failure zone. Instead his administration played by the political rules of a past era and was dogmatic about defense and enamoured of supply-side theory.

## Economics: The Public Interest

Thus far we have looked at spending from a "political" point of view—how leaders should respond to the wishes of their electorate. But is good politics—giving voters the level of expenditure they want—also good economics? The businessman's profit motive in a competitive market satisfies the needs of the consumers—for most goods such as cars, television sets, and bread—at the lowest overall cost. The market, however, cannot provide what John Kenneth Galbraith has called the right "social balance" between the supply of private goods such as cars and public goods such as roads, since the latter are collectively (and somewhat involuntarily) consumed and paid for. A reasonably good balance can be struck, though, through the trial and error of democratic elections. This balance is necessary not only for the reelection of leaders and the short-term gratification of voters but also to sustain long-term efficiency. Our economy can be starved by too little public spending or smothered by too much.

Public spending is needed to provide what are known as external economies—the roads, hospitals, schools, clean air, and water, which no individual exclusively consumes but whose availability contributes to everyone's productivity. And indeed it is difficult to imagine a modern economy getting by without these externalities: without roads there would be no General Motors and without education, no IBM. The safe operation of chemical plants requires good water and sewage facilities. Low-cost production in large centralized plants has to be supported by an extensive transportation grid of highways, harbors, and airports.

The rapid growth of Singapore shows how public spending can make an important contribution to the economy. In 1966 Singapore had no industry, little government, and 18 percent unemployment. Today the manufacturing sector is the backbone of its economy and labor shortages are so severe that the country imports guest workers. Big increases in government spending played a major role in this turnaround—the state built, from scratch, industrial estates where foreign investors set up shop, housing for workers to live near these estates, and highways and container ports for transporting the goods they produced.

It is not happenstance that public spending simultaneously provides political and economic benefits. Externalities help individuals help themselves to a better life and therefore make them more satisfied as voters. On the other hand, just as economic benefits accompany political benefits, so do costs. Paying taxes for public spending not only alienates individuals as voters, it also hampers their economic potential. For example, while better roads release citizens from the constraint of finding a job only in their immediate neighborhood, the higher taxes needed to pay for these roads reduce their ability to buy cars.

Fewer individuals buying cars is bad news for Detroit. The consumption of public goods limits the size of the market for private goods, which can hurt national competitiveness. For example, in Britain the cost of supporting a cradle-to-grave welfare system forces the public to sacrifice the consumption of consumer electronics goods; whereas Japan, which consumes a relatively lower level of public welfare services, can support a disproportionately large domestic electronics market. Japan's large home market for consumer electronics attracts the capital, inventiveness, and entrepreneurship that enables its industry to dominate the world's television and stereo markets. The U.K.'s National Health Scheme, on the other hand, cannot be exported.

The consumption of public goods hurts private enterprise on the supply side as well. Not only do higher spending and taxes reduce the market for TV sets and cars, they also leave the individual with less disposable (after-tax) income to save from. Lower savings in turn lead to lesser investment—fewer new factories, machines, computers, and buildings—and consequently, in the long run, to a weaker economy.

Public spending, undertaken by the government on behalf of its citizens, also reduces personal incentives in a fashion that personal spending does not: when individuals buy a car, they make a personal choice whether the benefits are worth the price. A taxpayer's purchase of road is not as voluntary—he may use it less than his neighbor, but no one offers him the choice to opt out of his share of the road. Taxes, therefore, can provoke in him a reaction different from the sticker price of a car: "Who am I working for, for myself or the government? The more I make, the less I seem to keep; and if I don't work so hard I don't lose much."

It is as important in the public interest to achieve the right balance between public and private expenditure as it is from a selfishly "political" point of view: private incomes must be taxed in order to provide externalities, but not so heavily as to choke off the activity that produces the incomes.

And it is not a coincidence that a reasonable* balance is reached at a politically rational level of spending, since voter satisfaction goes hand in hand with externalities that improve economic opportunities and electoral dissatisfaction is congruent with individual and collective costs. Pandering to voters contributes to economic efficiency. When leaders maximize their self-interest by keeping spending in a politically acceptable range, we hit upon the right mix of roads and cars and of schools and automobiles. And the psychological disincentive is tolerable—a small if annoying contribution to make to belong to the club.

Economic growth has been most robust when public expenditure has been in a politically reasonable range. In the twenty-five years between 1913 and 1948, when public expenditure was very low, world production grew at an annual rate of about 2 percent. As expenditure rose into a higher range in the next twenty-five years, this rate more than doubled, to 5 percent. Then in the failure-zone years between 1973 and 1983, the rate of growth fell by half, to less than 2.5 percent.

Not all countries suffered from low growth and failure-zone spending in the seventies. In countries like Japan, Korea, Taiwan, Hong Kong, and Singapore, government expenditure was held to the proportions it had been in the West during the the fifties. In spite of the slowdown in world trade and the oil shock, these robust economies of the East grew twice and three times as fast as their Western counterparts. Where factories fell silent and millions lost their jobs in the West, the Eastern economies accommodated a great exodus from farm to factory and yet there were jobs to spare. Consider too the comparative wage record: the real average industrial wage in the U.S. declined from $104 a week in 1969 to $99 a week in

*But not exact. Because personal values differ, there is no "perfect" level of spending. Committed individualists might be willing to forgo the economic advantages of externalities in order to keep the government as far out of their life as possible. I am talking about an approximate range that most people in a society would feel comfortable with.

1979,[49] notwithstanding the hard-bargaining United Auto Workers, United Mine Workers, and the Teamsters. And these are before tax numbers. In the U.K. too, notwithstanding the notoriously militant and unreasonable British trade unions, the average industrial paycheck crawled up at an annual rate of 1.6 percent a year between 1965 and 1975 and slumped thereafter. In contrast, during the same period, the compliant and exploited Korean worker received annual real-wage increases of over 9 percent.

Note, though, that the Far Eastern experience is not a testimony to the merits of inordinately parsimonious governments. These governments started with very low levels of expenditure, but had to increase it rapidly to provide the externalities they needed to support their booming industries. Between 1960 and 1977 public consumption increased by 4.5 percent per year in Taiwan, 6.9 percent per year in Korea, 8.6 percent a year in Hong Kong, and 9.8 percent in Singapore.

Spending in these countries thus quickly became comparable to U.S. spending of the 1950s, from a base that approximated the fiscal levels of the nineteenth century. Looking back to those low spending days, one does not find evidence of widespread prosperity. Economic growth was erratic— great busts and booms occurred frequently; inequality was great and the smaller fruits of prosperity fell into fewer baskets. If Lancashire slum dwellers had been informed about the joys of no government and low expenditure, they might well have been skeptical.

A democratic system can respond to the need for public goods in much the same manner as, if perhaps with less speed than, the market does for bread. Self-interested politicians can give voters the level of public spending they desire relative to their needs for private goods. But when politicians are unresponsive, when for reasons of class interest governments try to avoid incurring expenditure and levying taxes, or for reasons of ideology or free-vote tradition boost spending into the failure zone, they harm our economic welfare. Dogmatic politicians are responsible for too many roads and citizens without the means to buy cars or roads too crowded for the number of cars about, just as in the ideologically driven, centrally directed Soviet economy, where bakers are told how much bread they should bake (and consumers how much they should eat), there is always too little or too much bread compared to the proletariats' needs.

# CHAPTER 2

# Taxes: From Whom, and How?

THE RELENTLESS INCREASE in public spending has thrown taxation policies into turmoil. In their search for more revenue, governments have increased rates on existing taxes, devised new levies, raised their borrowings, and printed money. In addition, politicians have undertaken several tax experiments—reducing specific taxes like capital gains, or substituting taxes on consumption for taxes on saving—to revive their flagging economies.

The quest for more funds and the experiments have substantially altered the mix of government revenue. Popular, "progressive" policies have given way to a politically unattractive structure of regressive taxes and thus compounded the already serious political problems of spending in the failure zone. Tax-and-spend policies inadvertently increased the proportion of the revenue burden that the middle class and the poor had to carry in spite of the liberal commitment to progressive taxation; now conservatives are consciously accelerating the trend.

Progressivity cannot be easily reinstated without reducing the government's total need for funds. But neither will spending cuts be politically attractive unless the tax benefits are progressively distributed to a majority of voters. Hence the task for a vote-seeking politician today is to do both: to cut expenditure and to press for tax reforms that will put the greatest burden on the fewest voters.

## Tax Turmoil

From the beginning, the Reagan administration was marked by strife over the right revenue mix of the federal government: the supply siders insisting that the proportion of direct income taxes be reduced, at any cost, and the more traditional conservatives arguing that taxes were preferable to deficits.

Mr. Reagan is an ardent supply sider. In his view, high marginal taxes were choking the economy, and therefore cutting tax *rates* would so increase economic activity that total tax revenues would actually go up. So in February 1980 Mr. Reagan proposed an ambitious plan for a three-year, 30 percent cut in tax rates. The plan did not attract widespread support. Traditional economists and many conservative Republicans feared that cutting tax rates without matching cuts in spending would merely lead to higher deficits, not any miracle boom. Democrats attacked the plan for "unfairly" giving the rich a disproportionately larger share of the benefits. Opinion polls also showed that a majority of voters were opposed to the proposed cut in rates.

When it became clear by June that the tax proposals did not have much support, administration officials began to make deals. Fiscal conservatives were appeased by postponing the first stage of the tax cut and reducing it from 10 percent to 5 percent, and special-interest groups were lured by generous new deductions and allowances. Democrats who were offering their own tax proposals also began to court the various lobbies with tax breaks, and soon a bidding war broke out. "The hogs," as David Stockman put it, "were really feeding. The greed level, the level of opportunism just got out of control."[1] By August the President had gotten the tax cut he was determined to win and the lobbyists had earned their retainers. The revenue loss to the federal government in the tax legislation that was finally passed amounted to over $750 billion over the next five years.[2]

Supply siders like Professor Laffer were ecstatic. "The tax cut is marvelous, wonderful," he said. "It has improved incentives even more than did the Kennedy tax cut of the 1960s. It creates the conditions for a boom that will make those of the 1920s and 1960s look pale by comparison."[3] He also predicted that the boom (and therefore the higher tax revenues for the government) would arrive practically instantaneously. "How long," he asked, "does it take you to pick up a $100 bill?"[4]

The economy, however, didn't cooperate, and we entered a recession that, the President conceded, "none of us had predicted."[5] Interest rates grew along with worries about huge federal deficits. Fiscal conservatives, including Republican senators, OMB Director David Stockman, and the chairman of the President's economic advisors, Professor Murray Weidenbaum, joined forces to press for tax increases, which they believed were necessary to restore confidence in the bond markets and bring down interest rates. But Treasury Secretary Donald Regan and Assistant Secretary Paul Craig Roberts resisted, warning, in the words of Roberts, that raising taxes "might unravel the President's program."[6] After two months of internal debate the President announced in November 1981 that he had rejected the Stockman-Weidenbaum "revenue enhancement" proposals. "The train is a bit late in leaving the station,"[7] he admitted, but there was no need for any policy change.

As the recession deepened in 1982, however, and interest rates stayed high, pressures for new taxes to close the deficit gap continued to mount. Although it was an election year, a conventionally impossible time to raise taxes, there was strong support on Capitol Hill for a $98 billion tax increase bill fashioned by Republican Senator Robert Dole. The President, who had by then reluctantly come to accept the link between deficits and interest rates, supported the bill, which he described as loophole closings, not new taxes. With Mr. Reagan's help, Congress was able to pass before the summer recess in September what his critics called the largest tax increase in history. Supply-side spokesman Jude Wanniski complained that "Reagan is now acting like Nixon, Ford and Carter."[8] Again, before the Christmas recess in 1982, Mr. Reagan agreed to support a 5 cent per gallon increase in the excise duty on gasoline, accepting the argument that it really constituted a user fee for federal highways, not a tax.

## The Rational Standard: Progressive Taxation

The confusion and controversy was partly unavoidable. Even without the complication of supply-side experiments, there was no easy way to finance a budget that had passed $750 billion and was still headed up. Whatever the source tapped for more revenue—income taxes, user fees, or deficits—voters would complain and lobbies would fight. Nevertheless, the issue arises, what basic principles of tax policy could the President have adopted that would have caused the least possible political harm? Or was his week-by-week improvisation the only available course?

One thing is clear. The public prefers a progressive tax system—one that takes more from the rich. Voters believe that it is fair that those who can afford to shoulder a larger share of the tax burden should; perhaps the public is also jealous of the wealth of a lucky few. In any event, the Gallup organization has found consistent support for a progressive tax schedule. Starting in the mid-1930s, Gallup began asking the question: "About how much do you think a married man earning $3000 a year should pay in the form of taxes? What about a man earning $5000? A man earning $10,000? A man earning $100,000?"[9]

From the median responses for each income bracket, Gallup calculated a tax schedule, which as table 2.1 shows, was decidedly progressive. The public believed that no taxes should be collected from families with less than $2000 in income (over four-fifths of the population) and that the rate on the super-rich should be ten times the lowest rate. Gallup stopped asking this question in December 1962, but given the stability of the responses for over twenty-five years, there is little reason to believe that a schedule so constructed today wouldn't be progressive (or at least wouldn't be thought to be progressive).

The public's belief in its equity isn't, however, the principal reason for the political attractiveness of progressive taxation. After all, most voters don't have either the inclination or the means to monitor progressiveness, and it would be quite easy for politicians to create the illusion that the rich were paying high taxes even if, because of generous tax breaks, they really weren't. As Professor Benjamin Page writes:

Survey research indicates that people know little about the tax system. 'Don't know' responses are frequent, and most pollsters don't even bother to ask about really complex issues. Few Americans understand the differing effects

Table 2.1

*The Public's Income Tax Preference*

| Annual Income ($) | Tax Rate Favored (%) | |
| --- | --- | --- |
| | *1937* | *1962* |
| 2,000 | 0 | 0 |
| 3,000 | 1 | 0 |
| 5,000 | 2 | 3 |
| 10,000 | 5 | 7 |
| 50,000 | - | 10 |
| 100,000 | 10 | 20 |

SOURCE: *The Gallup Poll for the years cited.* George H. Gallup, *The Gallup Poll, 1935–1971* (New York: Random House, 1972).

of credits and deductions, let alone accelerated depreciation or intangible drilling expenses.[10]

But voters *are* intimately concerned with and aware of their personal tax bite. And it is primarily because of the voter's individual sacrifice that progressivity is politically attractive— it enables the tax burden to be so distributed that it pinches the fewest number of voters. The same total tax can be raised from fewer rich voters than poor voters. Progressivity cannot erase the political costs of public expenditure, but at least it can minimize them.

## Progressivity Through Direct Taxes

But how can progressivity be best implemented? Not through taxes levied "indirectly" on consumption such as sales, excise, or value-added taxes. Pechman and Okner have estimated that, for example, in 1966, sales and excise taxes equaled 9 percent of incomes between $0 and 3000, 4 percent of $25,000 and 30,000 incomes, and only 1 percent of incomes over $1 million.[11] Indirect taxes tend to be regressive (that is, their rates don't rise with incomes) since the items that yield the most revenue are those of the commonest usage, whose consumption is either proportional to incomes (such as clothes) or independent of income (such as bread). Some portion of the sales tax, which falls on goods purchased almost exclusively by the rich (such as diamonds and furs) is progressive, but the total consumption of such items and therefore the revenue derived from them is small.

Progressivity is more easily implemented through direct taxes on personal incomes and business profits. The advantage of personal income taxes is that progressivity can be simply and relatively accurately provided for by specifying higher rates for higher incomes. The disadvantage is that the tax laws have to be frequently modified to keep up with the cleverness of individuals who try to protect their earnings by receiving them in different forms—labor unions negotiate for fringe benefits instead of straight wages, sophisticated investors buy municipal bonds to avoid income taxes on the interest on regular bonds, and some British firms even arrange to lease business suits to their executives as a nontaxable fringe benefit!

Collection is less of a problem with direct taxes on corporate profits. There are far fewer companies than individuals (a few hundred of them account for over half of private GNP), and they keep their books better. The disadvantage of a corporate income tax is that its progressivity is hard to ensure—even widows and orphans own stock in the companies that are taxed. But this is not a crucial shortcoming if revenue needs are high (and a large number of voters would be taxed anyway), since the distribution of ownership of companies is similar to the distribution of income—the top 1 percent of the population owns 43 percent of all corporate stock,[12] and 60 to 70 percent of Americans don't own any stock at all.

But although progressivity can be achieved relatively easily through direct taxation, so can regressivity. Payroll taxes are the most common example of regressive direct taxes. Begun under the Social Security Act of 1935, payroll taxes are levied at a flat rate up to a ceiling of about $40,000, above which no tax is levied at all. Thus in 1977 payroll taxes were equal to 11 percent of an income of $15,000, 6 percent of a $45,000 income, and less than 1 percent on very high incomes. The progressivity of direct taxation can also be undermined by deductions, allowances, and credits. Deductions for charity, for example, are worth more to the rich than to the poor—a dollar's contribution gives a millionaire a 50-cent tax break but is worth only 14 cents to a low-income earner.

## Taxes or Deficits?

The alternative to levying taxes is to borrow, that is, to finance expenditure through deficits. Conventional wisdom holds that while deficits may be economically irresponsible, they are politically expedient: they allow public officials to escape the embarrassment of voting for tax increases and they defer to future generations the costs of expenditures that are incurred today.

But the conventional wisdom is seriously flawed. The public does not want politicians to incur deficits rather than vote for higher taxes. As the executive director of the Roper Center of Public Opinion Research writes: "on the question of balancing budgets, we are a nation of conservatives. . . . With a consistency rarely seen in public opinion polling, the populace for more than 40 years has indicated an abiding aversion to deficits every time and every way it has been asked."[13]

Nor did Ronald Reagan's election change the public's dislike for deficits: "If you had to choose," CBS/*New York Times* interviewers asked in January 1981, "would you favor a balanced budget or a large tax cut?" Three-quarters of respondents favored a balanced budget. In March 1982, in the midst of a deep and prolonged recession, Gallup asked: "There was a major cut in federal income taxes passed last year and it is being phased in over a three-year period. Would you be willing to postpone this tax cut in order to reduce the federal deficit?" Seventy-six percent of respondents favored postponement.[14]

Be that as it may, the critical political issue about deficits is really not how they are perceived but whether they hurt the voter more or less than taxes.* And here we must face the fact that the belief that deficits are a painless source of revenue, because the cost of borrowing can be deferred to future generations, is a myth. The money that the government borrows has to be extracted from the same public that would otherwise be paying taxes (except, of course, borrowing from foreigners), and this operation cannot be performed without hurting voters. The only "choice" that a government has is in how it

---

*The average citizen doesn't really care what goes on in Washington. Most voters don't know how much the federal government spends, taxes, or borrows in the aggregate. In 1983, for example, a third of all voters (and nearly 20 percent of college graduates) did not know that the federal government was running a deficit and only a tenth were aware that its size was on the order of $200 billion. Like the car buyer who is much more interested in the sticker price than in how GM calculates its production costs, average voters are primarily swayed by their personal "bottom line" rather than by debates about the national debt.

wishes to take its lumps: it can print money to finance its deficit and be blamed by voters for high inflation, or it can sell its bonds and court voters' displeasure over high interest rates and unemployment. In 1980 the public was upset with Democrats because of double-digit inflation, while in 1982 the Republicans were blamed for a severe recession. The Carter and Reagan budget deficits cost their parties votes, even though most voters did not understand how printing money led to inflation or why interest rates were forced up by the sale of government bonds. There are no free votes in substituting borrowing for taxes; deficits cannot be used by politicians as an underhanded device to trade away their country's future for their own short-term benefit.

Worse, the costs of deficits are erratic and excessive. Controlled progressivity is impossible to implement—the pain of recession and inflation is visited upon an unpredictable number of voters, without regard to their incomes. This unpredictability by itself can exact a higher toll than the actual economic loss to the voter. Voters are averse to deficits not because they know they are worse off with them than with an equivalent direct tax, but rather because they don't know and instinctively recoil from uncertainty.

## The Historical Evolution to Direct Progressive Taxation

It is natural to expect that progressive taxes, designed to restrict the revenue burden to the fewest number of citizens, are more likely to prevail where the majority interest is respected, and regressive levies are more likely to be found where government (and its taxation policies) is beholden to the rich. It is also reasonable to assume that if in the latter kind of society, the power of the rich is challenged, regressive taxation will become an important beachhead.

The history of taxation did follow this logical course. From ancient times to the middle ages, when power was concentrated in the hands of a few, taxes were regressive. State expenditure was financed either from tribute extracted from peasants or, under more sophisticated fiscal arrangements, from regressive consumption taxes. With the emergence of democracy, the tax structure began to change. As power passed from the aristocracy and landed gentry to populist politicians, progressive taxation gradually began to take hold. The elected representatives of the common people learned to exercise their growing legislative powers to shift the tax burden on their class enemies.

As it was difficult to actually replace existing regressive taxes (especially since public demands for expenditure were simultaneously growing), the strategy that evolved was to ensure that all new taxes were progressive. And as indirect taxation on goods was already quite heavy, it was natural that progressiveness be imposed through a tax levied directly on the incomes of the rich, rather than indirectly through the goods the general populace consumed.

In Britain such a progressive tax on incomes was first proposed in 1799, to finance the Napoleonic wars. The aristocracy who controlled Parliament saw in it the dangers of progressivity and only reluctantly allowed its passage.* After the defeat of Napoleon, the landed classes contrived the repeal of the income tax. Britain had the trappings of Parliament but was not quite yet a fully representative democracy; its lawmakers were beholden to the rich who elected them.

In the nineteenth century, as Parliament became more representative, a progressive income tax was again levied in 1842 as a "temporary" substitute for regressive import tariffs, in the teeth of vociferous objections from the rich.† Finally in 1909

*As Lord Auckland warned in the debate on the tax: "Graduation would be contrary to all the safety and rights of property; it would be worthy only of the French Council of Five Hundred and it would amount to neither more nor less than the introduction of a plan for equalizing fortunes and to the implied inference that, because a man possesses much, therefore more shall be taken from him than is proportionately taken from others."[15]

†The political din that the rich were able to make to abolish this tax led to the downfall of Prime Minister William Gladstone. In 1874 Mr. Gladstone found that his government had accumulated a large-enough surplus to dispense with the income tax. Misled by the sound and

the pretense that income taxes and other progressive taxes were temporary was directly attacked by then Chancellor of the Exchequer, David Lloyd George, when he presented his famous "people's" budget. Defending the introduction of an income-tax surcharge, which he called a super tax, he asked Parliament:

Why should the tax be treated as a reserve, as something which is of a temporary character, while other taxes are regarded as permanent? Why should not the other taxes have their turn as temporary taxes, the taxes on the food of the people for instance? Why should taxes on the necessities of life be regarded as permanent and the taxes on high income as purely temporary? If any taxes are to be treated as a reserve, I should say that the taxes which ought to be so treated are those which would press heaviest on the people who can least afford them.[16]

The people's budget was rejected by the conservative majority in the House of Lords. The rejection forced two general elections, and ultimately the Parliament Act of 1911 was passed, which severely curtailed the powers of the House of Lords.

At the time Lloyd George was battling the House of Lords, the French government was reacting to popular pressure for tax reform. As the general election of 1906 had produced a mandate for tax reform, the finance minister of the new government, J. Caillaux, proposed scrapping the existing structure of regressive taxation and levying a direct progressive income tax. The minister dealt with the accusation that the few who earned more than Fr 5000 would be unjustly penalized by the income tax thus:

Gentlemen, it is true that in this country there are not more than 500,000 or 600,000 taxpayers who have incomes of more than 5000 francs. But what then? Our friends on the right have tried to excite your sympathy on behalf of this class who are about to be called on to bear a small part of the public burdens. For my part I shall reserve my sympathy for the millions and millions

the fury of the agitation for its abolition, Mr. Gladstone prematurely dissolved Parliament and in the ensuing election campaigned on a platform that promised to finally get rid of the "temporary" income tax. In fact, the opposition to the tax was quite thin since most voters weren't income-tax payers. Gladstone lost and the income tax stayed on the books.

of Frenchmen who are not exposed to this peril for the excellent reason that they do not receive 5000 francs of income in the course of a year.[17]

In the U.S. the income tax was first levied during the Civil War. Like the British Napoleonic war tax, it did not survive the peace. Then, in 1894, Grover Cleveland, a populist Democrat, tried to revive the tax as a substitute for the regressive import tariffs that he had campaigned against. The income tax was opposed by Republicans who were dedicated to preserving the tariffs that protected the few industrialists and was declared unconstitutional by the Supreme Court.

The 1908 presidential plank for the Democratic party urged a constitutional amendment that would permit a progressive income tax. But a Republican, William Howard Taft, was elected, and in his inauguration speech he staked out his opposition: "The Democratic platform demands two Constitutional amendments, one providing for an income tax and the other for an election of Senators by the people. In my judgment, an amendment to the Constitution for an income tax is not necessary."[18] Pressure for an income tax continued to build, however, and in the very next year the president was persuaded to support a constitutional amendment. By 1913 two-thirds of the states had ratified the Sixteenth Amendment and a legal basis for a U.S. progressive tax was finally created.

## Failure-Zone Spending and Regressive Taxation

Since the total level of spending in that period was still within a very low range, few voters were affected by the newly instituted progressive income taxes and the rates they were subject to were low. In 1913, the year of ratification of the income tax in the U.S., the tax rate was 1 percent on incomes from $3,000 to $20,000 with surtaxes above $20,000—and the highest surtax was 6 percent, on incomes above $500,000. Income taxes in Europe were similarly low and affected only the richest 5 percent of the population.

Spending grew rapidly in the decades thereafter and was financed principally by progressive income taxes. By the 1950s spending was in a politically reasonable range and the economy was coasting prosperously. A large number (but still a minority) of voters were financing, without major financial sacrifice, the public goods that the prosperity of the community required. What followed, in the sixties and the seventies, was a headlong rush into the failure zone. In the scramble, not only were reasonable limits to spending exceeded but the whole rationale of progressive tax policy was undermined. The evolution toward simple, direct progressive taxes was reversed and was replaced by a vast muddle of regressive taxes.

The shift is quite startling. In President Eisenhower's times the tax system had begun to approach the populists' ideal— about 70 percent of federal receipts were from progressive income taxes and of these direct taxes, over half were taxes on corporate profits. By the time of President Ford's administration, as table 2.2 shows, regressive levies accounted for nearly 50 percent of total revenue and the share of corporate income taxes had dropped by half.

Table 2.2
*U.S. Federal Government:*
*Sources of Funds*

| Source (%) | 1955 | 1976 |
|---|---|---|
| Individual income tax | 42 | 36 |
| Corporate income tax | 26 | 11 |
| Total progressive | 68 | 47 |
| Payroll taxes | 12 | 25 |
| Excise taxes | 13 | 5 |
| Deficits | 4 | 18 |
| Other | 3 | 5 |
| Total Regressive | 32 | 53 |
| Total | 100 | 100 |
| Total funds raised (billion) | 68.5 | 366 |

SOURCE: Statistical Abstracts of the United States, 1971 and 1980.

The principal share of the regressive taxes was made up by social security payroll taxes, which grew twelvefold between 1955 and 1976 and increased their share of revenue from 12 percent to 25 percent. The social security tax became the highest tax paid by about two-thirds of the country's income earners. Although it is a "direct" tax, the rates aren't progressive—average voters pay 7 percent of their income, while millionaires pay less than 1 percent. Deficits were the other major source of revenue. In the twenty years between 1945 and 1965 the government ran deficits in nine years and surpluses in eleven. The net surplus for these two decades was about $15 billion. In the following decade, the budget was in surplus in only one year and the net deficit for the period was over $150 billion. In 1976 deficits equaled 18 percent of tax receipts, compared to only 4 percent in 1955.

Deficits were regressive because the costs they imposed on the public weren't graduated according to income. Inflation or high interest rates hurt the poor as much as they hurt the rich; in fact, it can be argued that the rich were actually better off because of their superior ability to take advantage of the disturbances caused by deficits.

The progressiveness of the income tax itself was undermined by a complex labyrinth of deductions and allowances through which an increasing number of taxpayers were forced to find their way: in 1952, 28 percent of taxable returns contained itemized deductions, while by 1970 the proportion was up to 60 percent. The tax code became a document over 1000 pages long and H&R Block offices opened in every neighborhood, like so many McDonald outlets. This proliferation of deductions, exemptions, and exclusions favored the rich. Deductions are regressive not only because every dollar off the gross is worth more to someone in a high tax bracket, but also because, in the words of Professor Page, "more is spent on deductible items by high income people than low income people."[19] Joseph Pechman, one of the nation's leading tax experts, has estimated that deductions reduce the tax rates of high-income individuals by 18 percent—more than a quarter of their scheduled tax rates.[20] This "Swiss cheese" tax system, according to IRS estimates, allows nearly 16 percent of the top decile of the population to be taxed at a lower rate than the mean tax rate of the bottom decile.[21]

Progressive direct taxation fared even worse in Europe than in the United States. By 1975 the ratio of taxes on income and profits to total government revenue was down to 44 percent in the U.K., 34 percent in Germany, 21 percent in Italy, and 17 percent in France. The principal substitutes for income taxes in the Old World were value-added taxes (VAT)—a modern strain of the regressive consumption taxes that the populists had fought against. In 1975 VAT and other sales taxes accounted for 25 percent of government revenue in the U.K., 26 percent in Germany, 28 percent in Italy, and 33 percent in France. (The other regressive component of taxation was, as in the U.S., made up of payroll and social security dues imposed proportionally rather than progressively on earnings.)

To some extent, this return to regressivity was inevitable as the U.S. government's appetite for funds grew by 366 percent between 1955 and 1976. In theory, a large proportion of the increase could have been financed out of the taxes paid by the well-to-do. But, in practice, it is virtually impossible to enforce an effective marginal tax rate of, say, 70 percent; the resistance from the rich is simply too great and the revenue burden inevitably gets passed down to lower income earners.

The higher the nominal tax rates on the rich, moreover, the greater is their incentive to invest in lobbying for loopholes. As spending entered the failure zone, lobbies for the rich spared no expense to protect their incomes. A study of organizations focused on tax policy shows that in the early eighties, the budgets of conservative groups were twenty-two times larger than those of liberal groups. Groups dedicated to reducing corporate taxes—the U.S. Chamber of Commerce's Tax Policy Committee, the National Association of Manufacturers, the American Business Conference, and the Tax Foundation, for example—spent over $4 million on questions of tax policy whereas liberal organizations—such as Citizens for Tax Justice and the Public Citizens Tax Reform group—spent only $365,000.[22]

The rich also spent heavily on tax lawyers and accountants to thwart the implementation of progressive tax laws. As Benjamin Page writes:

Just as the bar in England for centuries preserved the aristocracy's power to tie up land, so American tax lawyers seem to be able to invent new tax shelters, find new ways to take depreciation allowances and capital gains, no matter what Congress does. . . .

If Uncle Sam tries to capture some of the profits made by U.S. multinationals abroad, judicious shifting of gains from one subsidiary to another, or persuasion of foreign governments to assess "taxes" rather than royalties, may keep the tax collector at bay.[23]

Yet all the slippage into regressivity wasn't the inevitable consequence of high-income resistance to more taxes—politicians were willing accomplices. In countries with a strong Socialist establishment, like Sweden, politicians were in fact primarily responsible for undermining progressivity. Like the spillage of spending into the failure zone, the relapse into regressivity was the consequence of faith in economic theory, outdated political folklore, and free votes.

Deficit financing, for example, became popular because Keynesian economists convinced politicians that deficits (along with boosts in public spending) were useful in preventing recessions by keeping demand up; deficits were associated with Roosevelt's success; and politicians smelled a free vote—spend now (or cut taxes now) and let someone else take the odium of collecting later.

Deductions were spawned by similar beliefs. Economists would point to some far-reaching benefit that could be derived through a "targeted" tax break; and special breaks also fit with the political wisdom of the sort that Senator Russell Long (ex-chairman of the Senate Finance Committee) learned from his late Uncle Earl: "Don't tax you, don't tax me, tax the fellow behind that tree."[24] (The political costs of the fellow behind the tree, were, of course, to be disregarded.)

*Taxes: From Whom, and How?*

The economic argument for the indirect, VAT-type taxes that were imposed in Europe was that such levies were discretionary—an individual could choose not to buy certain goods and thus avoid the tax. Experts insisted that this discretionary element was desirable because it encouraged saving. Their pitch to politicians could be summarized as: "The economy is in a mess because the wretched plebeians don't save enough. Replacing income taxes with VAT gives workers more take-home-pay, but makes the automobiles and stereo sets they want to buy more expensive, so instead of consuming their income they will bank it instead. Besides, since indirect taxes are tagged on at the bottom of a sales receipt, they are virtually invisible and therefore politically painless."

## The Right's Frontal Attack on Progressivity

Liberals succumbed to the arguments for regressivity somewhat reluctantly, for it was against their basic ideology. Nevertheless and however gradually, they did cave in. This contributed to the conservative resurgence of the late seventies, which, because of the free-spending liberal policies, was perhaps inevitable (and even overdue). The rightists, however, see their victories in quite another light. They believe they have a stronger mandate to dismantle what remains of progressive taxation than to cut spending.

Unlike their spiritual progenitors of the nineteenth century, modern conservatives use the language of economic theory, not class interest, to justify their attacks on progressive taxation. For example, when President Reagan proposed a 30 percent income tax cut to Congress in 1981, he said:

Marching in lockstep with the whole program of reductions in spending is the equally important program of reduced tax rates. Both are essential if we are to have economic recovery. It is time to create new jobs, build and rebuild industry, and give the American people room to do what they do best. And that can only be done with a tax program which provides incentive to increase productivity for both workers and industry. . . .

Some will argue, I know, that reducing tax rates now will be inflationary. A solid body of economic experts does not agree. And certainly tax cuts adopted over the past three-fourths of a century indicate these experts are right. . . .[25]

Behind this facade of theory, however, was an unambiguously regressive proposal: 28 percent of the tax cuts would go to corporations, even though corporate taxes accounted for less than 10 percent of government revenue. Supply-side economics would thus reduce this percentage further, down to 8.4 percent by 1983. Moreover, as the president of the National Small Business Association complained, the business tax cut was skewed toward large corporations: "You have nearly 14 million businesses grossing under $2 million each and they employ about 58 percent of the workforce. They produce 43 percent of the gross national product—but they got only 25 percent to 33 percent of the total business tax cut."[26]

That portion of the tax cut intended for individuals was, as table 2.3 shows, skewed to favor the rich.

The less than 5 percent of voters who earned more than $47,500 per year would thus get more than half of the total dollar benefit of the individual tax cut. The tax cut for households with incomes of $10,000 a year would be worth $120, while the cut for the top 1 1/2 percent of households, with incomes over $80,000 a year, would be worth $15,250.[27] Ronald Reagan himself, it is estimated, saved over $40,000 on his 1983 taxes because of the tax cut.[28]

The regressiveness of these cuts was no accident. Influential

Table 2.3

*Distribution of the Proposed Tax Cuts*

| Income Bracket ($) | 0–11,500 | 11,500–22,900 | 22,900–47,500 | 47,500 & up |
|---|---|---|---|---|
| Tax Cut ($ billions) | 1.1 | 4.7 | 10.7 | 12 |

Source: Reprinted, by permission, from the *Wall Street Journal* 21 December 1981, p. 1.

figures within the administration like presidential counselor Edwin Meese believed that progressive income taxes were "immoral." Lowering the tax rates for the rich was, as David Stockman later revealed in an interview, a primary goal of the Kemp-Roth bill from which the President's plan was derived:

> The hard part of the supply side cut is dropping the top rate from 70 to 50 percent—the rest of it is a secondary matter. The original argument was that the top bracket was too high and that's having the most devastating effect on the economy. Then the general argument was that, in order to make this palatable as a political matter, you had to bring down all brackets. But, I mean, Kemp-Roth was always a Trojan horse to bring down the top rate.[29]

As time passed, tax policy continued along a regressive path. To overcome the widespread opposition to the tax cut, the President offered "ornaments," or regressive tax breaks, to corporate lobbyists. One such break was the safe harbor leasing provision that allowed money-losing enterprises to sell to other profitable entities the tax credits they had no use for. If a similar scheme were to be proposed for individuals—if, for example, the residents of New York's prosperous Fifth Avenue were allowed to buy the individual deductions of their less well-to-do neighbors who sleep on the benches of Central Park, the scheme would be laughed out of court. But conservative experts were willing to defend the safe harbor provisions as responsible economics.

Not long after the tax cuts became law, the original supply-side expectation that higher growth would pull in more revenues to compensate for the cut in rates lost all credibility. It became apparent that direct progressive taxes had been replaced by regressive deficits whose magnitude would more than triple in the course of the three-year tax cut.

The prospect of enormous deficits caused no small stir. Democrats in Congress such as House Majority leader James Wright seized the opportunity to point out that the President "who preaches so piously about deficits has produced the largest deficit in history."[30] Keynesian economist Professor Walter Heller wrote with barely concealed glee that "recoiling in horror from the trillion dollar debt of two years ago, Mr. Reagan is now presiding over a jump to $1.5 trillion by the end of his term. . . . In the messages unveiling his $200 billion a year deficits, one finds no word—not even a whisper—about a constitutional amendment for a balanced budget."[31] Even conservatives like Arthur Schlesinger, acting OMB Director and Energy Secretary in the Nixon Cabinet, referred to deficits as representing "the wreckage of the nation's fiscal structure inflicted by last summer's tax legislation."[32] But Mr. Reagan stood firm and threatened to veto any bills that tampered with his tax cut.

The Thatcher government's first budget, like the Reagan administration's opening fiscal program, was more exceptional for its frontal attack on direct progressive taxation than for major cuts in expenditure. In presenting his "opportunity budget" in June 1979, Chancellor of the Exchequer Sir Geoffrey Howe reminded members of Parliament: "We made it clear in our manifesto that we intended to switch some of the tax burden from taxes on earnings to taxes on spending. This is the only way that we can restore incentives and make it more worthwhile to work."[33]

Consequently he announced a $9 billion cut in income taxes and a compensating $9.4 billion increase in value-added taxes. Said the chancellor:

I fully realize that this increase in Value Added Tax will result in a rise in prices —in fact a rise of about 3 1/2% in the Retail Price Index. . . . But there never will be a time when it is easy to effect the switch from direct to indirect taxes and the present moment is no exception. This much-needed reform has been postponed too long already.[34]

Although less so than Mr. Reagan's cuts, Mr. Howe's income-tax reductions were also skewed toward the rich. Individuals in the top brackets, of $60,000 and up, could expect to see the amount of their total income taken in taxes reduced by over 40 percent, while the percentage benefit for low- and middle-income individuals was less than half this proportion. Mr.

Howe justified the regressive distribution of the cuts on the grounds that the high income earners were "people upon whom so many of our hopes for initiative, greater enterprise and national prosperity must depend." Progressivity, he continued, dampened their morale: "We have, over the years, spent too much time and effort trying to 'level down.' This is no good to anybody. It is much more important to have a successful and prosperous society. And we cannot have a successful and prosperous society without successful and prosperous individuals."[35]

The budget was, predictably, well received in certain quarters. Sir John Methven, Director General of the Confederation of British Industry, said: "The new chancellor has put together a package which will help Britain back on its feet again by restoring incentives all the way from the shop floor to the boardroom. He has made it worthwhile to work harder."[36] The Institute of Directors was pleased that the government "was attacking our penal tax rates as the only way of increasing national productivity."[37] It hoped the top rates would soon be further cut.

James Callaghan, leader of the opposition, was less sanguine about the switch to indirect taxation and called it "a reckless gamble" with Britain's economic future. It was "almost equivalent to the man who robs the gas meter in order to put money on a horse he is not sure is going to run and he has seen fail on previous outings." The Labour leader's own bet was that because VAT would increase prices, for most low- and middle-income earners, "these tax cuts are going to be eaten by inflation in the next few months."[38]

## Neo-Liberal Regressivity

If the current conservative wave subsides, can we expect liberals to reinstate the principle of progressivity? Not likely. Liberals have strayed far from their early progressive roots; it was in their heyday that complex regressive deductions were instituted for supposed political advantage, and it was the Socialists in Europe who pioneered supply-side tax experiments, slashing corporate taxes in the hope of stimulating investment. Mr. Reagan's "radical" proposals in 1981 to allow businesses to depreciate plants over ten years, machinery over five, and buildings over three pale in comparison to the depreciation schemes invented many years ago by liberal European governments that allow several categories of investment to be written off entirely in a single year. A Labour government in the U.K. once even toyed with a scheme for a 150 percent depreciation allowance for new investment!

Indeed there is a very good correlation (as table 2.4 shows) between low corporate contribution to state revenue and prolonged governance by parties of Socialist persuasion in countries like Sweden, Austria, Denmark, and the U.K. And liberal governments in Europe have long overcome their traditional ideological distaste for consumption taxes—Socialist regimes in Continental Europe relied extensively on VAT long before Mrs. Thatcher's government espoused their cause in the British Isles.

The diehard spenders like Olaf Palme of Sweden and François Mitterand of France, who have bucked the conservative wave, have used a variety of regressive revenues to finance

Table 2.4
*Percentage of Total Taxes (1977)*

|  | Taxes on goods and services | Corporate income taxes |
|---|---|---|
| Norway | 38.6 | 5.05 |
| Denmark | 35.1 | 3.10 |
| Finland | 34.4 | 4.18 |
| Austria | 32.4 | 3.37 |
| France | 29.9 | 5.58 |
| Italy | 27.0 | 6.34 |
| Germany | 23.5 | 5.48 |
| U.K. | 24.0 | 6.86 |
| Japan | 15.0 | 16.02 |
| U.S. | 15.0 | 11.54 |

SOURCE: Adapted from Revenue Statistics of OECD Member Countries, 1965–1978, Paris, 1979.

their growing expenditures—higher general VAT rates, special increases in the rate for alcohol and cigarettes, increases in payroll and social security taxes, and, of course, higher deficits. M. Mitterand's government pushed the budget deficit in France from Fr 24 billion in 1980 to Fr 100 billion in 1982, and Mr. Palme's in Sweden from SKr 76 billion in 1982 to over SKr 90 billion in 1983. From the numbers, therefore, M. Mitterand's and Mr. Palme's tax policies are practically indistinguishable from Mr. Reagan's—the middle classes and the poor paid for expenditure growth in all three countries.

If there is a difference, it is that Socialists like M. Mitterand don't mean to let off the rich. His government did propose a modest wealth tax from which it expected to raise about $1 billion a year out of the privately held wealth of the rich, estimated to be approximately $1500 billion. But when the time came to enact the proposal into law, the "revolutionary tax" became a damp squib, not because the new government lacked a sufficient majority in the National Assembly or felt constrained by public opinion, but because Socialist ministers let their cultural sensibilities and economic arguments cloud their political judgment. *The Economist* reports how the tax, which was "heralded as a first move to redistribute wealth in France," withered away:

The first exception was made for owners of companies who complained that the tax would be an intolerable burden. A personal intervention by President Mitterand, a culture buff, reprieved art owners. The government then agreed to virtually exempt farmers, including those who rent out their land, and owners of forests and woods. Finally the champagne, cognac and fine wine makers were exempt because, it was explained, they have to keep large amounts of wine and and spirits in stock while it is aging.

Leftists complain that the tax has been spiked as a social weapon. One ironic socialist suggested to the opposition conservatives that they could get away with the catch-all amendment reading: "Exempted shall be chateaux classified as historical monuments with cellars crammed with rare spirits and noble wines, walls draped with masterpieces and with the yacht anchored in the moat."[39]

The irony of this episode is that the objects of Socialist magnanimity had been overwhelmingly in favor of President Giscard in the presidential campaign of 1981 and their efforts later helped rout the Left in local elections of 1983. So much for going after the votes. . . .

In the U.S., the neo-liberal infatuation with VAT is on the increase. Talk about replacing income taxes with consumption taxes started with President Nixon, but the first concrete steps were taken by Democrats. In 1979 Democrats Al Ullman, chairman of the House Ways and Means Committee, and Russell Long, chairman of the Senate Finance Committee, initiated a set of proposals that would reduce direct taxes for individuals and corporations by $130 billion and recover the revenue through a form of VAT.

This was noted in the *New York Times* as quite a switch for liberal Democrats, who "shy away from a consumption tax on the ground that it is 'regressive,' that it takes a bigger percentage bite from a poor family's resources than from a rich family's." The *Times* continued that the very consideration of VAT, "in the face of this deeply felt objection, reflects a new feeling in Congress that Americans need fresh incentives to work, save, invest and take entrepreneurial risks."[40]

Mr. Ullman, a twelve-term Democrat, lost his seat in the House in the 1980 election after opponents made his sponsorship of VAT an election issue. VAT thereafter came to be known as the Al Ullman Memorial Tax on Capitol Hill.[41] But it hasn't been forsaken by all liberals. In 1982 the "consumption tax is good economics" thesis was being dusted off again by presidential aspirant Senator Gary Hart, who called the income tax "basically flawed" and proposed a substitute sales tax, which he claimed was "really true supply side economics, because it would immediately reward savings."[42]

## Regressivity Still Doesn't Pay

Whatever its economic merits (which will be examined in the last section of this chapter), regressivity makes no more political sense in a democracy now than it did a century ago. Take personal allowances: it is true, as poll after poll has shown, that voters are quite attached to their deductions and are most reluctant to surrender them. Nevertheless, deductions cannot win free votes, for as *The Economist* has observed, they get you "stuck in a vicious circle of penal tax rates which are then made less punitive by a succession of tax reliefs, which then lower the tax 'take' and so ensure that rates have to be kept high."[43]

The complexity of deductions that we have today also leads to voter resentment because, as Treasury Secretary Regan has observed, "it is only the well-to-do who can afford the lawyers and accountants needed to really pore over the whole matrix."[44] Consequently, as a Louis Harris poll found in 1983, 86 percent of Americans agree with the proposition that: "while most lower and middle-income people now pay their federal tax by taking standard deductions, most higher income people get out of paying much of their taxes by having clever tax accountants and lawyers who show them how to use loopholes in the tax law."[45]

Tax breaks given to corporations to stimulate investment also have high financial and political costs. These "tax expenditures" cost the U.S. government $38 billion in 1979. In the U.K., whose economy is less than a fourth that of the United States's, the corporate giveaways were worth $34 billion in the same year.[46] If the same sums had been applied to individuals instead, a staggering number of voting taxpayers would have benefited. In the United States about 70 percent of households could have been spared from paying federal income taxes altogether; in the United Kingdom, over 90 percent of British taxpayers would have been relieved of their tax burden.

Regressive consumption taxes are politically tempting because they are considered invisible—they are tucked away at the bottom of a sales slip, and the voter doesn't have to endure the annual ritual of computing and filing them. But actually consumption taxes aren't as painless as they are made out to be. Voters may or may not see a sales tax on their purchases but are certainly aware of changes in the prices of the goods they buy and are unhappy about increases in the cost of living that consumption taxes lead to. When inflation rose to 20 percent soon after the Thatcher government's "opportunity budget," the public wasn't thrilled (even if some voters may not have been aware of the contribution higher VAT had made to this rate).

Higher VAT also leads to painful second-order effects: as the opposition leader Mr. Callaghan had predicted, the 20 percent inflation rate pushed voters into higher tax brackets, and, except for the very rich who did see a real reduction in their tax burden, the average income-tax burden actually rose. Then, to reduce high inflation, Mrs. Thatcher was forced to apply such a tight money policy that nearly a fifth of British industry was put out of commission. So the principal "opportunity" that Mr. Howe's tax switch created was for bankruptcy receivers.

Cuts in direct progressive taxes that get made up by higher deficits are unpopular. When he took office, Jimmy Carter was determined to cut the prevailing 12.8 percent "misery index" by a program of stimulatory tax and spending increases. He proposed and Congress passed $31 billion worth of tax cuts in 1977 and $18 billion in 1978. White House advisers, writes his Treasury Secretary W. Michael Blumenthal, "had projected the computer runs to show how it would all come together. The economy would grow, while youth and urban unemployment declined—without inflation."[47]

The free lunch predicted by the econometric models failed to materialize. As the deficit produced by the tax cuts was financed by printing money, unemployment did temporarily decline, but Mr. Carter's reelection campaign was haunted by a 50 percent rise in the misery index, for inflation more than doubled. It is probably safe to conclude that Mr. Carter's tax cuts didn't win him many votes in 1980, even if he did list them as an important achievement in the campaign.

The Reagan supply-side deficit was financed through selling government bonds rather than by printing money, so its consequence was recession instead of inflation. But it was pain nonetheless, and more universal than the 10 percent rate of unemployment that was reached in the first full year of the tax

cut would indicate. An ABC-*Washington Post* poll of regis-
tered voters showed that 20 percent of households contained
at least one person who had lost a job; 16 percent of households
had at least one person who had taken a lower-paying job; and
19 percent had at least one person whose hours had been short-
ened.[48] In November 1982 the conservative swing in Congress
was abruptly arrested and Republicans suffered a net loss of
twenty-six seats in the House as well as surprise losses of numerous governorships and state houses. The fact that the deficits were caused by tax cuts skewed toward the rich didn't go
unnoticed either. By March 1983 an astounding 70 percent of
voters surveyed by *Time* agreed that "the President represents the rich rather than the average American."[49]

## Some Good Ideas

Fortunately, because the fears of the public and of Wall Street
about the deficit have forced lawmakers to look for more
sources of revenue, there is hope for a more progressive tax
policy. Although President Reagan was initially against any
new taxes to close the deficit (and when pressed favored only
regressive levies), he did support, in the summer of 1982, clos-
ing loopholes in corporate taxes worth $100 billion.

In Congress, where sensitivity to deficits seemed higher,
there was some willingness to take on "sacred" personal loopholes. One option being considered in early 1983 was to limit
the nonbusiness interest deductions individuals could take on
mortgages, car loans, and the like to $10,000 per year. Other
options included repealing tax credits for energy-conservation
improvements, increasing taxes on gains of home sales, and
lengthening the depreciation period for rental buildings.[50]

Outside the U.S at least one conservative leader openly endorsed increasing progressive taxes to reduce deficits. Chris-
tian Democratic Union (CDU) leader Helmut Kohl campaigned for chancellorship of Germany in February 1983

asking for reduced government welfare spending and, in spite of the opposition of his more liberal Free Democrat coalition partners, for a 5 percent income-tax surcharge for people earning more than $21,000 annually. (The CDU/Christian Socialist Union [CSU] won handsomely.)

Actually, it is not even necessary to raise tax rates for the rich in order to achieve a more progressive tax structure—elimination of loopholes would probably do the trick. And, if it is impossible to eliminate the loopholes overnight, they can at least be forced to progressively wither away. For example, in 1974, the Labour government in the U.K. limited tax relief on interest payments to mortgages under £25,000. The limit met with little opposition since it affected fewer than 2 percent of all mortgagors. By 1983 inflation had whittled down the real value of £25,000 to £8,000 so the loophole was practically closed. (In the 1983 budget, however, the Conservatives proposed raising the limit for the potential benefit of less than 4 percent of high-income voters.)[51]

Another avenue toward the restoration of progressivity lies in the redefinition of income to include more benefits and perks. For instance, most health insurance in the U.S. today is provided to employees as a fringe benefit. The premiums are treated as a tax-deductible expense for the employer but not as taxable income for the employee. According to Professor Martin Feldstein, chairman of the President's council of economic advisers, this subsidy is regressive because the largest benefits go to high-income families. It also cost the Treasury approximately $26.5 billion in 1983.[52]

It should be remembered, however, that restoration of progressivity by itself cannot be the answer to these unsettled political climes. In the failure zone, reduction of the overall tax burden is more important than its redistribution. But since real tax reductions require real, painful spending cuts, progressive distribution of the benefits of these cuts—higher after-tax incomes—can help rally the largest number of voters to the cause of austerity. Otherwise, spending cuts will be rightfully regarded as a device to help the rich. A populist taxation policy is the loyal handmaiden of a populistic spending policy.

# Taxes: From Whom, and How?

## Progressivity and Economics

But is good politics—maintaining a progressive tax policy—also good economics? Elitist economic theorists hold that we are all better off in the long run by being lenient toward the rich, because their entrepreneurship and investment are the fountainhead of economic prosperity. Progressivity, they claim, trades away long-term efficiency for short-term equity and "political" gains.

The claim is backed by little substance. It is undoubtedly true that high spending and taxes hurt individual initiative—high taxation can dampen an individual's incentive to hustle for the extra buck, since he is left with pennies for his pains. What is dubious is the assertion that the disincentives for the rich are the most debilitating. Actually, a regressive partiality toward elites is fundamentally at odds with the nature of a modern industrial economy. We don't live as the Romans did, off the tribute exacted by a few heroic warriors; a modern economy is a vast cooperative endeavor, by the people, for the people, and of the people. Only a progressive taxation system is consistent with its thoroughly plebeian character.

Ours is a mass-market economy. The health of the automobile industry depends upon the demand for Chevys, Mustangs, Toyotas, and Volkswagens, not on the Rolls-Royces and Lamborghinis that millionaires buy. The personal computer revolution is with us because Apple took its magic to Everyman. Underpinning the Nipponese conquest of the world electronics consumer goods industry has been the voracious and seemingly insatiable appetite of the average Japanese for TV sets, stereos, and videocassette recorders, a demand all out of proportion to income. (For every $1000 of national income in 1970, the Japanese bought 600 percent more TV sets than the Germans and 200 percent more than the Americans.)[53]

Progressivity minimizes the number of individuals who are taxed, bears down least heavily on the buyers of Chevrolets and most heavily on Rolls-Royce owners, and thus protects the breadth and depth of the mass market. Regressive taxes constrict mass consumption either by increasing the purchase prices of goods or by reducing the incomes of the middle and poor classes. Progressivity is good for McDonalds, the TV set in every living room, and the six-pack; regressivity is good for the business of chic French restaurants, opera, and champagne.

Ours is also a mass-production economy, in which the cost and productivity of the common man's labors are critical. Chrysler, Ford, and General Motors are (or were) in varying stages of crisis not because their top executives are denied the same incentives as Toyota's or Nissan's, but because their blue- and white-collar workforces are more expensive and less productive. I am not suggesting that the roles of the individuals at the top are not important or that risk takers aren't essential, but rather that plebeian motivation seems to be more of an endangered species and therefore in greater need of protection. Even with steeply graduated income taxes, An Wang (of Wang Labs), Ken Olsen (of DEC), Steven Jobs (of Apple), Howard Head (of Head rackets and skis), and Bob Hewlett and David Packard (of HP) appear to have done all right by themselves, and their firms have grown like gangbusters. It is the blue-collar workers—and industries whose success depends on the quality and cost of their labor—that seem to be in the most trouble.

Progressivity looks after the interest of John Doe, machinist, bricklayer, plumber, and bookkeeper. It lets him keep all or most of his income so that he doesn't have to agitate for higher wages to stay even with taxes; isn't disgruntled because he seems to be working to fill Uncle Sam's pockets; and doesn't take the day off because the after-tax loss of wages is so negligible. In the process of looking after many John Does, however, progressivity does have an adverse effect on the motivation of a few Steven Jobses. Regressivity implicitly plumps for the opposite choice—an elitist tax system holds it to be more important to reward the rich even if this means that the common folk are faced with higher inflation, a greater risk of unemployment, or lower take-home pay.

The many schemes to improve economic performance by

redistributing the tax burden away from the rich have been major disappointments. Either the elites don't respond as intended or there are unforeseen side effects.

Take the Reagan choice of higher deficits in order to achieve lower income taxes for the rich. The supply-side justification as provided by George Gilder was that the effect of "taxation with rates so progressive—graduated so steeply to capture increasing portions of larger incomes"—had been to smother "capitalist ferment and creativity," and a significant cut in the top marginal tax rate was imperative.[54]

We never will know how much entrepreneurial activity was unleashed among the taxpayers in the top tax brackets. But we do have on record what federal deficits, swollen by the tax cuts, did—they sucked away the funds needed for productive investment. According to preliminary estimates,[55] in 1982 households saved about $130 billion, corporate savings and retained earnings were $33 billion, and state and local government surpluses were $36 billion for a total of $199 billion that could have been used for private investment. But the federal deficit absorbed about $140 billion, or 70 percent, of the savings pool. Private borrowers competing for the remaining $60 billion drove up interest rates to astronomical levels and caused fixed investment and research and development spending to fall steeply. The tax cut did indeed lead to capitalist ferment —for more capital.

President Reagan's continued refusal to allow any tampering with his tax cuts to reduce deficits had a negative psychological influence on the financial markets. The persistence of high real interest rates in 1983, said Professor Feldstein, "stems mainly from widespread concern that very large budget deficits may continue for many years to come. If the government continues to borrow 5 or 6 percent of the gross national product to finance its budget deficits, the real interest rate must remain high in order to squeeze private borrowers down to the limited amount of funds that remain."[56]

The Thatcher policy of creating incentives to work and save by substituting VAT for direct income taxes didn't produce the advertised benefits either. A Gallup poll conducted in March 1980 showed that: "The large income-tax cuts in last June's budget have had only a limited impact on the public's attitude to work so far . . . Only 14 percent of those interviewed say the cuts encouraged them to work more hours. Some 6 percent say they are going to work fewer hours to earn the same money. More than three quarters say the cuts made no difference."[57]

The program didn't boost saving either. Tory economists had claimed that individuals who received larger pay packets (because of lower income taxes) wouldn't spend it away as they would be discouraged by the higher VAT rates. In fact, average Britons went on a shopping spree because the government failed to provide them with much of a positive incentive to save (an issue we will discuss in the next chapter). The savings rate dropped as the economy experienced a most peculiar kind of recession: during 1979 and 1980 manufacturing production fell by 14.8 percent and the construction industry's output was down by 13.6 percent, but consumer spending rose by 4 percent.

Tax incentives to corporations have produced disappointing results. The larger, more sophisticated corporations have been quick to squeeze every last benefit out of the investment incentives, but that has only made the capital shortage worse for the smaller firms that lack the necessary strike force of lawyers and accountants. Furthermore, since most tax breaks have been linked to fixed investment, the incentives have distorted the relationship between the cost of labor and capital—a new machine is subsidized by Uncle Sam but hiring another worker is not. This might make sense if capital was abundant and labor scarce, but it's absurd when unemployment is running over 10 percent. The distortions caused in the capital markets are even worse when tax breaks are "targeted" and expert whims (and corporate lobbyists) determine which industry is favored over another.

It is interesting to note that while regressive taxation schemes are catching on in the West, the successful economies of the East have been supporting sensible spending policies with progressive tax policies. The top marginal tax rate in Japan, for example, is 75 percent (compared to 50 percent in the U.S.), and corporate taxes as a percentage of revenue are the highest of any developed country. Taiwan, which has traditionally depended on indirect "commodity" taxes, has an explicit policy to make its tax system more progressive. Top marginal tax rates are higher than in the U.S. and since the 1960s the government has never deviated from a policy of balanced budgets. The government of Singapore has also been fanatical about balanced budgets (the first act of the Lee Kuan Yew government when it came to power was to raise taxes to avoid a deficit), and, being a free port and tourist shopping center, it levies almost no consumption taxes.

Progressivity won't cure the great problem of failure-zone spending—our greatest hopes must lie in reducing the government's total revenue needs, which will increase purchasing power and incentive for both rich and poor. But with high spending or low, some oxen will be gored. Steadfast adherence to progressive taxation ensures there are no wild-eyed sacrifices and that the motivation of the majority is protected to the utmost.

# CHAPTER 3

# *Monetary Policy:*
# *Chasing Shadows*

MONETARY POLICY has come to the top of the national economic agenda, because as with supply-side tax cuts and VAT, politicians and economists see in it a cure for the problem of excessive spending. So the Federal Reserve Board, whose independence is protected by law, has received intense scrutiny and advice from the White House, Congress, and freelance guardians of the public interest. If the Fed could get it right, its counselors have believed, inflation would be licked and the economy could be restored to a path of steady growth.

In February 1981 Mr. Reagan staked out his position in his first address to Congress:

Our plan requires a national monetary policy which does not allow money growth to increase consistently faster than the growth of goods and services. In order to curb inflation, we need to slow the growth in our money supply. . . . A successful program to achieve stable and moderate growth patterns in money supply will keep both inflation and interest rates down and restore vigor to our financial institutions and markets.[1]

## Monetary Policy: Chasing Shadows

With this apparently innocuous statement, the President threw his weight behind a historic change in the Federal Reserve's policy that had occurred in October 1979. Until then the Fed had focused primarily on interest rates and paid little attention to the growth of money supply; if it wanted to stimulate a slack economy, the Fed would aim for lower interest rates, and if it wanted to step on the brakes, it would push rates higher.

Monetarists had long criticized the Fed for its preoccupation with interest rates—the pace of economic activity, they claimed, was far more effectively controlled by managing the growth of money supply. Testifying before the Joint Economic Committee of Congress in May 1959, Milton Friedman had said:

the urgent need, I believe—and here I am venturing furthest from any academic ivory tower—is to keep monetary changes from being a destabilizing force, as they have been through much of our history. In my view, this can be done by assigning the monetary authorities the task of keeping the stock of money growing at a regular rate, month in and month out.[2]

Focusing on interest rates, monetarists argued, lead to uncontrollable increases in the money supply and therefore, to inflation.

Professor Friedman's had been a voice in the wilderness for decades until October 1979, when his direst prophesies seemed to be coming true. The Fed then announced that it would concentrate on controlling money supply and disregard changes in interest rates. Fed Chairman Paul Volcker explained:

What persuaded me was the need to somehow get a grip on the situation, and on psychology, and this seemed to me a way to do it.

We had taken some tightening moves in August through September that didn't seem to make much of an impact. So I thought, how can we change the approach a little bit here to get people's attention!

One of the things we did anticipate—that it would inject more instability into the market in the short run—was not considered altogether undesirable at that point. A little more uncertainty, we thought, might have favorable effects on psychology and behavior, speculative behavior in particular.[3]

And now in February 1981, the President was endorsing the Fed's monetarist conversion—never mind how high interest rates get, the administration was implying, get money supply under control and inflation out of the system.

Mr. Reagan's supply-side friends who did not like the idea of controlling either interest rates or money supply but favored a return to the gold standard instead were upset. "Paul Volcker cannot control monetary growth, and neither can Ronald Reagan," said prominent supply-side theorist Jude Wanniski. "You have to fight inflationary expectations by bringing Fort Knox into the battle." If the U.S. announced a return to the gold standard, interest rates, which had been raised by expectations of high inflation, would plummet immediately. "All you would have to do," Mr. Wanniski continued, "is have a public flogging of Beryl Sprinkel [at that time the leading monetarist in the administration]."[4] Failure to adopt the right monetary policy (that is, the gold standard) would jeopardize the benefits of the tax cut. "If spending cuts are 1 and tax cuts are 10, then monetary policy is 100," said Professor Laffer.[5]

In any event, although Mr. Reagan was sympathetic to the notion of a gold standard, he did not make it his major priority —too much was already happening because of the Fed's experiment with money supply targets. Inflation had fallen at a totally unexpected rate—from a roaring 18 percent to under 5 percent in less than three years. Unfortunately, the depth of the recession that the tight money policy had induced was also wholly unanticipated. The economy was thrown into reverse gear as consumers stopped buying and businesses cut output and laid off workers. Real interest rates, as Chancellor Helmut Schmidt of Germany put it, reached their highest levels since the birth of Christ. The national cost of disinflation—in lost profits and jobs—was estimated at $700 billion, or $3000 for every American.[6]

Republicans who had been promising an unprecedented boom took out their frustrations on the Fed, blaming it for a variety of errors. In February 1982, for example, Representative Jack Kemp criticized the Fed for keeping money too tight and insisted that "the President has to try to persuade Volcker to change, or he must ask for his resignation."[7] On the other hand, some stern monetarist officials and even the President said that the Fed was not restricting the money supply enough. Treasury Secretary Donald Regan blamed the Fed for the "volatility" in money supply and urged it to redefine the monetary base so that money supply would grow more "smoothly."[8] The "pragmatists" within the administration—the chairman of the Council of Economic Advisers Murray Weidenbaum, Chief of White House Staff James Baker, and Presidential counselor Edwin Meese—made unpublicized visits to Fed Chairman Volcker, asking him to ease up on the money supply.[9]

In Congress a rush of new legislation was introduced to curtail the independence of the Fed. Republican Senator Larry Pressler introduced a bill that would add congressional watchdogs to the Fed Board of Governors as ex-officio members. Democratic Senator John Melcher was pushing a resolution that would, in effect, order the Fed to lower the discount rate. Senate Democratic leader Robert Byrd offered a bill that would require the Fed to maintain real short-term interest rates at "historic" levels. The chairman of the House banking subcommittee on housing, Henry Gonzalez, introduced a bill of impeachment against Fed Chairman Volcker.[10]

In July 1982, faced with the prospect of an even deeper recession and pressure from the administration and Congress, the Fed blinked. It decided to go back to paying more attention to interest rates (that is, to seek lower rates) and be less rigid about money supply targets (that is, to permit faster growth). As usual there were mixed reactions in the administration—the Secretary of State, the chairman of the Council of Economic Advisers, and the Treasury Secretary were pleased, while the monetarists like Sprinkel made no secret of their unhappiness.

In countries where the monetary authorities don't enjoy the legal independence of the Fed, political leaders intervene even more vigorously. Conservatives in the U.K. had pledged before the 1979 election to give the Bank of England (the British equivalent of the Fed) "a more independent role." Bank officials were, however, less committed to monetarism than the Thatcher government and opposed Cabinet decisions on money supply targets. Relations between Mrs. Thatcher and Gordon Richardson, the governor of the bank, were soon strained. Sir Geoffrey Howe, Chancellor of the Exchequer, suggested sacking Mr. Richardson, but the prime minister took a different line. "It says on the plate outside my front door that I'm First Lord of the Treasury," she declared. "So Richardson must do what I say."[11]

Mrs. Thatcher did indeed succeed in wresting control of monetary policy. As the *Financial Times* wrote three years later:

> Overall, although her trappings may be as splendid as ever, the customary air of intellectual hauteur just as grand, the Old Lady [referring to the Bank of England] has been dislodged from her pedestal.
> Under a Prime Minister who likes to underline that she is First Lord of the Treasury as well, the Bank has come under a particular kind of personal domination from "the other end of town." There are those close to Mrs. Thatcher who say, with a touch of glee, that the interest rate and exchange rate policies which the Bank puts into effect are determined directly in Downing Street.[12]

## The Political Coin

Ardent supply-side bullionists and Chicago monetarists are often motivated to prove that their pet theories work. But when presidents, prime ministers, and chancellors who are required to face reelection as well as run their nation's affairs seek to wrest control of monetary policy from an independent Federal Reserve, Bank of England, or Bundesbank, politics is not far from their minds. The chairman of the Federal Reserve is deemed to have immense power—when "leaders in 30 fields" were asked, in 1982, to rank the most influential men and women in America, Paul Volcker ranked second after President Reagan.[13] Surely, it is presumed, such power can win or lose votes.

Conventional political wisdom has it that easy money— ample credit and low interest rates—wins elections. Presidents have been known to try to twist the Fed's arm to bring about such conditions just before an election. For example, in 1969 the Fed had embarked on a tight money policy, which caused the unemployment rate to nearly double. Business failures increased too, including the largest bankruptcy in business history, that of the Penn Central Railroad. President Nixon thereupon lobbied hard to get the Fed to relax its policies. As Professor Friedman tells it:

The threshold at which Nixon could rise above principle was very, very low. In the summer of 1971, before wage and price controls, I had a conversation with him. He was trying to get me to press Arthur Burns [chairman of the Federal Reserve] to increase the money supply more. I objected that that would be a bad policy because it would produce inflation. My recollection is that what I said was that there's no point in getting elected by means of making the country ungovernable after the election. Inflation now might help you get elected, but it would leave you with a situation after the election when it will not be worth having been elected. I recall Nixon having said, "Well, let's first get re-elected." That was typical.[14]

In any event, President Nixon did convince Mr. Burns. The Fed chairman duly told corporate leaders at a White House dinner that he would not let the economy collapse and quickly allowed money supply growth to double. And, as Professor Edward Tufte has demonstrated in *Political Control of the Economy,* the 1972 events were not special—the Fed *always* increases the money supply just before a presidential election.[15]

In 1982 it was politics too that sent Republicans scurrying off in all directions away from the tight money policies of the Fed. "Interest rates are the issue out in the Republican grass roots," said one top White House strategist before the November election, noting that the largest screams were coming from Mr. Reagan's core constituency of farmers and small business owners.[16]


## Leaving Well Enough Alone

But is it worth all that trouble—are there really great political dividends to be gained by arrogating the powers of Fed? Facts and logic suggest otherwise; unlike spending or taxes, monetary policy contains no vote-getting payoffs. Playing with monetary policy is, at best, a waste of time.

Consider the belief that easy money is a source of free votes. The theory is that a government can contrive an artificial boom before an election and deal with the inflationary consequences afterward. In fact, this is an impractical ploy. Today financial markets are in such a flux that the best economists are incapable of managing the fine timing that such a strategy demands. They don't really know how quickly an illusory boom can be induced by loosening monetary policy; nor can they accurately predict when the inflationary aftermath will materialize.

The unpredictability of the speed and extent of changes caused by altering monetary policies is illustrated by events of 1980, the final year of the Carter administration. In March the administration decided, as a stern, anti-inflationary measure, to clamp down on consumer credit. This induced, according to Chairman Volcker, an unexpectedly sharp reaction: "The economy had this abrupt fall and the money supply fell very rapidly with it. . . . Consumers suddenly thought they'd better not use their credit cards or consumer credit at all. But they had bills to pay, and so they drew down their cash balances. So you had this wild decline in the money supply for six weeks or so."[17]

The sharpness of the economic decline led to the credit controls being dismantled ten weeks after they had been imposed, for the presidential election was not six months away. Again, the economy's reaction caught the administration and the Fed by surprise. "It [the money supply] began bouncing back," says Mr. Volcker, "which we didn't mind for a month or two because it was just offsetting the decline. What we did not judge, we nor anybody else, was that the economic decline itself was going to be so short-lived."[18] The Fed's expectation that money supply growth would slow was belied, and the prime rate, which had come down to 11 percent by August (from nearly 20 percent in April), shot back up to 21.5 percent in December.

Could Mr. Carter have "managed" the preelection economy better if he had more prescient advisers? Unfortunately, no. As some distinguished economists admit, they can't make reliable predictions any more (for reasons that we will see in the last section of this chapter). To quote Professor James Duesenberry, former chairman of the President's Council of Economic Advisers: "Everywhere I go, these corporate and banking types are always asking me, 'What are interest rates going to do? What are interest rates going to do?' How the hell should I know what interest rates are going to do? The fact is *nobody* knows what interest rates are going to do."[19]

Experts who do venture to look into crystal balls rarely agree. For example, in the spring of 1983 when the Fed had relaxed its policy and interest rates had begun to decline, some advisers were urging the President to press Mr. Volcker for even more rapid growth so that the Republicans could enjoy the fruits of a robust economy in the 1984 election. Walter Wriston, chairman of Citicorp, was, on the other hand, warning his friend Mr. Reagan that the recovery was liable to peak too soon and that the President should press for a short spike in interest rates to prevent that. How was Mr. Reagan to know whose advice was politically more astute?

Politicians who try the preelection easy-money gambit are wasting their time chasing a free-vote myth, gambling in a game with highly unpredictable results. The sensible course is to leave well enough alone, downplay the importance of monetary policy, and not get into the hair of independent experts appointed to do the job. Monetary officials are usually competent, have a difficult job to perform, and it makes as little sense for a vote-seeking politician to badger them about the money supply as it does for a businessman to tell his plumber about how to fix his water supply.

Delegation is the better part of valor in nonelection years as well. For a politician to get involved in the choice between interest-rate targets and money-supply targets, or in how the Fed should define its monetary base, is a waste of time. The issues are highly technical and arcane, and it is impossible to figure out where the majority voter interest lies. How can a politician tell what difference it makes to the average voter if the Fed sets contemporaneous reserve or lagged reserve requirements?

Even the votes of university professors who have an emotional or intellectual stake in policies of their choice are difficult to come by. One would think, for example, that the recent trend toward monetarism would have made Professor Friedman happy. Far from it. In a memorandum submitted to the British Parliament, Professor Friedman supported Mrs. Thatcher's monetary strategy but complained that her monetary tactics were "egregious" and simply wrong. About the Fed's October 1979 monetarist experiment, he says:

It was terrible it wasn't carried out. One step forward and two steps back. You cannot get large bureaucratic agencies to move, period. . . . In both the British and American cases, you set out on the correct course of reducing the monetary growth rate. But in both cases, you did it in such an erratic and inefficient way that you did not get the assistance of any confidence that you were really doing it. The best image I can give you for both the Fed and the Bank of England is that they have been trying to drive a car down the center of a road with a defective steering apparatus. First they hit one wall, and then they hit the next, and back and forth. They have kept down that road, but with these gyrations, with the result that the car is not in very good shape.[20]

The satisfaction that conservative politicians get from taking control of monetary policy is therefore mainly ideological. As we saw in the case of Mrs. Thatcher, tight money policies are a reaction to the frustrations of failure-zone spending. Free spending by liberals, accompanied by deficits and easy money policies, lead to inflation. Conservatives have failed to cut spending, adopted tax policies that exacerbated deficits, and seized upon reversing the incidental circumstance of easy money policies as their central economic theme: "the evil of evils is inflation which must be exorcised by tight money." So the primary attack is on the availability of credit while spending or deficits are treated as secondary nuisances.

In time, the remedy has "worked"—inflation has indeed been brought down by starving the economy of money. But inflation is only a symptom of the underlying malaise of failure-zone spending, and stable prices are only a means to the end of the prosperity that the electorate hankers for. Tight money, by itself, only replaces the symptom of inflation with the symptom of recessions. The switch, while appealing to stern reflexes of conservatism, does not better the lot of voters.

## The Populist Exception

There is, however, an exception to this policy of circumspection: a politician should personally ensure that the average voter's savings are protected from the ravages of inflation and taxation and earn a "fair" return. That is, the humble $300 or $400 deposit in the neighborhood savings bank should pay a rate of interest, after tax, that is greater than the prevailing rate of inflation. This done, the populist can let experts (and the financial markets) decide what all other interest rates should be or how fast money supply should grow.

Protecting the value of small deposits is of direct value to an overwhelming number of voters—there are 40 million small accounts in the U.S. It is a policy that is easy to implement and monitor; it takes no great sophistication to figure out what passbook rate will give the average citizen a positive after-tax, real rate of return. And the number of "losers" from such a policy is relatively small—they are the few thousand financial institutions that have a real or perceived interest in obtaining cheap money from the many small depositors who lack the sophistication or the ability to earn higher rates of return elsewhere.

Politicians who are eager and willing to plunge into the intricacies of monetary policy are reluctant to discharge this simple responsibility that would provide value to so many voters. Consider 1981, the year in which most interest rates were well above the 8.9 percent inflation rate; the average prime rate for the year was 19 percent, the average Treasury Bill rate, 11 percent, and the average mortgage rate, 15 percent.

The one exception to this alarming schedule was the interest paid on passbook savings accounts set, by government decree, at less than 6 percent. Average Americans of modest means had invested approximately $300 billion in these accounts because they lacked the knowledge of and access to alternatives. More prosperous folk, with better advice and larger savings to invest, were able to earn 12 to 15 percent returns by putting their money into T-Bills or money market funds.

Why did the administration allow the economic interests of so many of its constituents to be injured? Why did Treasury Secretary Donald Regan, who announced in October 1981 that "it was time to strike a blow for the little guy," suddenly reverse himself a month later and vote to block a paltry half-percent increase in passbook interest rates that would have raised them to $5\frac{3}{4}$ percent?[21]

A partial reason lies in the conventional political tradition of sacrificing the interests of a large but silent majority to mollify a noisy minority; Mr. Regan succumbed to pressure from the savings bank lobby. By forcing the administration to withdraw its support for the half-percent increase in passbook rates, the few thousand savings banks saved themselves, or thought they did, between $350 to $500 million dollars. (Ironically, the gratitude of the banks turned out to be quite short-lived. In 1983 they orchestrated one of the most successful grass-roots campaigns ever to force Congress to repeal tax withholding of interest—a measure behind which the President had put his personal prestige.)

But special-interest politics wasn't the only reason. After all, the Reagan administration was willing, more or less, to let the prime rate rise to over 18 percent and hurt the equally powerful automobile and housing industries. The administration was also in favor of, at least in principle, higher interest rates on passbook accounts. It dragged its heels because of its ideological assumption that the "little guy" is naturally a spendthrift and won't appreciate or respond to economic incentives to save. Using up important political chips to push up the passbook savings rate just isn't worth it.

The propensities of the rich, conservatives believe, are a different matter altogether. They buy furs and yachts only because their saving isn't adequately rewarded. Give a few well-heeled individuals sufficient motive and they will so cut back on their consumption that an enormous increase in the absolute level of savings will result. Hence the passionate insistence on keeping the tax cut and the tolerance of money market funds, even though the latter hurt savings banks every bit as much as deregulating the passbook rate.

## The Economics of Discretion

The leader who delegates the conduct of monetary policy need not be concerned about neglecting a charge of great economic consequence. While monetary policy does need to be competently managed, it is only a peripheral function, like the maintenance of a plumbing system. And because bad monetary management isn't the source of our failure-zone problems, its exemplary conduct isn't going to solve them.

Monetary policy is a black art, an approximate alchemy. The targets that central bankers set are rarely achieved—in 1981, for example, none of them reached their goals for money supply growth. France and Britain overshot; the former had 12 percent growth compared to a target of 10 percent and Britain 13 percent against a target of 6 to 10 percent. Others fell short. In the U.S. money supply growth (M1B) was 5 percent against a target of 6 to 8 1/2 percent, and in Canada, where the target was 4.8 percent growth, money supply fell by 2 percent.

Furthermore, achieving targets seems to be of little practical import, for no one knows what economic growth or inflation rate will result if the Fed does ever meet its targets. As Fed Chairman Volcker testified before the Senate in 1983:

Our objective is easy to state in principle—to maintain progress towards price stability while providing the money and liquidity necessary to support economic growth. . . .

In practice achieving the appropriate balance is difficult, and a full measure of success cannot be achieved by the tools. . . .

The year 1982 amply demonstrated some of the problems facing monetary policy during a period of economic and financial turbulence, and the need for judgment and a degree of flexibility in pursuing the objectives we set for ourselves. . . .

In setting out our monetary and credit objectives for 1983, the Federal Reserve has had no choice but to take into account the fact that "normal" past relationships between money and the economy did not hold in 1982 and may be in the process of continuing to change. . . .[22]

Historical relationships don't hold because financial markets are not inanimate objects that always obey the same physical laws—they learn from experience and adjust to monetary policy. As Goodharts Law (after C.A.E. Goodhart of the Bank of England) holds: "When growth of a nation's money supply is effectively controlled, it will inevitably lead to the development of new kinds of money that are not so strictly controlled."[23]

An illustration of the law is seen in the growth of money market funds. The Federal Reserve includes checking accounts in its definition of M1B, the measure whose growth it restricted strongly in 1981. By the end of the year, money market mutual funds, which are used as a substitute for bank checking accounts but were not included in the Fed's definition of M1B, had grown to $183 billion. And banks were in the process of creating new substitutes for checking accounts to compete with money market funds, which would also be outside the M1B definition. So the historical statistical relationship between M1B growth and inflation failed to hold.

Another reason for the unreliability of "national" monetary policy is that money is now a freely traded international commodity. The size of the domestic money supply, held within U.S. borders (the order of $600 billion), is only about half of the volume of the dollars held abroad. These "Eurodollars" and "Asia dollars" are perfect substitutes for domestic dollars but are largely outside the jurisdiction of the Federal Reserve. Control of what is really a $1.5 trillion pool of money with regulations that directly cover only a third of that pool is naturally less than reliable.

The inherent limitations of monetary policy are increased by failure-zone spending and high deficits. The Fed cannot neutralize defective expenditure and tax policies—it can only make jerky, unpredictable substitutions of the symptoms: high inflation with easy money or recession with tight money. And, of course, it gets blamed for both. As one governor of the Fed says:

There is no room between Scylla and Charybdis. You can push the economy so hard with tight money to kill inflation that you discourage business so much so that there is no investment.

So you get the anti-inflation effects but not any expansionary effects and if you ease you get the inflation again. The dilemma is, whether you eased or you didn't no one is a winner.[24]

Countries that have their tax and spending acts in order have the luxury of ignoring the limitations of monetary policy. As Dr. Goh Keng Swee, deputy prime minister and chairman of the Monetary Authority of Singapore (M.A.S), says, "Nobody in the M.A.S. bothers if M1, M2, M3, or Mz is going up or down.

"We're in this happy position because the government's financial and economic policies have been successful."[25]

## Plebeian Savings

In the one area where a politician should take responsibility—
the passbook savings rate—long-term cause and effect is predictable: if a positive real rate of return is not offered, there is
an inevitable decline in the national savings rate. An expert
describes the consequences of U.S. regulations that kept down
interest rates on savings accounts:

> With inflation rates running at more than 10 percent, savers simply stopped
> saving. It did not take that much intelligence to calculate that holding money
> at zero interest in the case of checking accounts or 5 and 1/2 percent in a
> savings account is not a winning proposition. Surprisingly, the U.S. public was
> slow to realize this. Ultimately, however, the rate of saving in the country
> declined to a point that could only be called a national disaster—less than 5
> percent of the GNP and the lowest of any industrialized nation in the world.[26]

The "little guy's" savings (like his consumption and productivity) is a bulwark of a plebeian economy. His passbook account not only finances new investment, it also gives him a
stake in the system's stability and prosperity. His savings are
a node in the vast economic web of interdependence and
voluntary exchange. It is an elitist myth that common folk do
not like to save or that their savings are unimportant. The poor
and the middle class, like the rich, will save or consume according to the incentives provided to them. If one or the other class
is seen to have a higher propensity to save, there is usually a
good economic reason for its thrift. And it is good public policy
to provide this reason to all citizens.

In 1981 personal savings in the United States amounted to 4
percent of its gross national product. In West Germany the
savings rate was 9 percent, and in Japan, 13 percent. The
higher rates in Germany and Japan reflect a sustained effort to
mobilize grass-roots savings. In 1961 the German government
passed the Act to Promote Workers' Participation in Capital
Formation, which exempted workers from paying income
taxes on 600 DM of interest income. In addition, the act provided for an investment wage, secured through collective bar-

gaining, that was tax free as long as it was placed in a savings account or investment fund. Complementing these tax policies were interest rates on savings accounts that almost always offered a positive real rate of return. In Japan the tax and interest-rate incentives to small savers have been so attractive that there are three times as many small savings accounts as there are Japanese.

Singapore also provides an example of the importance of grass-roots savings. The average Singapore worker's earnings would put him below the poverty line in the U.S.; yet the average savings rate in Singapore is even higher than in Japan. And this thrift cannot be ascribed to Confucianism or Chinese tradition, for the savings rate was not always that high. It doubled in less than a decade because the government actively promoted savings through pension schemes and post-office savings accounts.

## Conclusion

Monetary policies have a major impact on the economy and on the pocketbooks of voters. The impact is, however, quite unpredictable; hence money supply or interest rates cannot be reliably manipulated to gain political advantage. Unlike the areas of spending and taxes, there are no rules to guide the politician to the right vote-winning policies. In particular, monetary policies offer no panacea to the problems of the failure zone. Therefore, an astute politician should not indulge in risky gambles with monetary policy but instead entrust its conduct to competent experts. An exception to this rule is the protection of the public's savings—the politician should ensure that these are protected against inflation and financial cartels.

# CHAPTER 4

# Trade Policies: Never-Never Land

THE LAST MAJOR WAVE of protectionism was set off, fifty years ago, by politicians seeking to ease the economic problems caused by underspending. Today protectionism is again on the rise, as politicians seek shelter from the poor economic performance caused by overspending. Knocking imports is becoming increasingly popular in campaign rhetoric. For example, John Connally, Republican candidate for President in 1980, warned the Japanese that if he was elected and Japan continued to run a trade surplus, they had "better be prepared to sit on the docks of Yokohama in your little Datsuns while you stare at your little TV sets and eat your Mandarin oranges because we've had all we're going to take."[1]

Candidate Reagan was less flamboyant, but he too promised during a swing through Detroit: "Japan is part of the problem. This is where government can be legitimately involved. That is, to convince the Japanese in one way or another that, in their own interest, that deluge of cars must be slowed while our industry gets back on its feet. . . . If Japan keeps on doing everything that it's doing . . . obviously, there is going to be what you call protectionism."[2] Mr. Reagan also promised the textile industry that as President he would consider "keying import growth to the growth of the American market."[3]

Campaigning in the 1982 congressional elections, Walter Mondale, Democratic aspirant for President, told steelworkers: "I believe in international competition but I am not a sucker . . . . The key task in the next few years is to stop flying the white flag, to start running up the American flag, to turn around and fight. We have to stop talking about getting tough in terms of international trade—we have to start acting tough."[4] Otherwise, he warned Americans, they would all be selling hamburgers to each other and "sweeping around Japanese computers."

Since protectionism is ostensibly directed against "foreigners," politicians find it easy to keep their election promises to domestic producers. Mr. Reagan kept his word to Detroit after he was elected. While touting the merits of free trade, his administration got the Japanese to agree to "voluntary" quotas on automobile exports to the U.S. For its supporters in the textile industry, the Reagan administration pushed the Multifiber Agreement (MFA) to clamp down on imports from Third World countries. Citing the national interest, quotas were extended on clothespins. The Commerce Department asked the International Trade Commission (ITC) for restrictions on imported flue-cured tobacco because it threatened the tobacco-subsidy program. Imports of auto parts, electrical goods, fertilizers, chemicals, and glassware worth $3.8 billion from Hong Kong, South Korea, Taiwan, Brazil, and Mexico were removed from a duty-free program. Quotas were imposed on imports of sugar from those very Caribbean basin countries to whom the administration wanted to extend development aid. The Commerce Department initiated an antidumping complaint against steel producers from five nations.

Perhaps the most thorough action against imports was taken in the case of semiconductor memories from Japan. The Commerce Department complained against the dumping of these microchips, but just to show how political the process had become, the Justice Department started a probe to determine whether the Japanese companies had formed a cartel to push up their prices in the U.S.

The only import restriction that Mr. Reagan ended was the quota on shoes imported from Taiwan. Presidential spokesman David Gergen cautioned, however, "I would not read it as a way he would come out on any case."[5] And, as one expert noted, "it may only be a coincidence that a major congressional advocate for U.S. shoe manufacturers is House speaker Tip O'Neill."[6]

Despite its professed free-market views, the Thatcher government in the U.K. also did not shy from protectionism. It forced the Japanese to limit car exports to the U.K. and under the aegis of the European Economic Community (EEC) won promises of "moderation" on a range of products that extended from quartz watches to forklift trucks to machine tools. It imposed quotas on synthetic fibers imported from the U.S., which it claimed were "as limited as humanly possible." The agriculture minister ensured that British consumers would pay 50 percent more for milk than their neighbors in Belgium and Ireland by banning the imports of ultra-high-temperature milk. The EEC Court of Justice ruled, after several years of litigation, that the ban was illegal, but the Thatcher government defied the court and maintained the restrictions.[7]

These conservative restraints on free trade are, however, mild, compared to what the liberals who are more beholden to organized labor in threatened industries would rather see imposed. According to *The Economist*, Edward Kennedy and Walter Mondale "are spouting rhetoric against Japanese goods that approaches to the verge of racism."[8] Liberal Democrats have been introducing a flood of protectionist legislation in Congress claiming as Representative Barbara Kennelly of Connecticut does that "the individual citizen is asking us to do something."[9]

The U.K. Labour party's manifesto in the 1979 general election was explicitly protectionistic: "We will not allow our industries to be wiped out by excessive imports before they have had a chance to recover their strength. The Labour Government will ensure that imports enter our market only within acceptable limits."[10] In the 1983 election, the party was committed to wholesale import controls.

The Socialist government in France is the most protectionist in Europe. Japanese automobiles are virtually banned—only three out of every 100 French citizens can choose a new Japanese car.[11] The government decreed in 1982 that all imports of videocassette recorders into France would have to pass through the small town of Poitiers, where five customs officials would inspect each set. (Poitiers was a symbolic choice, because the French had defeated the invading Saracens there in A.D. 732.)

## Symbols versus Pocketbooks

Protectionism is believed to afford considerable political advantages. It gives presidents and congressmen a chance to make speeches vigorously affirming their commitment to the American worker. Negotiating a "voluntary" quota, investigating dumping charges, or voting for a domestic content bill, politicians believe, sends a strong signal to constituents that their leaders mean what they say.

But although such signals may have an impact on politicians and political correspondents who are sensitive to symbolic nuances, do they really reach the average voter? The evidence is that a great majority of the public isn't tuned in to the signals that emanate from Washington—most people don't keep score of debating points or take heed of a new quota on clothespins. Nearly half of all voters, Gallup polls have found, do not know the name of their congressman and over three-fourths don't know how their representative votes on major bills.[12] Only 27 percent of Americans report that they "regularly follow accounts of political and governmental affairs,"[13] and 56 percent that they pay little or no attention to election campaigns. Americans aren't unique in their disinterest—only 23 percent of Britons and 34 percent of Germans follow accounts of political and governmental affairs; and 76 percent of Britons and 61 percent of Germans pay little or no attention to election campaigns.[14]

The public is, however, rather more sensitive when it comes to its personal well-being: housewives sniff out sales, five-hundred-dollar investors turn to the stock pages in their newspapers every morning, and small taxpayers have an accountant's knowledge of deductions. When pollsters ask respondents whether they are better or worse off than they were a year ago, "don't know" usually constitutes less than 1 percent of replies; and the responses of the 99 percent who answer correlate remarkably well with "hard" economic indicators.

Tariffs and quotas are net vote losers because they score symbolic points that few voters keep track of, while they hurt a great number of citizens where they feel it the most—in their pocketbooks. Protectionism is a regressive tax imposed on innumerable consumers of both imported and domestic goods. Quotas on Japanese automobile imports drive up the prices of the 1.73 million Toyotas, Datsuns, and Hondas that are allowed in; and, because of the reduced availability of Japanese cars, GM, Ford, and Chrysler can raise prices on their products too. So the quota imposes a hidden tax on the entire public for most of whom driving is a basic necessity—80 percent of Americans use automobiles to get to work.[15] And the "tax" isn't collected by the Treasury but is for the benefit of automobile industry profits and the wages of auto workers (even though wages earned by United Auto Workers members are more than double the average industrial workers' earnings). Protectionism thus takes from the many consumers to give to a smaller, richer group of workers and stockholders.

The political costs of protectionism are incurred whether or not voters know that their administration has negotiated a quota. An unaffordable sticker price on a car can be the last straw on a back that is already heavily loaded with failure-zone taxes, even for a voter who has not been educated in the benefits of free trade and feels great sympathy for the auto industry and its workers.

In any event, it is not true that people have been gulled into demanding protection and are through with free trade. "Americans hold free trade views," reports a *Business Week*/Louis Harris poll, "even though some 60 percent feel that imports hurt U.S. business and three-quarters believe that imports hurt workers." The pollsters found that voters "have solid reasons for being wary of a new structure of barriers to foreign goods"—81 percent of the sample agreed with the proposition that "Many foreign products are very good and American people should have the chance to buy them at reasonable prices." Two-thirds of the national sample voted for fewer impediments to the free flow of goods, and only 25 percent favored import restrictions.[16]

## The Liberal Irony

It is a historical irony that liberal Democrats, beholden to rich and powerful trade unions, are now the strongest advocates of protection, while Republicans, at least in theory, seem more committed to free trade. For the Republicans once were the party of protection. It was the *Republican Campaign Text Book* that said:

We renew and emphasize our allegiance to the policy of protection as the bulwark of American industrial development and prosperity. This true American policy taxes foreign products and encourages home industry; it puts the burden of revenue on foreign goods; it secures the American market for the American producer; it upholds the American standard of wages for the American workingman. . . .[17]

And it was Democrats who used to stand up for the majority consumer interest against the owners of domestic industry. In

1887 President Grover Cleveland, a Democrat, demanded that Congress reduce import tariffs. In the first annual message ever sent to Congress about a single issue, he said:

Our present tariff laws, the vicious, inequitable and illogical source of unnecessary taxation, ought to be at once revised. These laws, as their primary and plain effect, raise the price to all consumers of all articles imported and subject to duty by precisely the sum paid for such duties. . . .
    [Tariffs led to] a condition which, without regard to the public welfare, must always ensure the realization of immense profits. . . . So stubbornly have all efforts to reform the present condition been resisted by those of our fellow citizens thus engaged that they can hardly complain of the suspicion . . . that there exists an organized combination all along the line to maintain their advantage.
    We are in the midst of centennial celebrations, and we rejoice in American skill and ingenuity and in the wonderful resources developed by a century's national growth. Yet, it suits the purpose of advocacy to call our manufactures infant industries still needing the highest degree of fostering care that can be wrung from Federal legislation.[18]

Liberals who have forsaken their free-trade roots are not only on the wrong side of the majority interest, the political advantages they derive from the minorities they seek to protect are also dubious. Protection is often demanded by industries that are threatened by far greater problems than imports. While the Japanese are a thorn in the side of Detroit and Pittsburgh, the more serious problem U.S. manufacturers face is the overall decline in demand for automobiles and steel. Imports are often just a convenient bogeyman: between 1973 and 1980, writes Robert Lawrence of the Brookings Institution, only eleven out of the fifty-two sectors that constitute the U.S. manufacturing base suffered job losses due to trade. Leather and footwear were the only two sectors in which trade caused employment losses of more than 5 percent.[19]

With or without imports, however, some industries inevitably decline—employment shrinks and lower profit margins squeeze wages. When such industries have a history of high profits, lifetime employment practices, and generous wages, its workers find it difficult to make the transition to hard times.

They are frustrated, rebellious, and prone to behave self-destructively; for example, they resist wage concessions that might save their jobs. And although much of their anger is directed against the management of their companies, workers also blame the government for not doing enough to restore the good times. Protection, which barely scrapes the surface of their industry's problem, is naturally not regarded as being enough.

Workers from declining industries are, therefore, prone to vote against whoever is in power—in 1980 workers from smokestack America turned against President Carter and the Democrats. Mr. Carter lost every steel-and-automobile state except Minnesota. His share of votes from union households fell 13 percent from 1976. Many other Democratic politicians also took a similar drubbing in the Midwest. Two years later, in the 1982 congressional elections, the smokestack labor vote turned against Republicans. In good times, the steel-producing Ruhr region of Germany was a stronghold of the metal workers' union and the Social-Democratic Party (SDP). As the fortunes of the steel industry in Germany declined, life-long members of the metal workers' union ignored their leaders and handed the SDP its worst drubbing in the Ruhr in the 1983 national election.

So while politicians may find it useful to promise protection to get elected, it makes no sense to keep that commitment once they are in power. Barring miracles, the votes of workers from declining industries are more or less lost and should be treated that way. There is no percentage, for an incumbent, in pushing up prices and interfering with the majority's freedom to choose between domestic goods and imports.

## The Kiss of Death

But what of the argument that it is quixotic to oppose protectionism if it is supported by powerful union leaders; that a

Democratic presidential aspirant is forced to support restrictions on automobile imports not just for the sake of Detroit's vote but in order to win the all-important endorsement of the AFL-CIO, which represents the entire U.S. labor movement? It is true that the public considers unions to be important institutions: 76 percent of Americans believe that most unions "have been good forces," working for "desirable social ends," and 85 percent agree that "in many industries unions are needed so that the legitimate complaints and grievances of workers can be heard." But only 10 percent of the public has confidence in union leadership; nearly 60 percent believe that "most union leaders have become arrogant and no longer represent the workers in their unions."[20] The ability of a few union leaders to sway the labor vote with their endorsement is therefore quite exaggerated.

The issues director of Jimmy Carter's 1976 election campaign, Steven Stark, cites several reasons why "Labor's endorsement is a curse, not a blessing":

First, the clout of labor leaders, even in Democratic primaries, is vastly overrated. Unions are no longer cohesive political units, and most labor leaders can't even deliver their own locals.

Second, the labor endorsement is going to end up sinking the candidate who gets it because most voters don't like labor leaders. Even union members dislike the image of their vote being delivered to a candidate selected in the back room.

Equally as important, the labor-endorsed candidate will be an easy target. . . . Rightly or wrongly. Democrats are on the defensive because they are perceived as the party of "special interests"—labor, minorities and government workers. A campaign tailored to those interests only reinforces the notion that the Democratic party does not represent the interests of the average voter.[21]

A Gallup poll held in May 1983 supports the view that union support can be a liability. The question asked was: "Labor unions are going to announce their choice of a Presidential candidate before next year's primaries. Would the endorsement by labor unions of a Presidential candidate make you more or less likely to vote for that candidate?" Thirty-five percent of those queried said they would be less likely to support a candidate backed by the unions. Forty-one percent said an endorsement would make no difference, and only 18 percent said they would be more likely to vote for a union-supported candidate.[22]

Many leaders have ignored (or even confronted) big labor without incurring serious political costs. President Reagan has had no dialogue with the AFL-CIO and busted the air traffic controllers' union without making a whit of difference in his standing with voters. Mrs. Thatcher conspicuously broke several decades of tradition of inviting Trade Union Congress (TUC) leaders to 10 Downing Street for consultations on economic policy and introduced legislation in Parliament that threatened their power; that didn't win or lose the Tories many votes in the 1983 general election either.

Farmers are another minority group that can be dangerous to protect. French farmers, for example, contributed to the downfall of the Gaullists. Gaullist capitulation to pressure from agricultural interests turned France into a protected enclave for exorbitantly priced agricultural goods. Protection allowed French farmers to sell wheat in France at $5.50 a bushel, when American wheat was available at $3.50, and duties on American corn raised its price from $2 a bushel to $4. Cheap milk and butter from New Zealand were almost entirely blocked off. French food became as overpriced in the common man's supermarket as it is in Michelin three-star restaurants.

Though France has a large agricultural workforce by the standards of an industrialized country, farmers account for only 11 percent of the population. Chaban Delmas, former prime minister and Gaullist presidential candidate, once suggested to his colleagues that they risk the support of the relatively small farming bloc in order to capture the votes of the more numerous industrial workers by reducing agricultural protection. But the "farmers' vote" was too much of a security blanket to cast away, and M. Delmas's proposal was summarily rejected.

Gaullist obstinacy increasingly alienated them from the

working class and lost them the presidency to M. Giscard. As we saw in chapter 1, M. Giscard turned out to be a selectively tough conservative. His government shut down uneconomical steel mills, tried to freeze wages, and imposed a tight monetary regime. These policies might have been more palatable if he had concurrently cut taxes and spending or reduced agricultural tariffs—workers would at least have been able to buy more food with the same frozen wages.

The tough Giscard, who was unmoved by riots in steel towns and sat out months' long sit-ins in state-owned plants, did neither. His government didn't cut spending and didn't touch agricultural tariffs even though there wasn't much danger of the ultra-conservative farmers defecting to the Socialists or the Communists. Sources within the government said the question of agricultural protection would only be considered after the 1981 election. That opportunity did not arise. Food prices stayed high, and workers who were convinced that right-wing austerity meant decreasing living standards and rising unemployment voted the Socialist candidate, François Mitterand, into power.

## Standing Up for Free Trade

Consumers have the greatest need for the benefits of free trade in the difficult economic conditions of the failure zone, when their earnings are squeezed or inflation is high. But it is also in these very circumstances that special-interest pressures for protection are at their most intense. If politicians wish to avoid being overwhelmed by these pressures, if they wish to protect the majority's interests rather than the domestic steel or textile industry's market share, they must stand up and be counted for free trade and actively defend it.

The public, according to the Louis Harris poll on free trade cited earlier, has "trouble identifying the views of prominent politicians and political parties." For all his protectionist lapses,

Ronald Reagan, for example, is more of a free trader than Walter Mondale; yet, the poll found, almost half the public thought that Reagan wanted to restrict imports while only a third thought Mondale to be a protectionist. As for Mondale's closest Democratic competitor, Senator John Glenn, 59 percent of the public didn't know where he stood on international trade.[23]

Politicians should not be shy about advertising to the majority that they are on their side, particularly if they are running for reelection and have to write off declining industries as a source of support. Leaders should use the slick selling skills that politicians are claimed to possess to counteract the considerable and natural sympathy voters have for laid off auto workers and steelworkers; it is in the politician's interest to demonstrate to them the dollars-and-cents costs of translating this sympathy into restrictions on imports. Free trade is too often defended by leaders in abstract terms of economic efficiency and global interrelatedness.

Politicians should also promote free trade by actively manipulating special-interest groups and lobbies. Lobbies are to politicians what suppliers are to businessmen. They are a natural threat—they can rob politicians of their power just as a businessman's supplier can put him out of business by "forward integration." But they can be a valuable resource, especially if different lobbies are played off against each other.

Protection for the steel industry can be fought by harnessing Detroit's lobbyists, since the U.S. automobile industry consumes nearly 40 percent of domestically produced steel and General Motors, Ford, and Chrysler have a strong interest in buying steel at the same (or preferably lower) price as Toyota, Nissan, and Honda. (Today, because of protection, U.S. companies suffer an estimated 5 percent steel cost disadvantage.) Politicians should pit the consumer lobby against the textile and footwear industry—after all, the price of shoes and clothes is a legitimate consumer interest. And if the leaders of consumer groups don't consider the public's right to buy cheap imports to be important, politicians should not shrink from trying to "manipulate" the consumer movement, for the lobbies don't hesitate in trying to influence politicians' staffs and organizations.

Politicians must not be panicked by the seemingly calamitous destruction of certain industries. United Steel Workers' advertisements showing photographs of the demolition of blast furnaces to dramatize the effects of steel imports should be viewed in historical perspective. A healthy economy is always restructuring, the old constantly giving way to the new. Greater shifts in employment than we see today have occurred before without a political apocalypse or a revolution. Society has coped with the pains and dislocations of change and emerged stronger as a consequence. The U.S. has lived through its transformation from an agricultural to an industrial economy and accommodated massive migrations from the farm to the city. Between 1940 and 1960, a net of 21.5 million Americans left farming. Between 1951 and 1970, farm population as a percentage of U.S. population declined from 14 percent to 4 percent. Presidents, from Roosevelt to Nixon, weren't toppled by these changes, which involved many more people than the shrinking of the steel or the automobile industry.

For steel or auto workers who have to leave jobs they have held for thirty or forty years, find new employment, learn new skills, and perhaps sell a house and move to a new city, "restructuring" is certainly a wrenching experience. But politicians who would sacrifice the majority interest in order to impede the inevitable should remember that change, of jobs and homes, and the dislocations that go with such change are normal events for an average American. Home mortgages, for example, change hands, on the average, every six to seven years. Rental units turn over in about half that period. The average voter is mobile, either by choice or because of circumstance; it is the exceptional worker who keeps a job for two or three decades. Even Japan's much-touted privilege of lifetime employment is available only to the 30 percent of the workforce who work for the large *zaibatsu* companies; and the cost of "permanent" employment is borne by the other 70 percent who are paid significantly lower wages and don't enjoy such security.

## Renewal and Rebirth

A growing number of scholars, but still thankfully a minority, are adding the respectability of economic argument to the self-interested voices of protectionist lobbies. The "Cambridge group" of economists in the U.K. has called for wholesale import controls. Dr. Amitai Etzioni, a scholar with some influence during the Carter administration, has written: "Instead of chasing a free trade rainbow, our realistic goal should be tit-for-tat trading." The U.S., he says, needs "more trade protection," albeit "of the right kind."[24]

These protectionist arguments take a narrow and pessimistic view of the value of human labor and cooperation. Trade between individuals, firms, and nations is not a zero-sum game with "winners" and "losers." Free trade makes for international specialization from which the world benefits—we can produce more and better goods with fewer resources, and without trade we all lose. The Depression of the 1930s came with tariff wars; the reduction of tariffs after World War II helped sustain two and a half decades of prosperity; and failure-zone stagflation has been accompanied by even steeper declines in world trade.

"International specialization" is not just a slogan. The decline of inefficient enterprises is a tangible blessing that accrues immediately to the majority and ultimately to everyone. Germany, recognizing its inability to produce cheap food, put its farmers out of jobs and became one of the world's largest import markets for agricultural commodities. Food imports helped Germany to concentrate on the production and export of engineering goods, while France, which coddled her farmers, remained a bucolic backwater.

Much is made of the demise of the U.S. television industry. In fact, the "loss" is no more lamentable than the disappearance of the buggy-whip industry—it has freed up scarce electrical engineering and design talent (which is in worldwide short supply) to work in such high-technology areas as personal computers and word processors, in which American firms have established a dominant position. Zenith's $300 TV set loss has been Apple's $3000 personal computer gain.

Then there is the greatly misunderstood case of Japan, which is often portrayed as a bastion of protectionism. Japan industrialized rapidly after the Meiji Restoration of 1867, when Western powers prohibited its government from imposing tariffs higher than 5 percent. After World War II it reconstructed and rose to be an industrial giant with the help of vast imports of technology, capital goods, and raw materials. Although the Japanese bureaucracy reflexively resists free trade (for example, they tried to deny Sony import licenses for transistor technology), import policies have been quite liberal compared to other countries in similar stages of industrial development (for example, India) and "self-sufficiency" has never been a national goal. Since 1867 the Japanese have concentrated only on those products and processes where they had unique advantages and brought in everything else from the best international suppliers.

When, after the 1973 oil shock, the Japanese government decided to restructure the economy toward high–value-added goods, imports of low–value-added goods from Korea, Taiwan, Hong Kong, and Singapore were substantially increased. Between 1974 and 1976, for example, Japan's imports from its Asian neighbors increased 1100 percent in transistors and diodes, 1300 percent in radios, and 9800 percent in TV receivers. Today, when the U.S. and the EEC are jeopardizing big-ticket capital goods exports to China by limiting imports of cheap garments, Japan is increasing its imports of slacks and shirts from China at about 10 to 20 percent a year. These imports help the Japanese export to China and, more important, help keep down the Japanese inflation rate by providing consumers with cheap garments.[25]

Imports continue to be important to Japan at the high end too. Japan's personal computer revolution is following hard on the heels of that in the U.S. The architecture of these machines, the microprocessors (or microprocessor technology), the operating systems, and much of the applications software is all imported from the U.S. Overall, Japanese imports from the U.S. in 1982 were $204 per capita, while U.S. imports from Japan were $156 per capita.[26] (The Japanese had even higher per-capita exports; hence the trade deficit.)

Countries that refuse to give up their areas of comparative disadvantage and protect inefficient industries do themselves grave injury. First, tariffs and quotas promote inflation by raising the prices of imported and domestic goods. Second, protectionism hampers the regeneration of an economy. The trigger-price mechanism that brings up the price of cheaper imported steel to the higher domestic level transfers profits from healthy steel-using companies to aging, obsolete steel plants.

Ironically, protectionism can even make the very companies against whom it is directed more dangerous long-term competitors. As the *Wall Street Journal* noted on the first anniversary of the quota forced on the Japanese auto industry:

The quota has accelerated the transition of Japanese automakers into higher-priced models that compete more directly with the American cars where Detroit makes the most money and where it has the strongest chance for comparative advantage. Sales of $12,000 Toyota Cressidas and Datsun Maximas rose in 1981 to 30,000 and 35,000 from 12,000 and 9,000 in 1980. Sales of low-priced Corollas and B-210s dropped. . . . This is what usually happens with quotas: The importers shift to the higher-value products that count most. The steel quotas of 1969 to 1972 wreaked havoc on the U.S. makers of high-value-added specialty steels. TV-set quotas led Sony to shift from low-priced to premium sets.[27]

Protection of inefficient producers hurts wherever it is imposed. As it has in France, agricultural protection has led to high food prices in Japan. The Japanese telecommunications equipment market is a closed domestic oligopoly; consequently, the Nippon Electric Company (NEC) is a less aggressive and successful competitor in international markets than

Sweden's LM Ericsson, which isn't given much local business by its government.

## The Bogeys of Security and Dumping

Considerations of "national security" are sometimes claimed as a justification for protecting domestic industry. Some of these claims are palpably ludicrous—the fifty-odd Florida farmers who control much of the country's tomato production and demand protection against Mexican imports on the grounds that the U.S. could be held to ransom by a "tomato OPEC" cannot be taken seriously. But it is hard to justify, from historical experience, protection for more strategic sectors on the grounds of security. For the threat sought to be protected against—embargoes and boycotts—has never succeeded in practice.

Napoleon's blockade of Britain's foreign trade was a failure. Fidel Castro survives in Havana in spite of a two-decade-long U.S. trade boycott. OPEC's attempt to enforce an oil embargo against the U.S. failed. Rhodesia, a small, landlocked country, flourished economically for years in spite of international trade sanctions, until its regime was dislodged by armed guerrilla warfare. Taiwan's international trade flourishes even though it has diplomatic relations with barely a dozen countries. Its businessmen even carry on a flourishing business with the People's Republic of China through Hong Kong intermediaries. President Carter's ban on U.S. grain exports to the Soviet Union didn't prevent it from buying all the wheat it needed on world markets. And President Reagan in turn had to give up his attempt to prevent European countries from selling pipeline technology to the Russians.

Another bogey raised against free trade is "dumping"— price cutting by unscrupulous foreign exporters that "unfairly" damages domestic industry. Actually, it would be a terrific boon if a country could become the "victim" of a prolonged dumping assault. The British textile industry thrived because it could force its colonies to dump cheap cotton on it. (Today it foolishly restricts imports of U.S. synthetic fiber.) Hong Kong thrives because China sells it cheap food. The Soviet bloc countries are cushioned against the follies of agricultural collectivization because the EEC practically gives away its dairy produce. In Ireland there are companies based solely on subsidized British steel and coal. Korea and Taiwan took full advantage of the plant and machinery that Japanese companies eagerly sold them on easy terms. Now the Japanese complain bitterly about the "boomerang effect" as these plants produce products that compete in common export markets.

Unfortunately, with these few exceptions, consistent dumping is difficult to arrange. Few countries will systematically sell goods to another and not demand real payment in return. OPEC wouldn't dump oil in the U.S. in order to make the automobile and chemical industries happy. Koreans export shoes and garments to the U.S. not because of animosity toward U.S. industries but because they want the dollars to buy wheat or machine tools.

## Conclusion

Henry George said a hundred years ago: "What protection teaches us is to do to ourselves in time of peace what enemies do to us in times of war." A protectionist politician is a foe of his constituents who blockades his own ports and besieges his own castle. Moreover, he rarely derives any benefit for injuring the majority interest: industries that demand protection are usually in the throes of some deep-rooted structural change —stagnant or declining demand or the need to adjust to new labor-saving technologies. The votes of the workers who have to face the problems of such change cannot be "saved" with the Band-Aids of tariffs or quotas.

Economically, protectionism is a stultifying force. We are on the verge of a high-tech revolution; it will succeed only if the hungry new industries are given the capital and talent that is trapped in smokestack sectors. Free international trade can help this transfusion; protectionism will throttle it. Japanese imports of low–value-added goods are a key to its progress. European barricades around their aging textile factories will imprison them in the past.

# PART II

# Escaping the Failure Zone: Setting Priorities for Cuts

SPENDING PRIORITIES weren't important in the New Deal. Since public expenditure could be financed out of the taxes on a few rich people, virtually all programs were politically attractive. Politicians could "tax and spend" without much regard to what they were spending on.

When the cost of financing spending began to pinch the middle class, politicians ought to have started worrying about priorities—favoring programs that gave voters value for taxes and weeding out those that didn't. But politicians didn't adjust to the changed realities—as David Stockman suggests, they couldn't or wouldn't judge claims for more benefits and therefore gave into them all. This helped push expenditure into the failure zone.

If the spending genie is to be put back into its bottle, some cuts will have to be made in all programs; the public demand for real tax cuts simply cannot be satisfied otherwise. Nevertheless, priorities are crucial: a package of tax and spending reductions should cut deepest into programs that are the least popular and only modestly curtail programs that voters have reason to want to retain.

Drawing up a hit list is an unpleasant but necessary chore for a politician who wishes to survive in office. Conventional wisdom is of little help in this task because it treats all programs as sacred. In the next four chapters, therefore, we will use logic and real-world evidence instead. We will analyze four categories of spending programs—programs to generate and maintain employment; public services like health and education and defense; welfare programs; and capital investment projects. We can thus identify the weakest links in the spending chain and figure out how the "impossible" goal of spending cuts might be most popularly achieved.

# CHAPTER 5

# Employment Programs: Tilting at Windmills

TELEVISION did not exaggerate the misery of the nearly 12 million unemployed Americans in the winter of 1982. Pictures of the jobless standing in long soup lines, of their houses being auctioned off because they couldn't make the mortgage payments, and of their families packed into cars and vans for hopeless journeys in search of nonexistent jobs in the Sunbelt only touched the surface of their despair. TV cameras couldn't really capture their loss of dignity and self-worth, the fear that sets in after months of not finding work: "Will I ever find a job?"

When unemployment is as widespread as it was in 1982, the anxieties of the jobless are reflected in the minds of those who are employed: "What if it happens to me? Is my job safe?" Unemployment becomes an issue of serious concern to the entire public, not just the jobless. Politicians who feel the need to do something about their constituents' worries propose jobs bills, employment creation schemes, and bailouts of failing

companies. Liberals support such programs both because they
think they are popular and because they believe that the state
should be the employer of last resort. Conservatives who hold
the opposite ideological view often go along for "political"
reasons, heeding reminders in the press that "The last time
[unemployment] was above 7 percent in the first 6 months of
a congressional year, the Republicans who had the White
House lost 17 seats in the House of Representatives. That was
in 1958. Two years later they were voted out of the White
House as well."[1]

But are jobs programs really good politics? Can a politician
significantly reduce the public's disaffection with high unemployment by spending public money? Or should a president
concentrate on issues that he can influence—for example, cutting spending and reducing tariff barriers?

## Bucking a Rising Tide

Rising unemployment is no longer, as it was in the 1950s and
1960s, a temporary, cyclical problem; joblessness has been
gradually rising, almost without interruption, for a decade.
Unemployment accelerated after 1979, when the Federal Reserve decided to tighten money supply to fight inflation. As the
inflation rate was brought down, prior records for unemployment were broken. By Christmas 1981 there were about 25
million people out of work in the developed world, with 9.5
million of them in the U.S. By the winter of 1982 another two
and a half million were jobless in the U.S., making a total of 12
million unemployed, the highest ever recorded since the government started keeping statistics. The overall unemployment
rate of 10.8 percent was the highest since 1941. Joblessness in
the Midwest was at Depression levels—17.2 percent in Michigan and 14.2 percent in Ohio.

Germany, which had avoided serious unemployment in the
1970s by expelling guest workers and reducing its labor force
by 1.7 million people (7 percent), began to witness serious

joblessness of its own citizens. The number of unemployed grew by over 50 percent in 1982 and reached a twenty-eight-year high. Even greater job losses occurred in Britain.

In the winter of 1982, the future looked bleak. Martin Feldstein, chairman of the President's Council of Economic Advisers said that even with the expected recovery in 1983 and 1984, it might take five or six years for the U.S. unemployment rate to drop to the 6 to 7 percent level that prevailed during the early months of 1980.[2] The OECD predicted that unemployment in the Western world would probably reach 35 million in 1985, up from 10 million in the 1974–75 recession.[3]

Inevitably, rising unemployment spawned jobs bills. The Carter administration took office just as the U.S. economy was recovering from the 1975 recession and immediately spent $10 billion to create public sector jobs. The unemployment issue subsided in 1978 and 1979 as the economy recovered, but then joblessness headed up again. By 1980 unemployment was once more a serious issue, and the Democratic program for the November election pledged a $12 billion program to create at least 800,000 jobs.

The program was forgotten in 1981 because of President Reagan's opposition to "make-work" programs and in the excitement of the supply-side experiment. But, as hopes in Reaganomics faded and the grim reality of unemployment grew, jobs programs crept back into Congress. In the winter of 1982 House Democrats proposed a $5.4 billion emergency jobs bill. President Reagan condemned the bill as "a pork barrel" filled with "make-work" jobs. Faced with the threat of a presidential veto, Democrats scrapped the bill. "It's just a case of recognizing reality," said Appropriations chairman Jamie Whitten.[4]

When a new Congress reconvened in January 1983, that reality had changed. Democrats, with a net gain of twenty-six seats, were in a stronger position to reintroduce a jobs bill, and even Republicans who had so far stood with the President were running scared of the unemployment issue. Republican House leader Robert Michel said: "I don't want my troops cast in the role of naysayers about any Democratic initiative that comes along."[5] Republican Senators Dan Quayle and Orrin Hatch introduced their own jobs bill in the Senate.

In early February the White House proposed its version of a jobs package, half of which, according to the administration's briefing sheets, was borrowed virtually wholesale from the Democratic bill Mr. Reagan had threatened to veto the previous December. With such all-round, if reluctant, support, a final $4.65 billion bill soon cleared the House by a margin of 329 to 86 and the Senate by 82 to 15. The President signed the bill a few hours after he received it. "It was damage control," one administrative official said. "You don't seriously think anyone in this administration believes in this crap."[6]

In Britain, a Conservative Thatcher government implemented the Labour party's rhetoric. In the 1979 general election Prime Minister Callaghan had said, "A vote for Labour is a vote for your job—that is the issue. . . . I have argued and will continue to argue, that in the present state of world recession it is not possible to rely purely on the free market to ensure full employment." The Conservatives' "do-nothing policy would be as out of place in the competitive world as a cavalry charge against tanks," he warned. "The truth is that Conservative theorists are out of date, out of touch, and dangerous on these matters."[7]

The Thatcher government belied Mr. Callaghan's fears. In 1981–82 the Department of Employment spent over $2 billion to provide a grabbag of schemes to the unemployed. "The supposedly Thatcherite employment secretary, Mr. Norman Tebbit," reported *The Economist* in 1982, "is now custodian of an employment relief programme of a size and comprehensiveness which makes Mr. Michael Foot's Labour effort in the mid-1970s look positively Scroogelike."[8]


## Indirect Payrolls

In addition to job programs, politicians have tried other means to turn back unemployment. Workers are indirectly put on the taxpayer's payroll by subsidizing investment to create new jobs and keeping lame ducks alive to protect old ones. As Mr. Callaghan says: "Public expenditure means creating new industries, saving jobs, helping firms."[9]

Politicians have been so eager to be seen creating new jobs that few large investments are now undertaken without generous help from the public coffers. You wouldn't guess from the prominently advertised blandishments to new industry that governments are strapped for money. According to one newspaper advertisement: "Vermont wants industry. We offer 4 percent interest plant financing, . . . state-financed manpower training, and a fiscally responsible government."[10]

Although Philadelphia doesn't claim fiscal responsibility in giving away public money, its terms are even more generous. A large advertisement in the *Wall Street Journal* has a picture of a plant, and the caption below says: "Philadelphia financed 100 percent of the cost of this project. And we will do the same for your company. Few cities, if any, can offer you the scope and variety of financing packages available in Philadelphia."[11]

Investment grants operate as if in a different world. In its news columns the London *Times* reports that: "So far, as the prime minister and her attendant knights are concerned, the main thrust of the battle against inflation and excessive money supply will be made by attacking the financial demands of the public sector."[12] Four pages away, the government-owned National Research Development Corporation (NRDC) advertises: "Through our joint venture financing, we can contribute half the cash flow required and carry half the risk. . . . Joint venture financing is unsecured and off the balance sheet. The funds received from NRDC can be treated as income to the profit and loss account."[13]

Ireland, the poorest country in the EEC, offers the most generous investment incentives. The Irish Development Authority donates half the cost of a new project and the government offers a tax holiday for export-based companies. Such companies, however, cannot take advantage of the 100 percent depreciation that is also allowed in the first year of investment (since they pay no taxes); so, instead of buying the equipment they need, they lease it from banks at low or even negative inflation rates. Banks have been able to offer such rates because $100 of equipment only "costs" the banks $5: $50 is received as a capital grant and $45 is the value of the 100 percent depreciation to the bank. Until some of these loopholes were closed, the Irish government was financing up to 120 percent of the cost of projects through capital grants and lost taxes on bank profits in order to create jobs.

Governments protect existing employment by chipping in when companies cannot pay their bills. Lockheed was saved from bankruptcy during the Nixon administration with the aid of vast federal loan guarantees. U.S. aid was also given to Conrail and Penn Central to protect railroad workers' jobs. In 1980 Chrysler was on the brink of bankruptcy. Luckily for the company it employed 100,000 workers, and it was an election year. Republicans and Democrats therefore cooperated to expeditiously arrange a $1.6 billion loan-guarantee program to bail out the automobile company.

The precedent for bailouts in the U.K. was set by the Conservative Heath government when it nationalized the ailing Rolls-Royce company. Write Professors Kenneth D. Walters and R. Joseph Monsen, "The rescue established nationalization as a legitimate British industrial policy to save firms and jobs." In 1974 the Labour party rescued British Leyland.

Although the price tag was far higher than that of Rolls-Royce, Leyland employed 250,000 workers, was a major exporter, and represented the last major British-owned auto manufacturer. A conservative government would almost certainly have nationalized it had it been in power.[14]

Aid to ailing industries prevented the Thatcher government from achieving its spending reduction targets. In 1980 the government had wanted nationalized corporations to switch from a loss of £ 2.7 billion in 1979–80 to a net surplus of £700 million in 1983–84. But employment politics interfered. Mrs. Thatcher caved in to the miners' veto on pit closures in the coal industry. British Steel management was told by the government to keep open uneconomic plants at Ravenscraig in Scotland. By 1983 British Steel, British Rail, British Shipbuilders, the National Coal Board, and others had blown a £5 billion hole in the 1980 plans.

The Conservative government in Sweden rescued and nationalized more companies in four years than the Socialist Social Democrats had in forty-four. The entire shipbuilding industry fell into state hands. With the establishment of Swedish Steel, into which the loss makers were merged, the steel industry became a full ward of the state. The government took over the two largest clothing and textile concerns and bailed out the two largest pulp and paper manufacturers.

The Italian public sector, which accounts for about half of the nation's industrial investment, lost $3 billion in 1982.[15] Instituto per la Riconstruzione Industriale (IRI), the state-owned conglomerate charged with bringing jobs to the traditionally high-unemployment Mezzogiorno region in southern Italy, has gone down in national folklore for constructing "cathedrals in the desert"—"cathedrals," writes one observer, "without congregations of local entrepreneurs, of markets, or efficient credit structures."[16]

## Job Subsidies Don't Win Votes

What is the political bottom line of jobs bills, investment subsidies, and bailouts? High unemployment is an unpopular condition, not a cause; the source of the problem is excessive public spending. Subsidizing jobs can no more turn back joblessness than King Canute could order back the tide.

Direct employment by the state is ineffectual and dangerous. Public jobs can barely make a dent in the enormous numbers of unemployed. It would take a 33 percent increase in the number of federal employees to bring about a 1 percent decrease in the unemployment rate. To hire down the 10 percent unemployment rate of 1982 to a 1960s "full employment level" of 4 percent would require a 200 percent increase in U.S. government employment. If the federal payroll expanded proportionately, it would require over $120 billion in additional taxes or deficits.

Few leaders have the gumption, in these times, to try raising that kind of money, so their jobs programs are symbolic and make little difference to the unemployment rate. President Carter's 1977 public employment program was aimed at creating three-quarters of a million jobs—a 0.75 percent unemployment rate equivalent. President Mitterand's "ambitious" program to create 54,000 jobs could, at best, have reduced the unemployment rate in France by about 0.3 percent.

Since only a few of the unemployed can be given jobs, the politician is faced with setting thankless priorities. Who is to benefit—black teenagers among whom unemployment exceeds 50 percent or white adult women among whom unemployment is "only" 8 percent? Should jobs be given to those who have been unemployed for two months or two years? How about those people who have been "discouraged" and dropped out of the labor force?

Giving jobs to a small number of the jobless doesn't touch the principal source of public discontent with unemployment. Unemployment becomes the number-one public issue not because of the distress of the 10 percent of the workforce that is jobless but because the other 90 percent worries about the stability of its own livelihood: "Am I going to be laid off next, or are my wages going to be cut?" A state-funded lottery in which a few lucky winners get jobs doesn't go very far toward calming the anxieties of the working majority.

Politicians can't even count on the gratitude of those who are given employment. Typically the programs create white-collar positions, such as those for caseworkers or teachers, because many such jobs can be created without fixed investment. Wages are kept low in order to maximize the number of positions offered. The relatively young and better educated people who are best qualified for the kinds of jobs created have high expectations and resent the wages they are paid and the government that pays them. The politics of finding someone a job in an age of high social and economic awareness and universal availability of welfare benefits is different from that during the Depression era, when any job was welcome.

The cost of creating many new public jobs reduces the government's ability to pay good wages to the existing "core" employees, such as firemen, policemen, nurses, and sanitation workers. Low wages can provoke these employees to stage strikes, which cause enormous inconvenience to the public. Voters usually don't care about the specific issues behind these strikes (the illegal strike by $40,000 per year air traffic controllers was an exception)—they want their fires put out, their streets patrolled, their hospitals functioning, and their garbage removed; and if these services aren't being provided, politicians are held responsible.

Several political leaders have been burned for creating new public jobs while underpaying existing employees. Two years after he tried to lick unemployment by increasing jobs in public services, President Mitterand had a near mutiny by the police on his hands. Edward Heath, former Conservative prime minister of Britain, who increased government employment by 400,000 jobs and promulgated a national wage freeze, was toppled by striking miners from the nationalized coal industry. The Labour government that succeeded Mr. Heath's continued to expand public jobs. A few weeks before the 1979 general election 530,000 white-collar civil servants went on strike, making a mockery of Prime Minister James Callaghan's "social contract" with the unions. Michael Dukakis, who was elected governor of Massachusetts in 1974, increased the number of state employees to compensate for flagging employment in the private sector.[17] In the 1978 election public workers organized a "Dump the Duke" campaign that helped topple him.

Government protection of jobs in the private sector does not pay off either. Bailouts are ineffectual because bankruptcies and contractions of business are so widespread, frequent, and natural that government aid couldn't possibly prevent more than a small fraction of business failures that routinely occur. Every business that serves a competitive market is vulnerable —its customers' needs may change, the technology it uses may become obsolete, or a competitor may devise a better widget. And as firms die, jobs are lost—it is estimated that approximately 50 to 60 percent of all jobs disappear every ten years.

Fortunately, in a healthy economy new businesses (and jobs) are born as quickly as the old ones die. Unemployment is not simply due to the death of businesses—it is the net result of deaths, contractions, births, and expansions of firms. An economy is in poor shape only if more firms die or contract than are born or expanded.

David Birch of M.I.T., who analyzed the histories of 5.6 million businesses (collectively encompassing 82 percent of all private-sector employment) between 1969 and 1976, concluded that high unemployment in declining regions is not due to excessive business failures but rather to a low rate of business formation ("births"). He writes:

The rate of job loss due to . . . (deaths plus contractions) is about the same everywhere and is quite high—8 percent per year. Northern cities are not losing jobs faster than southern ones, nor are cities losing jobs particularly faster than suburbs. This shows up quite clearly . . . [when] states are grouped according to their rate of growth. Most of the variation in net change is due to variation in the rate of job generation [births and expansions], *not* to variation in the rate of loss.[18]

Studying the life cycle of firms in his data base, Birch found that:

The odds of an establishment dying over this seven-year period (1969–76) were quite high, especially for new firms—63.9 percent of new firms did not survive four years.

The odds of dying versus contracting were quite sensitive to size, with a sharp break around twenty employees—57.8 percent of small firms did not survive the seven-year period.

Of those that do survive, small firms were four times more likely to expand than contract, and larger firms are 50 percent more likely to shrink than to grow.

Birch concluded: "It is no wonder that efforts to stem the tide of job decline have been so frustrating—and largely unsuccessful. The firms that such efforts must reach are the most difficult to identify and the most difficult to work with. They are small. They tend to be independent. They are volatile."[19]

Bailouts of a few large companies like Lockheed or Chrysler ignore the bankruptcies of hundreds of thousands of smaller firms and the precarious existence of millions of others. Like jobs bills, they don't make a dent in the unemployment rate or reassure the employed. State-financed rescues don't even assure the votes of the employees of the firms that are saved. As with firms that demand protection from imports, the decline in the fortunes of firms that ask to be bailed out can at best be slowed. Even with gifts of taxpayers' money these companies continue to shed workers, and the wage increases they offer are below the historical expectations of their employees.

The Labour party in the U.K. got nothing but trouble for nationalizing and rescuing British Leyland. The company was a labor-relations nightmare to start with—collective bargaining was conducted through 220 separate bargaining units. The strike record of the company grew worse after nationalization. Billions of pounds of public money had to be poured into a company whose employees never seemed satisfied with what they received; the government was forced to repeatedly violate its own wage guidelines. Then in the May 1979 elections automobile workers ignored the high subsidies their Labour government had arranged for them. Over twelve conservative members of Parliament were elected from "safe" Labour constituencies around British Leyland's plants.

It is difficult to estimate how many more seats were lost indirectly. When British Leyland was being "saved" in 1975 there were over 6000 recorded bankruptcies, and tens of thousands of other businesses disappeared without filing bankruptcy petitions. They too had products, services, and employees. Their fault was obscurity; and their anonymous revenge was a Conservative victory.

Some lame ducks, it is true, do recover because of the subsidies they receive. As of 1983, for example, Chrysler had been miraculously steered back to profitability. Owners of the automakers' equity had seen the value of their stock rocket up from under three dollars to thirty, and the company had paid off its federally guaranteed debt seven years ahead of schedule. Lee A. Iacocca, chairman of Chrysler, was voted the most respected business leader in the U.S. and was even urged to run for President. But what did President Carter get for his role in favoring Chrysler over the thousands of other businesses that went bankrupt in 1980? After the Carter administration had seen the Chrysler aid package through Congress and the president of the United Automobile Workers (UAW), Douglas Fraser, had been made a director of Chrysler Corporation, Fraser endorsed Edward Kennedy for the Democratic nomination. In the November presidential election Jimmy Carter was trounced in Michigan. (David Stockman, who had voted against the bailout, was reelected to Congress from the same state.) He may also have lost the votes of the businessmen who were too small to have been bailed out and he probably didn't win the support of conservative investors who owned Chrysler stock.

Although the rescue eventually worked, it didn't help save jobs. The $1.6 billion credit that was given to Chrysler could have kept other businesses that employed more, lower-paid workers afloat. In any event, Mr. Iacocca turned Chrysler around by getting rid of two-thirds of its 100,000 workers. A good bankruptcy receiver could conceivably have saved more jobs: a firm in Chapter 11 is freed from its collective bargaining contracts and can make deeper wage cuts to help keep more of its business going. (The only real concession the UAW had made when the rescue package was arranged was in the area of paid days off.) And at worst, if Chrysler had stopped making cars, it would have meant more work for the other auto makers who had by 1982 over 200,000 workers on permanent layoff.

Investment grants also create few jobs and are biased toward large corporations. Large companies have more glamour—

politicians will move heaven and earth to attract a Ford plant that creates fifty jobs and ignore a hub-cap supplier that employs the same number of workers. Also, the administrative ethos will tolerate the loss of public money through poor business judgment but not through hasty procedures; hence capital grants flow to established companies with large staffs to handle the necessary paperwork, rather than to small lean companies. Even the flamboyant John De Lorean had to spend nearly a year negotiating his financial package with the British government; the infeasibility of his grandiose proposal didn't bother the authorities as long as the right procedure was followed.

Unfortunately, as David Birch found, it is the small businesses that create employment. Writes Birch:

Of all the net new jobs created in our sample . . . two-thirds were created by firms with 20 or fewer employers, and about 80 percent were created by firms with 100 or fewer employees. Smaller businesses more than offset their higher failure rates with their capacity to start up and expand dramatically. Larger businesses, in contrast, appear rather stagnant.[20]

No responsible government can give investment subsidies to small new firms, for there are millions of such startups with highly uncertain prospects. Furthermore, many small businessmen are suspicious of government money and the inevitable government bureaucracy. As Walter Kane, chairman of the Small Business Association, the American Electronics Association wrote in response to an initiative to help small business:

Would the nation's largest association of small high-technology companies actually oppose a bill to subsidize 80 percent of its members? You bet they would!—and here's why:

H.R. 4326, the Small Business Innovation Development Act, would require all federal agencies with large research budgets to set aside 3 percent of their R&D budgets for small companies. . . .

This form of mandatory set-asides has led to much fraud, waste and abuse in other industries and can be expected to do the same this time. . . . We don't want this kind of scandal in our industry.

By the time the full [3 percent] set-aside is allocated to the government-wide small business program, the federal government would be funding about 30,000 proposals a year. In order to administer such an incredible number of research proposals, the agencies would have to hire a massive number of contracting officers, make only cursory reviews of proposals and results, or both. The result promises to be a combination of expensive bureaucratic buildup and a waste of R&D funds.[21]

## A Target for Cuts

Since direct and indirect job subsidies provide such negligible political benefits even in times of high unemployment, a politician should make them a prime target for spending cuts. As a government can't realistically expect to free voters from the anxiety of losing their jobs, it should at least allow them to keep a higher proportion of their income when they are employed.

Doing away with job subsidies is easier than getting rid of tariffs and quotas. It is not necessary to make any promises about jobs bills even at election time—the public isn't impressed by them. Voters in the U.S. weren't swayed by the jobs program on the 1980 Democratic platform. In two general elections the Labour party in the U.K. hasn't succeeded in convincing the electorate of the importance of creating new public jobs. The Social-Democratic Party in Germany also failed to win support in the 1983 elections for its public employment schemes. Even committed liberals recognize that the mood is against new spending on jobs; in 1977 left-wing Democrats in Congress enthusiastically supported President Carter's $10 billion jobs bill; in 1983, when unemployment had doubled, they made do with a $4.6 billion program (worth under $3 billion in 1977 dollars).

Reversing the growth in the number of public employees is not a pipe dream—the Thatcher government did reduce the number of civil servants in Britain by 12 percent between 1979 and 1982.

Investment subsidies can be avoided through self-control.

Large companies (and the workers they haven't yet hired) can't afford to lobby too openly for handouts.

Politicians can warn companies seeking to be rescued that the money won't be forthcoming. International Harvester, for example, was effectively discouraged by the Reagan administration from asking for federal money in 1983 even though its financial condition was as precarious as Chrysler's had been in 1980 and it was as large an employer. Harvester, it was said, is an example of "the dog that didn't bark."[22]

The experience of British Leyland demonstrates that with good management backed by firm political will, even the sorriest nationalized lame ducks can be weaned away from public subsidies. In 1979 Sir Michael Edwardes was made chairman of British Leyland by the Thatcher government with a strong mandate to turn the company around. He submitted a "recovery plan" to the unions that involved several plant closings, layoffs, and subinflationary wage increases. When union officials rejected the plan outright, it was sent directly to all the workers, who were asked to mail back their opinion. When the votes were counted, Sir Michael had won the approval of 87 percent of his workers. By early 1983 the company was back in the black.

## Too Few Producers

Job subsidies hurt the long-term health of economy as they do the short-term self-interest of politicians. Make-work jobs programs increase the number of "passengers" that the productive members of society have to pull along—they don't produce goods or services that are needed by the market; nor do they support productive activities with necessary public services (as do policemen, firemen, teachers, and so forth). Paying for these "pure consumers" saps an economy's ability to make the savings and investment necessary to generate productive jobs.

135

Employment saved through bailouts only appears more productive than make-work public jobs—workers produce goods that customers don't want, or at a price they cannot afford. Bailouts, like protectionism, also hinder what Joseph Schumpeter described as the "creative destruction" that "incessantly revolutionizes the economic structure from within."[23] The deadwood isn't cleared away, so there isn't room for new saplings to grow.

Investment subsidies don't increase total investment, which today is severely limited by the shortage of savings; they merely distort the availability of capital. Investments are made by large "respectable" firms instead of small entrepreneurial companies. Capital is awarded more for making up the best story about job creation than for having the best product to take to market.

Europe's dismal position in high technology illustrates the danger of corporate handouts. In spite of having a large, sophisticated market and an early technological lead in many products (for example, Phillips made many of the important innovations in videocassette recorders), Europe lags behind Japan in consumer electronics, the U.S. in office automation and computers, and both in semiconductors. This is because critical resources of capital, engineering skills, and distribution channels are controlled by large bureaucratic companies— dinosaurs that governments won't allow to become extinct, protecting them from fleet-footed foreign predators and feeding them subsidized capital. Consequently, the young entrepreneurial talent, like Adam Osborne of Osborne computers and Terry Mathew and Michael Cowpland of Mitel, must flee to the New World to add to the already rich hoard of ingenuity and inventiveness there.

## Conclusion

High unemployment is unquestionably unpleasant and unpopular. Spending public money to create or preserve jobs is, however, not a politically sensible solution to the problem. Creating a token number of low-status jobs in the public sector does not allay the fears of the much larger working majority, from whom the real political problem derives. Similarly, bailouts of private companies are ineffectual because the government has the means to save only a fraction of the thousands of businesses that routinely go under. And providing investment subsidies to large firms fails to reach the myriad fledgling enterprises that really make the difference. Hence the pursuit of a theoretically popular objective—reducing unemployment—only accomplishes the unpopular result of raising taxes.

# CHAPTER 6

---

# *Public Services: With a Tight Fist*

UNLIKE JOB SUBSIDIES, which benefit only narrow constituencies, several services that the state provides are of interest to the public at large. All governments play a role, for example, in providing education, health care, housing, and security to their citizens. But there is great dispute about how that role should be fulfilled: liberals believe that the federal government, in the interests of promoting equality and protecting the weak, should provide and administer a broad range of public services. Conservatives, who are more concerned about fiscal prudence and limiting the role of the state, argue for a limited federal role, preferring that more public services be provided by private profit-making organizations or by states and local communities. As we will see in this chapter, a "political" approach falls between these two extremes: a vote-conscious government will play a major part in providing public services, but with a tight rein on costs; and with a primary emphasis on serving the needs of the largest number of constituents rather than on pursuing ideological goals.

## The Liberal-Conservative Divide

The Reagan administration's policies in education and health have reflected its conservative aims of a reduced federal presence. Mr. Reagan had pledged, in 1980, to abolish the Department of Education, and in his first year in office instituted several budget cuts in federal education programs. The control and financing of the public school system, he said, should be decentralized. "We've proven that throwing money at it is not the answer, and the Federal government can never match the funding of schools at the local and State level, where we created the greatest public school system and then have let it deteriorate, and I think you can make a case that it began to deteriorate when the Federal government started interfering in education."[1] He claimed that past administrations had "seemed to forget that education begins in the home where it's a parental right and responsibility."[2]

Mr. Reagan was also a strong advocate of private education and sought ways to help parents pay tuition costs. He proposed, for example, that parents be given tax credits to offset tuition payments and vouchers that could be used to obtain either public or private education for their children.

In 1981 Education Secretary T. H. Bell appointed a National Commission on Excellence in Education, which concluded in 1983 that "a rising tide of mediocrity" was eroding the educational system. The federal government, the commission said, "*has the primary responsibility* to identify the national interest in education. It should also help fund and support efforts to protect and promote that interest. It must provide the national leadership to ensure that the Nation's public and private resources are marshalled to address the issues discussed in this report."[3] Mr. Reagan called the commission's report "masterful" but insisted "education is not the prime responsibility of the Federal Government" and that "what they are talking about can be corrected without money."[4] "The focus of our agenda," he said, "is, as it must be, to restore parental choice and influence and to increase competition between schools."[5]

Regarding health, Mr. Reagan was opposed to government-mandated limits on hospital costs, all forms of national health insurance, and supported tax credits for private health insurance programs. Medicaid, he said in his first speech to Congress, was not "cost effective" because

right now Washington provides the states with unlimited matching payments for their expenditures. At the same time we here in Washington pretty much dictate how the states will manage the program. We want to put a cap on how much the Federal government will contribute but at the same time allow the states much more flexibility in managing and structuring their programs. I know from our experience in California that such flexibility could lead to far more cost-effective reform.[6]

Later, as Medicaid costs continued to rise, he proposed that the elderly pay more for the benefits they received from the program through higher deductibles, co-payments (patient's daily share of hospital costs), and monthly contributions.

The opposite liberal objective of broad and generous public services is reflected in the U.K. Labour party's 1979 election manifesto:

Under this Labour Government, the proportion of 3- and 4-year-olds in nursery classes and schools has doubled. Local authorities will be encouraged to do much more. We will provide a universal scheme of education and training for all 16- to 19-year-olds, if necessary, backed by statute. We will remove the financial barriers which prevent many young people from low income families from continuing their education after 16. Further education places have increased by 25,000 under Labour. Labour will substantially increase the opportunities for people from working class backgrounds, particularly adults —to enter further and higher education. We want to see more workers given time off work for study. To this end, the places at the Open University have increased from 42,000 in 1974 to 80,000 in 1978.

Labour will end as soon as possible the remaining public subsidies and public support to independent schools.[7]

## Public Services: With a Tight Fist

### The Political Perspective

The conventional political view coincides with liberal ideology: more schools and hospitals mean more votes. Conservative leaders, as politicians, are therefore quite hesitant about advertising or implementing their desire to cut public services. In the 1983 general election in the U.K., for example, the Labour party alleged that the Conservatives had plans to undermine the National Health Service (NHS). Labour leader Dennis Healey said that the proposed Tory health service would mean "a big new private hospital doing facelifts for the rich next to a run down, overcrowded building where you wait for hours for someone to treat your sick child."[8] These attacks did not elicit a spirited conservative defense of private medicine. Instead Tory ministers pointed out that their government had increased real spending on health by 7.7 percent and Mrs. Thatcher avowed that she was as committed to the National Health Service as she was to the British Defence services.

In general, the liberal view has held greater sway in Europe than in the U.S., where conservative opposition has checked the growth of public services. U.S.-financed Medicare, for example, covers only 26 million senior citizens and about 3 million disabled; 160 million Americans are covered by private, employer-paid health insurance, and as of 1982, 30 million had no coverage at all. In Europe, state-operated health schemes cover all citizens and provide generous benefits. The U.K. NHS, which began to operate in July 1948, entitles every man, woman, and child to medical treatment of every sort, free at the moment of need. Patients are at liberty to choose their doctors, and 98 percent of general practitioners and nearly all dentists are in the service. The goal of the Italian national health scheme is to provide *tutto per tutti*—"everything for everyone." The German government offers, in addition to basic care, frills like *kur*, or a health-cure program whereby patients can be sent to stay for a month at a *kurot*, or spa. There are approximately 250 state-registered *kurote* in Germany, located in attractive parts of the country with social and recreational as well as medical facilities.

Similarly, in education: privately financed institutions for higher education thrive in the U.S. whereas in Europe they are virtually extinct. In the U.S. many individuals have to borrow heavily to attend college and some cannot afford to go at all. In European universities, admitted students not only pay no tuition, they also receive a living allowance from the government.

## Vote-winning Potential

Compared to other categories of expenditure, spending on public services has high vote-winning potential. Funding a hospital or a school for the benefit of the community at large is, unlike a jobs program, a reliable way of taking from a few to give to the many. This Robin Hood popularity of public services is naturally most pronounced when spending is in a low range and declines as the total level of expenditure increases. But even when the middle class has to pay for the services it receives, a government can still create value for voters by correcting the "inefficiencies" of the market. Politicians can, in other words, help their constituents by providing them with services that private profit-seeking businesses won't or can't provide at a reasonable cost.

Education, for example, is a public need that markets cannot easily finance. Education is an investment—money spent now on improving an individual's knowledge, skills, or contacts yields an enhanced stream of income in the future. Unfortunately, private financial markets are not capable of making loans for investments in human capital, where "paybacks" can extend over forty-year periods and the risk of investing in a particular knowledge or skill is difficult to evaluate. The educational investment in a student cannot be financed by selling "equity" in the individual either: the stock issue would be difficult to structure, the investors would have a hard time collecting, and most people would find selling themselves off distasteful.

Since markets won't supply the capital, investments in education have traditionally been made by rich individuals, who have sought to perpetuate the prosperity of their heirs rather than to maximize their returns. Some rich individuals also invest, as Milton and Rose Friedman point out, in "monuments" —by giving libraries, university chairs, or endowing scholarships,[9] but their generosity has not been on the scale necessary to ensure equality of opportunity to the children of all citizens. Hence by investing public money in education, politicians can win the favor of the many middle class and poor citizens by offering their children the same opportunities available to the children of the rich.

Most voters believe that tax revenues devoted to education are well spent. While public support for many other categories of spending plunged in the failure zone, education stayed in favor. (See chapter 7 for a discussion of how support for welfare plunged in the same period.) Although federal outlays grew rapidly through the 1960s, in 1973, 57 percent of Americans believed that the federal government should be spending even more on education (barely down from 60 percent in 1961), while only 7.7 percent thought that government should be spending less.[10] The Gallup poll reported that in 1975 the public's second most important priority for public spending was education (just marginally behind the first, health care).[11] In a 1982 Gallup poll, education was the number-one priority, way ahead of defense and welfare. The Presidential Commission on Excellence in Education noted that these polls "strongly supported a theme heard during our hearings . . . very clearly the public understands the primary importance of education as the foundation for a satisfying life, an enlightened and civil society, a strong economy and a secure Nation."[12]

Governor William Winter proved the point in Mississippi recently. His top priority after his election in 1979 was the expansion and improvement of the public school and kindergarten system, financed by raising the severance taxes on oil and gas. Mr. Winter's initiative was blocked in two consecutive sessions of the legislature, but he persisted. He organized statewide town meetings to mobilize support for his educational program and then called a special session of the legislature to deal with the issue.

"He had the worst possible combination against it," said Representative Jim Simpson, the floor leader for the bill. "The oil interests opposed the tax measures. There was another group who were committed not to vote for any new taxes. And I would be less than truthful if I told you race was not a factor."[13] (An estimated 45 percent of the children in Mississippi public schools are black.)

Nevertheless, the educational program was passed. "Governor Winter is an old style southern gentleman," Simpson said. "He is not a street fighting politician. It is not within his nature to be a bargainer. He does not like to pressure people. He's uncomfortable with it. But on the educational bill, he did it the other way. He prepared unbelievably well, he went out to the grass roots and brought out an awareness like has never been done before."[14]

Winter won considerable acclaim for his initiative. Even conservative legislators in Mississippi who had voted against the educational bill conceded that "in the aftermath of the previous administration, Winter has substantially changed the image of the State."[15]

Health care also is an area in which a government can be profitably involved since the private medical industry seems incapable of delivering a reasonably priced service to the public and for several reasons the health care market is not efficient: consumers can't make intelligent choices about the service they desire and are entirely in the hands of their physicians. As economist Victor R. Fuchs notes, "the doctor exercises primary control over the quantity, type and cost of most services utilized by his patients from drugs, tests and office visits to hospital admissions, lengths of stay and courses of treatment."[16] And physicians tend to use their control to provide high-quality and expensive service because of dedication to the high professional standards, fear of malpractice suits, and, unavoidably, to maximize their incomes. The option of cost-efficient treatment therefore isn't available to patients.

The medical profession's preference for expensive quality over cheap essentials is also seen in the supply of doctors. If many were trained quickly, there would be numerous cheap physicians around but with questionable skills; whereas long apprenticeships for few students makes for high-quality but expensive doctors. This trade-off between the number and quality of new doctors is not freely determined by the market but is regulated by associations of existing practitioners, such as the American Medical Association. The goal of these associations isn't to provide the public with the most cost-effective care but rather to maintain the high-quality of professional standards and, implicitly, to protect the incomes of their members by restricting the number of practitioners.

Although there is no explicit conspiracy, there is considerable circumstantial evidence of an artificial scarcity, in the high ratio of applicants to available places in medical schools, in the long hours that doctors work, and in the fees they charge. Taking a cynical view of the number of immigrant doctors in the West, one might conclude that the supply of doctors has deliberately been kept well below demand and the "gap" has been filled, especially in the less attractive jobs, with doctors imported from developing countries.

The medical profession's preference for high-cost care is reinforced by the rapid growth of private insurance schemes; as of 1982 third-party payments covered 91 percent of hospital costs and 63 percent of physicians' services.[17] These insurance schemes free consumers from cost concerns and ease physicians' qualms about overprescribing and overcharging. Since hospitals are reimbursed on the basis of their costs, there is an incentive for administrators not to risk lowering income by cutting costs. As Samuel Davis, director of Mount Sinai Hospital, writes, "the more efficiently we run our institution, the more we are financially penalized by the system."[18]

The health-care industry has become, as Stanford University economist Alain C. Enthoven puts it, "a classic example of market failure. We have allowed it to evolve in a direction in which waste, overuse and an upward spiral of fees are encouraged, while efficiency and economy are discouraged."[19] Voters are paying through the nose for inefficiency. Between 1967 and 1982 overall medical costs more than tripled and hospital rates more than quintupled. Overall medical costs in 1982 represented 9.8 percent of the gross national product, compared to 5.3 percent in 1969 and 7.5 percent in 1970. More than one month of the average American's yearly work effort now goes to paying the nation's health-care bill through hidden taxes and insurance premiums.[20]

Although most voters don't understand why health costs are high, they expect their government to help control them—even by spending tax money, if necessary. Public support for health-care expenditures runs neck and neck with that for expenditures on education. Between 1961 and 1973 the percentage of voters who thought the government should be spending more money on hospitals and health care rose from 49 percent to 59 percent, while the percentage of people who favored less spending fell from 8.7 percent to 7.3 percent.[21]

## Disciplined Priorities Are Missing

When spending is in a low range, most public services are net vote winners, since they can be funded from the taxes levied on a few rich. At higher levels of total spending, where public services are financed out of more painfully extracted taxes, a more disciplined and fiscally cautious ordering of priorities is necessary. Vote-seeking politicians should fund services that are attractive to the largest number of voters and be alert for opportunities to help the public without spending its money, by correcting market deficiencies and putting individual private initiative to better use.

## Public Services: With a Tight Fist

Many politicians, however, equate abundant universal services with votes, ignoring the political costs of raising the taxes to pay for these services. They avoid setting priorities or considering trade-offs; few attempts are made to determine whether voters really want the services provided and many opportunities to help the public without spending its money are neglected.

An unsystematic, free-vote mentality has caused politicians to spend tax revenues on providing special services to small groups at the expense of basic services used by the public at large. Consider, for example, the funds and attention lavished on expanding the capacity of colleges. College enrollment in the U.S. quadrupled from 3 million in 1960 to 12 million in 1980. The growth was principally through public money spent on public colleges; by 1980 there were four times as many students enrolled in government institutions of higher learning as in private institutions; and direct government grants accounted for more than half of total expenditure on higher education.

Expenditures on higher education are a subsidy to middle- and upper-income families whose children are two to three times as likely to attend college as those from lower-income groups. Several studies have shown that spending on higher education transfers income from the many to the few. A study in Florida compared the benefits four income classes derived from public spending on higher education with the taxes they paid. The top income class got back 60 percent more than it paid; the bottom two classes paid 40 percent more than the benefits they received, and the middle class was out of pocket by 20 percent. A study in California showed that families with college-going children received a net benefit ranging from 1.5 percent to 6.6 percent of their income, with the highest benefit going to those with the highest average income. Families without children in public higher education incurred a net tax cost of 8.2 percent of their income.[22]

The money and attention lavished on higher education could have been devoted to improving the quality of public schools to which a much larger number of families send their children—for example, in 1983, of the 60 million students in the U.S., only 20 percent were enrolled in institutions of higher education.[23] The public school system, to which a majority of families send their children, is much in need of attention and repair. As the Commission on Excellence in Education put it:

If an unfriendly foreign power had attempted to impose on America the mediocre educational performance that exists today, we might well have viewed it as an act of war. As it stands, we have allowed this to happen to ourselves. We have even squandered the gains in student achievement made in the wake of the Sputnik challenge. Moreover, we have dismantled the essential support systems which helped make those gains possible. We have in effect been committing an act of unthinking, unilateral educational disarmament.[24]

The political attractiveness of other public services has been wasted by not ensuring that the benefits reach the broadest number of voters. Federal spending on health care jumped from $3 billion in 1960 to $70.9 billion in 1980; the government now picks up nearly 40 percent of the nation's health-care bill but provides benefits to less than 15 percent of the population.[25] The U.S. pays for nearly 50 percent of the nation's hospital costs, where, as Drs. Francis Moore and Christopher Zook found, 1.3 percent of the public consumes over half of all hospital resources.[26]

Mass transit is another heavily subsidized public service that benefits a few relatively better off citizens. To build Washington, D.C.'s, "solid gold Cadillac of mass transit," $7.2 billion was spent. The Washington area happens to be the wealthiest metropolitan area in the U.S. and contains two of the richest counties in the nation—Montgomery County, Maryland, and Fairfax County, Virginia. And the $7.2 billion tab was at least $550 million more than the combined cost of all the other rapid rail systems that were built in the U.S. in the 1970s.[27]

These anomalies often arise because of an ideological commitment to a powerful state role in the provision of public services. A gleaming subway car in Washington, D.C., warms the cockles of liberal hearts even if its well-to-do riders are being subsidized by the taxes paid by the owners of millions of beat-up Chevys; a bustling state university, "almost as good as Harvard," is an egalitarian's delight, even though Harvard admits and supports a greater proportion of minorities and students from poor families and government spending on state universities leads to neglecting the needs of inner-city public schools.

## Ignoring Market Needs

An ideological emphasis on symbols also leads politicians to ignore opportunities to correct deficiencies of the market and can in fact increase public dissatisfaction. Consider, for example, spending on higher education: the main political value of state investment in higher education lies in the gratitude of poor and middle-class families whose children are offered an opportunity to get ahead. This benefit is lost if colleges graduate more students than the job market can absorb or impart skills of dubious economic value. Parental gratitude cannot be won by subsidizing a college education that palpably does not improve their childrens' earning prospects. A popular government must exercise careful control over the type of education it supports. This requires anticipating long-term labor market trends—a government must know roughly how many engineers, architects, microbiologists, and history majors are likely to be needed. And it must ensure that public funds are directed toward meeting these labor market needs, not toward promoting learning for learning's sake. Subsidizing intellectual curiosity with taxpayers' funds does not make political sense.

In practice, politicians have either been indifferent to market needs or so much in awe of educational institutions that they have failed to set necessary limits on the choice of programs funded with public money. Departments of labor draw up projections of manpower needs up to the year 2000; departments of education ignore them. In fact, it is the private schools and colleges, which need contributions from alumni and therefore have a vested interest in the economic advancement of their graduates, that tend to be more concerned about educating to market.

The failure to tie higher education to market needs has made college degrees an economic liability for millions of students. Too many places have been created—a college enrollment of 12 million is clearly excessive for an economy that generates only about 1 million net new jobs a year (and indeed a disproportionate number of the unemployed are college graduates). A high proportion of students are enrolled for courses of questionable market value—for example, in 1983, out of nearly a million bachelors' degrees that were granted, less than 75,000 were in engineering.[28] The most popular programs in liberal arts are rather quite open-minded in their conception of education. As President Reagan says: "We've seen a time in which you can get credits toward graduation for cheerleading. . . . Or how would you like to graduate by getting straight A's in bachelor life?"[29]

A lax educational policy increases the risk that students will bite the hand that feeds them. Students who have to work hard in professional colleges and have good jobs to look forward to are docile and averse to risk; those with undemanding courseloads, generous scholarships, and dismal employment prospects are natural recruits for campus rebellions. Student disturbances that shook many countries in the 1960s were fueled by uncontrolled growth in college enrollment, financed by public money.

A striking example is that of France. The number of students in French universities grew from 247,000 in 1960 to 612,000 by 1968.[30] While all of them were offered nearly free tuition, only 5 percent of the students—those admitted to the elite *grand Ecoles*—could look forward to a rigorous education and later to bright careers in industry and government. The rest were herded into universities like the Sorbonne where lecture halls designed to seat 500 were crammed with twice that number.

The courses themselves were "heavily theoretical and academic" which "limited career outlets" for the students who
had to take them.[31] French students were therefore receptive
to the radicalism of extremists like Danny Cohn-Bendit
(Danny le Rouge), and demonstrations in French universities
sparked off the May revolution in 1968 that nearly brought
down the government. The Gaullist response to this near miss
was a "reform" in the 1970s that increased the number of
universities from 22 to 65 and the number of students to nearly
one million.[32] Conservative politicians thus funded an intellectual and organizational base that helped elect the Socialists in
1981.

In health care the emphasis has also been on spending public
money; opportunities to help the public by promoting competition in the health-care industry have been largely ignored.
U.S. administrations, which have destroyed PATCO, the Professional Air Traffic Controllers Association, and confronted
the Teamsters, have steered clear of the American Medical
Association, which the Friedmans describe as "one of the most
successful unions in the country." For decades, they write, the
AMA has "kept down the number of physicians, kept up the
costs for medical care and prevented competition with duly
apprenticed and sworn physicians by people from outside
the profession—all, of course, in the name of helping the
patient."[33]

The only U.S. government agency that has tried to promote
competition among doctors, the Federal Trade Commission
(FTC), began examining professional conduct only in 1975; the
$6.8 million it spent in 1982 to investigate "anti-competitive,
unfair or deceptive conduct" is minuscule compared to the
U.S. government's $70 billion spending on Medicare and Medi-
caid.[34] The FTC's biggest victory so far was in 1978 when it
decreed that eyeglasses could be advertised—a ruling said to
have saved consumers $20 per pair of eyeglasses. And even
these feeble forays have been endangered by the conservative
crusade against federal regulation. In 1983 a coalition of special-interest groups representing doctors, dentists, veterinari-

ans, and ophthalmologists pushed an amendment though the Senate Commerce Committee to exempt their business practices completely from FTC scrutiny and succeeded in attaching such an exemption to the agency's budget.

## Testing the Value

Some services (for example, Washington's mass transit) identifiably provide no benefit to a majority of voters and therefore do not deserve priority in the allocation of public resources. But evaluating the political utility of other services that *are* used by much of the public (free prescription glasses provided by the U.K.'s National Health Service, for example) can be tricky. Consumption is not a reliable guide; the subsidized supply of public services can create its own demand, whether or not people value or need the services they use. Several writers have noted, for example, how free medical care has turned many European countries into nations of hypochondriacs where drugs are compulsively consumed, without any improvement in public health.

The real test of political attractiveness is whether or not most voters value a service more highly than the cost of the taxes they pay for it. It is useful, therefore, especially when the taxes are high, to exact some financial charge from the users of a service in order to estimate its true value. The higher the cost of a prescription patients have to pay themselves, the less likely they are to demand unnecessary medication. Making users pay for a portion of the costs of the services they consume also has other advantages: the money raised can be used in offering the service to more voters. User fees can also help prevent inadvertent many-poor-to-few-rich type of subsidies. Solid-gold subways are less likely to be built, for example, if they are required to break even.

Singapore's housing program is an example of the virtues of making public services pay their way. "Public housing is an area of pride in Singapore," says its deputy prime minister, Dr. Goh Keng Swee. "Half the population is housed in urban housing estates and some 40 percent of these are owner occupied."[35] The program *is* politically motivated. The housing projects have not been spontaneously constructed by market forces—the government has forced investment into them and slum dwellers who have been provided decent housing have become staunch supporters of the ruling People's Action Party.

The program has been successful, says Dr. Goh, because although the government directed investment into housing:

[we] insisted that public housing must pay its way. This means that tenants must pay rents adequate to cover interest on capital, property taxes and depreciation as well as current administrative costs. When a tenant defaults on rent, the Housing Authority dispatches a team of bailiffs to evict the family and remove the furniture and belongings onto the pavement. Invariably, there is an uproar in the Press and the Housing Authority is roundly condemned for heartlessness. Pictures of pathetic children squatting on the roadside, even of allegedly unemployed consumptive fathers, emphasize the pitiful condition the family is reduced to. However, such episodes invariably have a happy ending. Newspapers start a fund and readers' contributions quickly add to between five and ten years' rental. The money is handed over to the Housing Authority and the status quo is restored amidst much rejoicing. So the Housing Authority can proceed to build more new homes untroubled by fears of funds drying up.[36]

Dr. Goh insists that it is not difficult for government leaders who are prepared to take the trouble "to convince the electorate that public enterprises—utilities, housing, telephones, sea and airports—must be managed on sound business principles. Failing this, the continued existence of these services would require annual subsidies on an increasing scale which in turn would mean more and more taxes."[37]

Dr. Goh's contention that "you cannot run a public housing program under a soft approach" is borne out by U.S. experience. The Department of Housing and Urban Development does not lack resources. In 1980 it had a staff of 20,000 and a budget of $10 billion—but its programs "have been a conspicuous failure." Public housing has been virtually given away and therefore has been treated with disrespect, as being without real value. Units have "frequently become slums and hotbeds of crime, especially juvenile delinquency."[38] The Pruitt-Igoe public housing apartment complex in St. Louis, for example, won an architectural prize and was once the toast of the liberal establishment; unfortunately, it was so badly vandalized that it had to be dynamited.

User charges are especially important in the area of higher education. There is a great tendency to take advantage of cheap college education simply because it is there. Subsidized higher education that does not enhance career prospects can still attract many students "because fees are low, residential food and housing are subsidized, and above all many other young people are there."[39] Exacting a real financial cost can quickly deflate bloated enrollment and the associated problems thereof.

It is also necessary to eventually recover from a student the full cost of his college education in order to avoid a from-many-to-few type of subsidy. Higher education, unlike basic schooling, is almost by definition received by a minority. The political attractiveness of a government role in higher education does not lie in providing free education to a few students, but in correcting the failure of the financial markets to provide equal opportunity to the children of all families. A loan program is, therefore, preferable to outright grants because it helps create equal opportunity without permanently giving away the public money to a talented minority.

Politicians, especially those of liberal persuasion, often reflexively oppose tough repayment terms for student loans, higher transit fares, and other means of reducing the tax revenues needed to fund public services. Many Democrats criticized President Reagan's plan to reduce U.S. spending on Medicare by passing on some of the costs to the program's beneficiaries. The U.K. Labour party denounced in its election manifesto "Tory proposals for higher prescription charges and charges for seeing a doctor or being in hospital. Our aim is to abolish all charges in the NHS."[40]

## Public Services: With a Tight Fist

The reflex is an anachronistic vestige of a low spending era. Then, user charges were unpopular because they interfered with redistribution of income from the upper classes to the masses—a "free" hospital or school, from the point of view of most of the public, was truly so and user charges would only reduce the taxes of the rich. Today the avoidance of fees only implies higher taxes on the incomes of the many, often for the benefit of relatively few beneficiaries.

### Keeping the Baby

The conservative revival and the public agitation for lower taxes has brought some necessary consolidations and trims. In Mrs. Thatcher's first term, her government slashed grants to universities, chopped off over 47,000 places from higher education, closed 109 hospitals, raised NHS prescription charges, and reduced the burden of public housing to the taxpayer by selling off council houses to tenants. In New York City Mayor Ed Koch has won considerable popularity by breaking with the tradition that was set by Mayor Robert Wagner, who announced in 1965: "I do not propose to permit our fiscal problems to set the limits of our commitments to meet the essential needs of the people of the city."[41] Mayor Koch was more responsive to the public—he determined that his administration would deliver a level of public services that New Yorkers were willing to pay for. Tough priorities were set: hospitals had to be closed and the level of fire and police services were scaled back. Several liberals accused Mr. Koch of insensitivity and inhumanity. But once it was explained to New York's overtaxed voters why cutbacks in public services were in their interest, they bore the inconvenience with equanimity.

There is a danger, however, that ideological conservative zeal to reduce services (unlike ex-liberal Koch's calculated cuts) will throw out the baby along with the bath water. Although shrinkage may be the most popular priority in Europe, in the U.S. the emphasis should be on rationalization. Along with discarding some of the liberal excesses of the past, a vote-seeking administration should also be open to the many opportunities that exist to expand its role. In health care, the administration should broaden its focus from helping the elderly, the poor, and the disabled to shaking up the medical industry so that all Americans have the option of cheaper care. As of 1983, the Reagan administration had done little other than talk about the need to increase the competitiveness of the health-care industry. The only radical action had been taken by Governor Jerry Brown and the California legislature. In July 1982 California appointed a "czar" empowered to negotiate with hospitals and doctors to get the best rates for the state's Medicaid (called Medical in California) business. The state also went beyond helping the poor; it changed the health-insurance laws to increase the negotiating flexibility of insurance companies with the providers of health care.

A U.S. administration sensitive to the interests of its constituents should not leave such popular initiatives to be undertaken by a few sophisticated state governments. It should make restructuring of the health-care industry a high-visibility effort, under the responsibility of an individual of ability and stature, like the Carter administration's deregulation of the airline industry under the forceful Alfred Kahn. The rising cost of health care is a problem for all Americans, and the causes of this problem (for example, the artificial shortage of physicians, especially in unappealing state hospitals) are national. So taking on the health-care industry is a legitimate federal concern and one that could yield handsome political benefits.

In public schooling too there are several reasons why the federal government should expand its role in order to provide the educational opportunities that voters desire for their children. First, there is the growing importance of "computer literacy." As Senator Frank R. Lautenberg, who made a fortune by building the largest data processing company in the U.S., warned in his maiden Senate speech: "The concept of computer literacy defines a new type of illiteracy, and the potential for new and distressing divisions in our society." Almost 70 percent of schools in wealthy districts, he noted, had microcomputers; almost 60 percent of poor schools did not. "In an age that demands computer literacy, a school without a computer is like a school without a library," Mr. Lautenberg said. There was also the issue of home computers, which were "being acquired by the affluent, reinforcing disparities in opportunity."[42]

Huge numbers of computers are going to be needed in the schools. "We don't have more than 200,000 microcomputers in schools," says a U.S. Department of Education official. "If you arbitrarily say that every kid is entitled to 30 minutes a day on the computers, we would need four million in U.S. schools."[43] Educational agencies that are beginning to deal with computers at the state and district level are strapped for funds; the U.S. government, which could pay for all 4 million microcomputers with less than 1 percent of the Department of Defense's budget, has so far not played an active role.

Another reason for a greater federal role in education is the changing structure of the U.S. and the world economy. Local control and autonomy was appropriate to the nineteenth century when the U.S. consisted of many relatively loosely linked regional economies. It makes less sense today, now that integration of the national economy is three decades past and a "global" economy is evolving. Local school boards cannot independently and autonomously respond to the needs of a world economy. They don't have adequate information about future needs or about what is happening in the rest of the country or the world. The federal government, therefore, must plan, coordinate, and, where necessary, control. Diversity is an emotive catchword but uniformity is often more useful. The use of one language, English, has played a great role in American prosperity; standard computer languages taught uniformly in all schools could be of equal importance.

Then there is the public concern with quality. President Reagan has struck a popular chord, calling for merit pay for teachers (rewarding good teachers with more money), a return to academic basics, required courses in mathematics and science, more homework, and longer school hours. "The President is on the winning side of this issue as it is being played," said one Reagan aide. "The question is of quality and not quantity."[44]

Making the right speeches, however, is only part of the political battle won; parents who believe in basics want to see them actually returned to schools, not merely talked about. Some federal muscle has to be put behind educational reform—presidential exhortation will not change teaching practices, increase homework, or institute merit pay in the thousands of schools around the country. Blaming Washington or praising the virtues of local control and independence is an unrewarding cop-out.

President Eisenhower responded to the Sputnik challenge by taking personal responsibility for reforms like the National Defense Education Act, which authorized federal contributions to college loan funds and federal grants for strengthening science instruction in schools. Federally financed summer workshops retrained a whole generation of math, science, and language teachers. These reforms had a measurable and recognized impact on achievement scores. An administration today that desires the public's respect for its response to the decline in educational standards must similarly be willing to shoulder its responsibilities. It must make choices, set priorities, and initiate and implement reforms; an administration must administer!

## Enhancing Human Capital

Good public services contribute to a country's overall economic prosperity by enhancing the productive capabilities of individual citizens. A good public school system, for example, is a critical resource. As the National Commission on Excellence in Education wrote:

## Public Services: With a Tight Fist

We live among determined, well educated and strongly motivated competitors. We compete with them for international standing and markets not only with products but also with the ideas of our laboratories and neighborhood workshops. America's position in the world may once have been reasonably secure with only a few exceptionally well-trained men and women. It is no longer.

The risk is not only that the Japanese make automobiles more efficiently than Americans. It is not just that American machine tools, once the pride of the world, are being displaced by German products.

It is also that these developments signify a redistribution of trained capability throughout the globe. Knowledge, learning, information and skilled intelligence are the new raw materials of international commerce and are spreading today throughout the world as vigorously as miracle drugs, synthetic fertilizers and blue jeans did earlier.[45]

Japan's exceptional school system has contributed greatly to its economic success. That nation, which requires nine years of compulsory schooling, has the lowest illiteracy rate in the world and high proficiency in its schools in mathematics and sciences. Japanese higher education also educates scrupulously to market. Though Japan's college enrollment is only 2 million compared to 12 million in the U.S., the two countries produce approximately the same number of engineers. The number of liberal arts majors and lawyers is strictly limited. There are 30,000 applicants every year for 500 places in a three-year government-run apprentice program that produces Japan's lawyers. (In the U.S., over 40,000 students are admitted to law school every year, and there are already more lawyers in Philadelphia than there are in Japan.)[46]

The quality and cost of health care is also a factor in economic prosperity. A healthy worker is a more productive worker, and lower health costs moderate wage demands and keep inflation under control. And, for all their inefficiencies, the national health insurance schemes and services in Europe seem to do a better job in controlling the cost of health care than the more private system does in the U.S. In 1980 the ratio of health spending to gdp was 5.2 percent in Britain, 6.7 percent in Germany, 7.5 percent in France, and 9.4 percent in the U.S. "It is amazing," writes Professor Paul Starr of Harvard, "that we can spend more on medicine than any country in the world and yet get less value for our money."[47]

## Defense: A Special Case

On defense, liberals and conservatives switch roles. Conservatives became free spenders because they refuse to believe that national security interests can ever be too securely protected. Liberals, on the other hand, are committed to turning all swords into plowshares, that is, taking from the Department of Defense and giving to the Department of Health, Education and Welfare.

Public sentiment is prone to shift rapidly between the liberal and conservative positions. In 1976 Mr. Carter's promise to cut the rate of growth of military spending was popular—36 percent of voters believed "too much" was being spent on defense compared to 22 percent who thought "too little" was being spent. The public mood, however, shifted rapidly—by 1980, the "too-much" defense spending category dropped to 14 percent and the "too-little" group rose to 49 percent. Mr. Carter reversed himself and decided to ask for higher rates of spending growth, but his conversion was apparently not quick enough. So when President Reagan proposed a major increase in the defense budget in February 1981, with polls showing that 51 percent of voters thought defense spending was too little, liberal Democrats didn't dare object too loudly. But just over a year later, the public mood shifted again. The too-little category was down to 16 percent and the too-much one up to 41 percent.[48] As Senator Richard Lugar, head of the National Republican Senatorial Committee, said in April 1983: "In 1980, people felt we were falling behind the Russians and they did not like that. That is not so now. All the polls we see say that people feel we're spending enough on defense. And anybody who has been going up and down his home state for the last few weeks has heard that in spades."[49]

## Public Services: With a Tight Fist

Voters have reason to be confused about defense spending. They have no way of knowing how much expenditure is really needed to assure national security—conservative politicians discreetly aided by Pentagon officials are always warning them that the sky is about to fall down, and liberals have no way of proving otherwise. There are few sources of objective opinion; most experts who are capable of determining whether or not a certain level of resources is adequate are directly or indirectly on the military payroll and have a vested interest in more defense spending.

Defense spending does bring other benefits to voters besides assuring their security—people get a macho or nationalistic satisfaction from having a strong army. Paying for the Pentagon is a bit like supporting the local football or baseball franchise. But this psychic value of defense spending (unlike the more tangible benefit provided by a public school or hospital) is volatile and apt to disappear from the voter's mind when it collides against the reality of higher taxes.

Since public support for defense budgets tends to be erratic, a politician should talk like a conservative and spend like a liberal; speak loudly and carry a discount stick. To make speeches warning the Soviets about dire consequences or to shoot down a couple of Libyan jets is cheap—it is the MX missiles and B-1 bombers that cost real money. The funds saved by curbing hardware extravagances can be more popularly used to give voters tangible benefits of lower taxes or better hospitals and schools.

Curiously, former generals have often been the ones who have prevented voters' economic interests from being sacrificed in the name of national security. President Eisenhower popularized the unflattering term military-industrial complex to describe the Pentagon-defense contractors lobby. In 1954, when he was urged to take up the fight against the Vietminh that the French had lost, Mr. Eisenhower refused to do so because he felt General Matthew Ridgeway's estimate of a $3.5 billion cost would create too large a budget deficit.[50] A decade later, President Johnson had no such fiscal qualms.

In France the left-wing politicians of the Fourth Republic fought and lost a bloody eight year war to deny independence to Vietnam. The experience did not prevent them from trying to hang on to Algeria. By early 1958 more than half a million French troops had been installed there. In May 1958 right-wing extremists who believed that this was not commitment enough brought down the Fourth Republic and installed, as the first president of the Fifth Republic, General Charles de Gaulle, leader of the resistance in World War II.

Unfortunately for the plotters, de Gaulle realized that France was being bled by the Algerian war of independence and that he had to choose between the interests of the one million French *colons* settled in Algeria and the more than 44 million citizens in France. He chose to support Algerian independence and took the costs of his choice on the chin. Many of his supporters immediately broke with him and high-ranking military officers mounted an insurrection in Algeria. When the revolt failed, the rebels turned to terrorism and made several attempts to assassinate de Gaulle.

De Gaulle survived the crisis and became immensely popular. A referendum on the agreement of independence he had negotiated was approved by over 90 percent of voters. Soon thereafter, another referendum to amend the Constitution was passed that gave the president virtually complete power over all branches of government.

## Conclusion

Public services are, in general, popular items of government spending. While many other categories of expenditure have fallen from favor, voters continue to support outlays on health and education. And rightly so; judicious public expenditure can provide real value to the public. On the other hand, public services cannot be given away to win votes. Politicians should concentrate on basic services that are of value to the public at large and avoid funding the frills that benefit small groups. The most advantageous political position is in the center, between the ideological extremes of liberal extravagance and conservative parsimony.

# CHAPTER 7

# *Welfare Benefits: The Halo Effect*

CLOSELY LINKED with the expansion of cheap public services for the elderly and the disadvantaged has been the growth of a variety of "welfare" programs—food stamps, Aid to Families with Dependent Children (AFDC), unemployment and sickness benefits, and social security—designed to protect and improve the standard of living of those citizens who are considered to be not quite capable of earning a decent income. Although the costs of welfare programs are enormous, they have been protected from serious cuts by the halo effect—because some of the programs are very popular, conventional wisdom holds all welfare to be sacred. As we shall see in this chapter, such beliefs are questionable; to get spending out of the failure zone, welfare *has* to be cut. And the most sensible way to bring this about is to "unbundle" welfare spending and pick off the weakest strands.

## Folklore and Reality

Political legends about the invulnerability of welfare abound. Ireland's Fine Gael party is still taunted about an attempt in the early 1920s by Finance Minister William T. Cosgrave to reduce the old-age pension by one shilling per month. The uproar, the apocryphal story goes, pushed Mr. Cosgrave into a different public career—director of Dublin's Abbey Theatre. According to Milton and Rose Friedman, social security in the U.S. "is a sacred cow that no politician can question—as Barry Goldwater discovered in 1964."[1] President Carter's vain attempts at welfare reform are supposed to have contributed to his administration's reputation for incompetence.

These legends have deterred many conservatives from attempting to cut welfare. President Reagan was urged by David Stockman in the first few months of his term to go on national television to explain the need for reductions in social security payments. On the advice of White House staff who said that such a move would be suicidal, the President demurred. He even felt compelled to disclaim knowledge of proposals for social security reform that were being floated by the OMB director and other members of his administration.

In 1982 a British conservative think tank privately debated the wisdom of big cuts in the welfare state. "When this thing was leaked," says a senior Cabinet minister, "every vested interest came out of the woodwork and had a bash." Mrs. Thatcher's government promptly disassociated itself from the think tank's proposals. The minister says that the Cabinet felt "the welfare state in principle is not something we can do much about at present."[2]

A government cannot really afford *not* to cut welfare spending—the programs are a primary obstacle to the real tax relief that voters are agitating for. Welfare spending accounts for over 40 percent of U.S. federal outlays and over a quarter of public spending in the U.K. Growth in welfare has been a principal cause for pushing public spending into the failure zone. For example, federal spending in the U.S. grew by $380 billion between 1970 and 1980; 60 percent of that growth came from welfare and social security spending. In the U.K. welfare spending accounted for three-fourths of the increase in government spending between 1973 and 1979. Obviously, a government that wants to pull back to a popularly acceptable level of taxes and expenditure cannot avoid cuts in welfare.

Conventional wisdom exaggerates the costs and the dangers of cutting welfare. Generous welfare benefits are too recent to be considered an inalienable right by the public; although modest welfare programs were started over fifty years ago, the explosion in outlays began only in the late sixties. The joint federal-state unemployment insurance system and the AFDC program, for example, were enacted in 1935, but until the mid-sixties these and other income maintenance programs grew slowly. Writes Harvard economist Elizabeth Allison, "Comparatively stringent eligibility requirements kept total outlays on income maintenance programs below 2 percent of GNP and recipients limited to 1.5 percent of the population."[3] The Eisenhower administration took few social welfare initiatives. Liberals formulated many proposals, but their legislation was either defeated by conservative congressmen or was vetoed by the President.

Then came the Great Society legislation that "led to an enormous expansion of the number and range of income maintenance programs."[4] Spending on public aid, for example, which had been $3.1 billion in 1940 and $6.2 billion in 1965, shot up to $40.5 billion in 1975; similarly, expenditure on unemployment compensation, which was $0.5 billion in 1940 and $2.6 billion in 1965, zoomed to $14.4 billion in 1975. Benefits were expanded particularly sharply in the older cities of the Northeast. In New York, for example, the benefits potentially available to a four-person family in 1971 totaled $9,004—a fivefold increase over 1955; and since eligibility requirements were simultaneously relaxed, the number of welfare recipients expanded eightfold. (It is interesting to note that over the same period, average weekly earnings, net of taxes, in New York's largest manufacturing industry, apparel, increased by only 35 percent and equaled, in 1971, $3,900.)

In Europe also the growth of generous, universal welfare is quite recent, although the tradition of providing limited benefits is quite old. Between 1883 and 1889 German Chancellor Otto von Bismarck set up state insurance schemes against sickness, accident, old age, and permanent disability. "One who can look forward to an old age pension is far more contented and easier to manage," the chancellor said.[5] The normal principles of insurance were strictly applied, with benefits adjusted according to the number and level of premiums collected. Legislation on unemployment insurance was first introduced in 1927 under the Weimar Republic, with the aim of relieving the bitter poverty of the time. It was not until 1969, after the liberal Social-Democrats came to power, that the legislation was completely replaced by the *Arbeitsforderungsgesetz*, or labor promotion law. The new law provided for generous unemployment benefits, related to the individual's previous earnings and family status. Thus a married man with two children would receive about 70 percent of his last wage for nearly a year, after which unemployment benefits would drop to 60 percent of the last wage.

Elizabethan England had a poor law that only just protected the indigent from starvation. An Old Age Pensions Act was passed in 1908 and a National Insurance Act in 1911. A social security system was established in 1948 that paid retirement pensions to the elderly and cash benefits to the sick or unemployed. But welfare did not come into its own until the second half of the sixties. Until 1966, for example, unemployment insurance paid a relatively low, flat-rate benefit and a flat-rate dependents allowance. In 1966 an earning related supplement was introduced that provided for an additional payment equal to one-third of the claimant's previous weekly earnings. It proved to be immediately popular—the claims for unemployment compensation rose from 340,000 in September 1966 to 436,000 in October and 543,000 in November.

The sudden growth in welfare spending in Western economies during the late sixties was not set off by popular public demand. No extraordinary need had arisen—the unemployment rate in the U.K. in 1966 was 1.6 percent, and the U.S. economy was racing ahead at full capacity at the time of Great Society legislation. Nor was there any sudden upsurge in public sympathy or interest in the lot of the disadvantaged. In 1966, for example, Gallup found that only 38 percent thought favorably of the antipoverty program, 25 percent disapproved, and 37 percent hadn't heard of the program or had no opinion.[6] The growth in programs came about because of the fervor and concern of a handful of leaders, bureaucrats, and scholars. The welfare state was nourished by ideology, not votes.

The Great Society was Lyndon Johnson's personal dream. He had no illusions that his fellow Americans shared his vision or that there was a strong popular demand for his programs. Shortly after his inauguration in January 1965 (following his landslide victory over Barry Goldwater), he called a meeting of the congressional liaison officers of the various departments and, according to Wilbur J. Cohen, Secretary of HEW, said to them:

Look, I've just been elected and right now we'll have a honeymoon with Congress. With the additional congressmen that have been elected, I will have a good chance to get my program through. . . .

So I want you guys to get off your asses and do everything possible to get everything in my program passed as soon as possible, before the aura and the halo that surround me disappear.

Don't waste a second. Get going right now. Larry, Wilbur—just remember I want this program through fast, and by fast I mean six months, not a year.[7]

President Johnson put his legendary persuasion skills to work for his program. "I would be amazed," recalls Hugh Sidey, "at some of the devices he would use. He would lie, beg, cheat, steal a little, threaten, intimidate. But he never lost sight of that ultimate goal, his idea of the Great Society."[8]

By August 1965 Senator Tom Wicker was observing,

they are rolling the bills out of Congress these days the way Detroit turns superslick, souped-up autos off the assembly line. . . . The list of achievements is so long that it reads better than the legislative achievements of most two-term presidents, and some of the bills are of such weight as to cause one to go all the way back to Woodrow Wilson's first year to find a congressional session of equal importance.[9]

The momentum of the Great Society carried through to the Nixon administration, which proposed a guaranteed income (the Family Assistance plan) and greatly increased benefits under food stamps, Medicaid, and social security.

The growth in welfare took place while public support for such spending was declining rapidly. While, in 1961, 64 percent of the public thought the government should be spending more money on welfare and only 7 percent thought it should spend less, by 1973, 22 percent thought the government should spend more on welfare, while nearly 50 percent favored cutbacks.[10]

What was enacted without popular support can be undone without stirring mass discontent. True, the need for welfare is higher now than it was when the programs were established; nevertheless, the public has shown great forebearance for the cuts that have been made. In 1983 Garret Fitzgerald's government became the first in Ireland since the Cosgrave incident of the 1920s to "nick" the old age pension, by postponing previously promised inflation adjustments. Public reaction was muted—there was no uproar comparable to the mass demonstrations that had been held against taxes in 1979 and 1980. An eighty-year-old pensioner understood the finance minister's problem: "The money isn't there, he hasn't got it."[11]

In the U.S., ever since the 1980 recession began, welfare programs have been cut by several financially strapped state governments. Michigan, which was hard hit by slumping auto and truck sales, dropped 18,519 persons from its general-relief rolls during fiscal 1980 after they had refused to accept work. In 1981 it eliminated about 500 Welfare Department social workers and cut general relief benefits by 5 percent. Utah stopped giving general relief to unemployed single persons and cut the level of general relief benefits and AFDC checks by 9 percent.[12]

Welfare programs were also hit by the Reagan budget cuts of 1981. For example, under new eligibility rules a family of four did not qualify for food stamps if its gross income from all sources, including unemployment insurance, exceeded $916 a month, or if it owned more than $1500 worth of liquid assets. Extended state benefits (which supplement twenty-six weeks of regular state benefits) were restricted to individual states with high unemployment rates. Previously they were triggered in every state when the insured unemployment rate topped 4.5 percent.

As these cuts took hold in 1982, the erstwhile beneficiaries were undoubtedly hurt. But as Linda McMohan, the administration's welfare chief, noted, the political fallout was limited: "We're not seeing riots. We're not seeing people rushing the doors of Congress and the White House."[13] In 1983 even the sacred cow of social security was bled a little, as a bipartisan agreement was reached to postpone cost-of-living benefit increases by six months.

Benefits are being rocked even in Europe, the cradle of the welfare state. Fiscal difficulties are forcing governments to scale back their programs. In the wake of its reflationary fiasco of 1981, the Socialist government in France agreed to a "surprisingly severe program of cuts." The government determined, for example, that starting in 1983, welfare payments would be linked to the current inflation rate, not to that of the previous year—a change expected to save $2.4 billion. French workers who retired early would have to pay the standard level of social security contributions instead of the reduced rate. Holland, whose natural gas revenues had paid for one of the most generous welfare states in Europe, was "embarking on a savage cutback" in 1982. *All* social security benefits were to be frozen in 1983; several were to be cut. In Denmark a new rightist coalition led by the country's first Conservative prime minister in the twentieth century submitted a plan in 1982 to abolish the indexation of all transfer incomes. The government hoped to cut public spending by about 7 percent in 1983, almost entirely at the expense of social welfare programs.[14]

## Welfare Benefits: The Halo Effect

These trends, however, indicate little more than the vulnerability of a system that was thrust upon electorates by ideologues; they do not presage drastic reductions in the welfare state. Welfare programs are being trimmed because of the financial difficulties governments are facing, and the cuts represent the minimum that needs to be done to avoid bankruptcy. However, the myth that welfare is an ancient immovable institution is well accepted. "Nobody is going to cut the social net," says Wolfgang Schroeter, a West German official. "It's far too important, far too ingrained in our life. Do what we must to maintain it, it will be maintained."[15] The welfare state has become a leaky ship that is being patched up; it's not being rebuilt or scrapped. Politicians are not contemplating the deep cuts in welfare needed to get public spending out of the failure zone. Moreover, since emergency repairs are being made, there is little by way of a strategy or thoughtful priorities for the cuts.

## Divide and Rule: Unemployment Benefits

"Fundamentally, people are ambivalent about welfare," the Harris survey reports. "They have compassion for the less privileged, but they are also disturbed by the operation of the welfare system."[16] In the 1980 election, the *New York Times* found: "When Americans do talk about what they want cut from government spending survey after survey indicates they would like to cut welfare. But welfare appears to be used as a code word for profligacy, by government or individuals."[17] The same polls, noted the *Times,* often found considerable support for individual programs. It quoted Theodore Gray, a Republican state senator from Ohio, as saying: "Welfare is the guy in Cleveland who's cheating the government. People never use it to refer to the little old lady next door who needs it to exist."[18]

Since voters have widely different attitudes about different programs, a popular strategy to cut welfare spending must discriminate between categories and focus reductions on the least popular ones. To this end, we can divide welfare programs into three groups: first, the programs intended to protect individuals against temporary adversity such as unemployment or sickness; second, programs intended to ameliorate dire and extreme poverty; and third, programs to provide retirement benefits to the elderly.

Programs in the first category, which provide unemployment or sickness benefits, are the least attractive politically. Unemployment benefits are somewhat unnatural. Uncertainty of income and temporary adversity has been a part of the human condition since the time man was a nomadic hunter. People have always saved, first food and later money, for unforeseen difficult times. Over the last fifteen years visionaries have tried to substitute state-provided unemployment compensation for the age-old system of personal savings. Instead of putting their money into their own bank accounts to be drawn on in times of need, workers have been forced to pay higher taxes, which the state has used to support the jobless or the sick.

It is an unpopular substitution. Voters are denied the freedom to choose the level of savings they want to put aside from their income and the circumstances and the speed with which they wish to draw them down. The tax rate and the benefit levels under the new system are mandated by the government. The new system entails a "use it or lose it" game: unlike personal savings to which an individual retains title, taxes disappear into a vast anonymous pool and workers who avoid unemployment or illness "waste" their contribution.

Since at any time nine or more employed voters "lose it" for one jobless worker who uses it, unemployment benefits are a net vote-losing proposition. Moreover, the users don't become grateful supporters—between 70 to 80 percent of the jobless are dissatisfied with the compensation they are provided by the state.

The repercussions of cutting unemployment benefits aren't

significant; since joblessness is dispersed and usually temporary, unemployment compensation is not protected by a permanent, organized lobby of beneficiaries (as, for example, agricultural subsidies are by farmers). As Sidney Verba and Kay
Lehman Schlozman write in their study of the political attitudes of the unemployed, "the lack of a job creates a severe
personal strain on the individual but that strain is not translated into politically meaningful activity."[19] The participation
of the unemployed in elections tends to be low. "It's a real
challenge to get these people to the polls because they become
so alienated, especially if they have been unemployed for any
length of time," said a labor official in Michigan before the 1982
congressional elections. Even a politically active union like the
United Auto Workers, he predicted, would have trouble getting its 200,000 unemployed members to the polls.[20]

"The evidence appears to be that they don't vote very heavily," concurred Gene Eidenberg, director of the Democratic
National Committee. "One reason is that losing your job is such
a devastating blow both economically and psychologically that
people are depressed and focused on getting more work rather
than voting."[21] In 1978, reports the Bureau of the Census, only
27 percent of the jobless voted, compared to 47 percent of the
people with jobs; in 1980 voting was 41 percent among the
unemployed against 62 percent among the employed.[22]

## Antipoverty Programs

The second category of benefits, those intended to relieve dire
poverty, is more popular. Most voters who earn a reasonable
living do feel guilty about the evidence of poverty in their
midst and are upset by hunger, by the homeless freezing to
death in winter, and by children brought up in disease and
squalor. Over 90 percent of voters, the Harris survey reports,
believe "it is not right to let people who need welfare go
hungry," and 74 percent believe that "many women whose

husbands have left them with several children have no choice but to go on welfare."[23]

So to the extent that welfare programs antiseptically assuage the public's guilt, their political benefit extends beyond the relatively small number of direct recipients of state aid. Like the "macho" value of defense spending, however, the "moral" value of antipoverty programs to voters is volatile; public support for such programs tends to evaporate if the cost gets out of hand. There is no political reward for unrestrained compassion—in appealing to a voter's heart, a politician must not lose sight of his pocket. Nicolo Machiavelli has pointed out the dangers of excessive generosity in chapter 16 of *The Prince:*

I say that it would be well to be reputed liberal. Nevertheless, liberality exercised in a way that does not bring you the reputation for it, injures you; for if one exercises it honestly and as it should be exercised, it may not become known, and you will not avoid the reproach of its opposite. Therefore, anyone wishing to maintain among men the name of liberal is obliged to avoid no attribute or magnificence; so that a prince thus inclined will consume in such acts all his property, and will be compelled in the end, if he wishes to maintain the name of liberal, to unduly weigh down his people, and tax them, and do everything he can to get money. This will soon make him odious to his subjects, and becoming poor he will be little valued by anyone; thus, with his liberality, having offended many and rewarded few, he is affected by the very first trouble and imperiled by whatever may be the first danger; recognizing this himself, and wishing to draw back from it, he runs at once into the reproach of being miserly. Therefore, a prince, not being able to exercise this virtue of liberality in such a way that it is recognized, except to his cost, if he is wise he ought not to fear the reputation of being mean, for in time he will come to be more considered than if liberal, seeing that with his economy his revenues are enough, that he can defend himself against all attacks, and is able to engage in enterprises without burdening his people; thus it comes to pass that he exercises liberality towards all from whom he does not take, who are numberless, and meanness towards those to whom he does not give, who are few.[24]

In order to satisfy the public demand for lower taxes as well as a minimum level of compassion toward the poor, welfare programs must be few in number, capped by fixed budgets, and focused solely and directly on poverty. "Mixed" programs are not effective; unemployment compensation, for example, which liberals claim is also an important safety net for the poor, is an ineffective antipoverty device. Only 27 percent of temporary disability benefits and 20.8 percent of unemployment benefits go to people below the poverty line.[25] According to Professor Feldstein, the poverty-stricken unemployed are often ineligible for benefits because they are "more likely to work in uncovered occupations, to have worked too little to qualify for benefits, or to have quit their last job."[26]

The more numerous and complex the web of antipoverty programs, the less likely they are to reach the poor. There are well over one hundred programs in the U.S. to help the poor, ranging from the well-known social security, to obscure programs such as Urban Rat Control and Special Supplemental Feeding for Women, Infants and Children. In 1978, $90 billion was spent on these programs, excluding the $130 billion spent under the largest program, social security. This, as the Friedmans write, is "clearly overkill."[27] They point out that in 1978 there were 25 million persons living below the poverty level, defined to be about $7000 for a family of four. If $90 billion of welfare expenditures had actually been reaching the 25 million poorest people, each would have received $3,500 and a family of four about $14,000—twice the poverty-level income.

The poor actually receive only about 30 percent of the funds spent on programs aimed at reducing poverty.[28] A Census Bureau study in 1982 found that 40 percent of households below the poverty line did not receive *any* benefits from food stamps, Medicaid, housing assistance, or school lunches.[29] Some funds earmarked for antipoverty programs, write the Friedmans, "are siphoned off by administrative expenditures, supporting a massive bureaucracy at attractive pay scales." Some go to people "who by no stretch of the imagination can be regarded as indigent." And some are appropriated by "welfare cheats."[30]

An expensive, complex system of welfare bears down heavily on the average voter who has to pay for it without receiving the moral satisfaction of contributing to a compassionate society. And the poor are not too happy about not receiving the benefits intended for them. A consequence of the welfare maze seen in the 1980 election was that "the Democrats were unable to keep the wholehearted support both of the union family that benefited from New Deal reforms such as social security and unemployment compensation as well as that of the poor who were helped by Great Society programs—blacks, single women with children, the aged."[31]

Cutting, consolidating, and focusing welfare spending on antipoverty programs is politically practical. The poor are, thankfully, a minority and far less numerous than they used to be. Depending on the definitions used, the percentage of the population living below the poverty line is between 5 to 15 percent, compared to the 40 percent in 1929. Like the unemployed, the poor have no organized lobby of their own—poverty programs are pushed by organizations of their administrators, whose vested interest a politician can expose. And finally, if welfare programs are consolidated and focused on the poor, then there might actually be fewer people living in poverty than there are today.

## Retirement Benefits

The third group of welfare payments, retirement benefits to the elderly (or the Old Age and Survivor's benefit component of the U.S. social security system) are the toughest to reduce. The government became responsible for retirement benefits because of the Depression, which wiped out the savings of millions of older individuals. There was considerable support for a modest retirement scheme. Gallup reports that in 1936, nearly 90 percent of voters supported government old-age pensions for needy persons. The average amount favored was $60 a month for an aged husband and wife; 96 percent of the public disapproved of the Townsend plan to pay each aged husband and wife $200 a month.[32]

## Welfare Benefits: The Halo Effect

The public did not favor pensions for all aged people—77 percent thought they should be given only to those who were needy.[33] A "universal" social security program was enacted principally because the Roosevelt administration wanted it. There was also no compelling reason why social security could not have thereafter built up a trust fund and paid all its beneficiaries out of the interest on the accumulated capital. But the hard reality is that it did not—the trust funds are negligible compared to the system's unfunded liabilities, and payments to the elderly are paid out of the taxes of those at work.

This basic reality isn't going to change. The "pay as you go" nature of the system can't be done away with because to do so would require an enormous infusion of capital. Social security is not going to be replaced by private pension plans, as some conservatives and libertarians periodically suggest, because the elderly are extremely sensitive about attempts to "tamper with the system" and they constitute a large and vocal group with high turnout in elections. Even the working people whose taxes finance the benefits that the elderly receive would be upset by attempts to entirely dismantle the system because they believe that the money they have paid in over the years entitles them to some benefits when they retire.

If it is virtually impossible to change the basic structure of social security, it is still politically important to reduce the total benefits that are being paid out. Social security now absorbs 26 percent of the federal budget. Social security taxes take a hefty bite out of incomes and have been rising faster than most other categories of taxes. In 1950 the rate was 1.5 percent of income up to a maximum total tax of $45. It is now 7 percent with a maximum total tax of $2499. And since social security is a regressive, flat-rate tax, its burden is especially severe on low incomes.

True, the number of elderly who receive the benefits is large and they are well organized—there are 36 million beneficiaries, or about four times the number of unemployed—but they are still a minority compared to the 108 million working people who pay social security taxes. And although the 108 million working people are not making their social security payments for altruistic reasons, they have reached the limit of the sacrifice they are prepared to make now in the expectation that succeeding generations will continue to pay high social security taxes to support their retirement.

To roll back the working majority's tax burden, politicians will have to create and exploit differences within the seemingly solid bloc of the elderly. First, a vote-seeking government should discriminate between rich and poor retirees. Approximately 20 percent of the elderly are wealthy enough that the social security payments they receive are not their primary source of income; sharp cuts in benefits to these rich retirees (say by a steeply graduated tax) can be popularly made if the money saved is split between the working taxpayers and the less well-to-do senior citizens.

The second difference that should be exploited is age—whereas most eighty-five-year-olds can't earn a living, many sixty-five-year-olds can. Moving back the eligibility age as life expectancy increases and better health allows older people to work for more years can yield significant savings (part of which could be used to pay higher benefits to the older senior citizens).

Sixty-five is now an unrealistically low retirement age. Congress recognized this in 1978 when it legislated an end to mandatory retirement at sixty-five. Hence there is no reason why the eligibility age for benefits should not be correspondingly changed. As Frank Bane, described as the "father of Social Security" and the executive director of the Federal Social Security Board at its inception in 1935, says, sixty-five was chosen by "mistake"; he had not foreseen that Americans would live (and receive social security checks) for as long as they now do. In 1930 American life expectancy was 59.7 years. Though he knew it was growing, he says no one could have reasonably projected it would be 73.8 in 1980.

"If I had to do it all over again," he says, "I would make several changes. I believed old man Solomon. He did not know what he was talking about. Three score years and ten? He was way off base. I would change the age situation." Instead of three score years and ten, Mr. Bane would start by pushing back the time of retirement—moving the eligibility age from sixty-five to sixty-eight and the early retirement age from sixty-two to sixty-five: "I would change it 6 months every year. So you would not lose money. I would emphasize, as I do all the time with these old folk here, that no one under any conceivable circumstance is going to lose a dime of what they are now, underscore *now* getting."[34]

In early 1983 a bipartisan agreement was enacted in Congress that contained both elements of a popular cost-control strategy—reducing payments to the rich and raising the retirement age. But since the objective of the plan was to rescue social security from bankruptcy rather than to reduce the burden of the system on the working population, the measures were rather mild and the package contained new taxes "to shore up the financial position" of social security: the retirement age was to be raised but only very gradually—first to sixty-six by 2009 and then to sixty-seven by 2027; some benefits received by those with high taxable income outside social security (more than $25,000 for an individual or $32,000 for a married couple) would be taxable; payroll taxes paid by both employers and employees would be increased; and taxes paid by self-employed people would be raised to equal a combination of the employee and employer rates.[35]

"Because of this bill," said House Speaker Thomas O'Neill, "Social Security is secure for the next 25 or 30 years."[36] Perhaps it is, in an accounting sense; but the political problem is not going to be solved unless a president devises a bolder scheme that promotes the majority interests (while increasing payments to the senior citizens most in need), sells the plan honestly and forthrightly to the public, and pushes it through Congress with the intensity of a Johnson lobbying for his Great Society legislation.

According to Peter Drucker, radical reform, such as rapidly increasing the eligibility age:

. . . actually may be fairly easy. There would be a good deal of support for such changes among the elderly and perhaps even more among the middle-aged. For there is growing fear among the middle-aged, the working people over 45 or 50, that there will be no Social Security system left when they reach retirement age—and they know perfectly well that patchwork won't save the system. By now, everybody—excepting perhaps only Claude Pepper—has come to realize that our current Social Security system can't be maintained unchanged. And to give courage even to the faintest-hearted politician, when Congress a year ago raised full vesting age for Social Security by one year, there was no "outcry" and no "avalanche of wrathful letters" from the constituents —contrary to what even the advocates of Social Security reform had predicted. Putting Social Security on a demographically sound and enduring foundation actually may be a good deal easier than stumbling from one crisis to the next. It might even be popular.[37]

## Smothering Motivation

The political step of reducing the size and scope of welfare programs in order to reduce the public taxes will also provide long-term economic benefits by reducing the disincentives to work and saving that generous benefits have created.

The greatest harm has been done by the politically weakest programs—unemployment and sickness benefits. These benefits have reduced the incentive to find and hold employment: a jobless individual living off his own savings is more likely to be anxious to find a job quickly than someone who is being supported by the state. The disincentive is reinforced by the tax system, because income from the new job is taxable whereas unemployment benefits are not. As Professor Feldstein writes:

Because the cost to himself of additional waiting time is so very low, the unemployed worker is encouraged to wait until there is almost no chance of finding a job.

For example, since finding a job that pays as little as 5 percent more means an increase in net income of approximately $200 per year, even an additional 10 weeks of unemployment would pay for itself in less than a year. It is clear that individuals who are actively searching for a better job in this way are neither loafing nor cheating; they are trying to increase their long-run income. Their search is economically rational from their point of view but wastefully long for the economy as a whole. Unemployed individuals lose valuable productive time to achieve a slight gain in future income because taxpayers provide a $1,000 subsidy during the ten weeks of increased search.[38]

Many jobs in low-wage industries (like textile and garments) actually pay less after tax than what an unemployed individual can get from welfare. If this anomaly has not caused such industries to shut down altogether it is because of the heavy use of illegal immigrant labor and because many persons still prefer slightly lower incomes to the loss of dignity of unemployment.

The phenomenon of "voluntary unemployment" induced by generous welfare is widespread in Europe. As Tory Chancellor Sir Geoffrey Howe told the British Parliament:

The net extra reward to a low earner from going out to work can be so close to the benefits he can get when on social security as to extinguish his incentive to find or stick to a job. Indeed there are people whose incomes out of work exceed what they could reasonably expect to get in work. There is undoubtedly widespread and justified public concern about this disincentive.[39]

In Ireland the rapid growth of unemployment benefits has created a class of "nixers"—welfare cheats who collect the dole while holding a job in the underground economy. An Irish economist calculated in 1978 that "the real income gap" between working and not working was only $20 for a man with a wife and two children who was drawing benefits based on a former weekly pay of $120. Textile and garment factories in Dublin, he observed, "always have a sign outside offering employment. Unfortunately, this work can pay only £35/week, as at any higher rate their goods are not competitive. They are always short of staff."[40]

In Denmark a program of disability benefits was introduced in 1968 that provided workers with lifetime support at 80 percent of their full wage even if their disability was not job related. A worker could hurt his back skiing and collect over

$20,000 per year until he reached retirement age. The program was "so widely abused," writes Jon Nordheimer, "that some 800,000 people or nearly one out of six of the workforce are now officially listed as disabled. The figure does not include an additional 600,000 regarded as disabled for other causes."[41]

Retirement benefits paid to those who have completed their working lives don't have the disincentives associated with unemployment compensation. But the failure to adjust the eligibility age for benefits as people are capable of active work for many more years does. When Congress did away with sixty-five as the mandatory retirement age, most experts thought that many older Americans would stay at their jobs; yet only 200,000 did. In spite of the fact that many of the elderly could stay on longer, "people are retiring at earlier ages," says Phil Rones, a government economist. "There has been an improved financial ability to retire, through social security indexed to inflation and supplemented by a growing number of private pension plans."[42]

Although people above sixty-five account for 19 percent of the U.S. adult population, they account for less than 2 percent of the workforce. Older citizens who could be working but are not, because social security is available, represent a loss to the economy; their skills and experience are wasted, and as "pure consumers" they are an additional burden on the "producing" members of society.

## Conclusion

Politicians cannot offer meaningful tax cuts to the public without reducing the costs of welfare. Welfare programs span a wide variety of objectives and beneficiaries, so separate strategies need to be followed for the different categories. Radical cuts should be made in unemployment and sickness benefits since these provide the least benefit to most voters. Antipoverty programs need to be consolidated and reduced; although such programs do help the public get poverty off its conscience, their costs have gotten out of hand. Retirement benefits are the toughest nuts to crack, but they too can be reduced by focusing cuts on the relatively richer and "younger" senior citizens.

# CHAPTER 8

# Public Investments: Their Money's Worth

ADAM SMITH'S invisible hand, some savants claim, is often guided by a myopic eye whose vision does not extend beyond domestic shores, next quarter's earnings, or yesterday's technology. And even when the eye is farsighted, the hand often lacks the muscle to steer the right course. Managers may know the importance of new technology, modern plant, or global market share only too well but lack the resources to do anything about it. Hence, say these experts, government must step in and invest in critical industries to ensure their long-term health. Since shortsighted businessmen can't or won't, government must finance the research, development, and plant that important industries need.

As the importance of high-technology industries in our daily lives has grown, many politicians have followed the prescribed course of high economic statesmanship. Their investments have, however, failed, economically and politically. Public investments can win votes; but not if they are made in risky high-technology areas. As we will see in this chapter, politicians and voters are much better off with stodgy, unglamorous investments in infrastructure.

## Reaching Out

While many leaders have put public money into high technology, few have done it on the scale of President Mitterand of France. In one stroke, soon after its election, the Socialist government nearly doubled the amount of French industrial output under state control, from 18 percent to 32 percent. Paying lavish compensation to stockholders, the state gained control of 70 percent of the country's advanced electronics firms, 63 percent of its metal works, and 75 percent of its defense industry. The government bought industry leaders such as Compagnie Générale d'Electricité, France's largest electrical, electronics, and nuclear engineering group and the third largest European concern in the field; CIT-Alcatel, France's telecommunications specialist; Thomson- Brandt, an electrical, electronics, and arms manufacturer with over one hundred subsidiaries and thirty production plants outside France; Dassault, an aircraft manufacturer; and Matra, a missiles, guidance, watches, and electronics group.

The government claimed the nationalized companies had a bright future but were foundering because of underinvestment and indecisive leadership. According to Pierre Dryfus, the industry minister, nationalizations "are the most appropriate way to enable French industry to meet the international challenge which has placed it in difficulty."[1] Francis Lorentz, managing director of France's state-owned computer company, agreed: "Conditions for financing companies in France are absurd. Self financing is low by international standards; the equity market hardly exists; industry interest rates are high and the tax and social security system penalizes the corporate sector. The Government's willingness to channel funds to industry marks a change of attitude—a revolution in France."[2]

In the U.K., the first proposal for large-scale public investment in industry was made in the Labour party's Programme 1973, which called for the state purchase of the top twenty to twenty-five manufacturing companies in order to capture the "commanding heights" of the economy. Although such sweeping nationalizations were not accomplished, the government did acquire several aerospace companies including Hawker Siddeley Dynamics, Hawker Siddeley Aviation, and the British Aircraft Corporation. Unlike Rolls-Royce and British Leyland, which had asked to be rescued, these companies were growing and profitable and fiercely resisted acquisition.

The Labour government also set up the National Enterprise Board (NEB), a step Prime Minister Harold Wilson called "the biggest leap forward in economic thinking and policy since the war."[3] The NEB was given a budget and the power to make unfriendly tender offers for the stock of private companies. In the seventies, it mainly acquired and helped small companies, but if Labour had been elected in 1979, it would probably have played a more important role. Prime Minister Callaghan had spelled out Labour policy for the 1980s in the election campaign thus:

> It is now more than ever vital that we have a government able and willing to intervene positively to ensure that Britain gains and does not lose from the new industrial era.
> The amount of effort, the volume of investment, the financial and technological resources required are far beyond the scope of individual firms.[4]

In the U.S., support for high technology has so far been principally through research subsidies—the federal government today pays for over a third of all industrial research and development. It started with the Johnson administration changing the National Science Foundation's emphasis from sponsoring basic research to supporting "research applied to national needs."[5] The Nixon administration set up the New

Technological Opportunities program to promote innovations thought to be neglected by private companies. The program's director was William Magruder, who had previously been in charge of the supersonic transport (SST) project, scrapped by Congress after the federal government had invested a billion dollars in it.

After the oil crisis of 1973, the government asked half a dozen agencies and a dozen federal laboratories to remodel the nation's energy technologies. In 1975 these programs were consolidated into the Energy Research and Development Administration (ERDA), which later became the nucleus of the Department of Energy. Under the Carter administration, the Department of Energy in turn spawned the Synthetic Fuels Corporation, which was to invest $88 billion in projects to develop unconventional energy sources.

On the whole, however, U.S. government investment in future-oriented industries has been small compared to the spending by European governments. "Atari Democrats" and academics like Robert Reich are urging a much expanded role for government in allocating capital—a national industrial policy, as it is called. Their proposals are often inspired, sometimes explicitly, by warmed-over recipes for corporate resource allocation. Just as it was once fashionable to believe that the ideal corporation consisted of a portfolio of businesses centrally orchestrated by master strategists who "milked" mature businesses to invest in growing enterprises, now the government supposedly should treat the economy as a financial portfolio and supply capital to the high-technology growth sectors. What is good for ITT is good for the U.S.

The Japanese Ministry of Trade and Industry (MITI) paradigm is usually cited by advocates of an activist investment policy. Japan's high productivity and growth, we are told, is due to MITI, the strategic planner par excellence of Japan Inc. MITI figures out tomorrow's winners and provides Japanese companies with subsidized capital to invest in chosen businesses without regard to immediate profits. Hence, in the long run, Japanese firms always beat their shortsighted Western competitors.

## The Voters' Perspective

What is the political effect of statesmanly investment? Leaders believe that advancing the national interest in important industries also wins points with voters—jobs are created and influential legislators rewarded with projects for their constituencies while earning a reputation for farsightedness and responsibility.

The voters' perspective is, however, quite different—average citizens have little reason to be excited by public investment. Most don't expect to be employed on state-funded high-technology projects, and few are aware of or impressed by posturing in Washington—industrial policy leaves Peoria cold. Nationalization or investment by the government doesn't make average voters feel richer—60 percent of the French public, for example, said in a poll taken after Mitterand's nationalizations that the takeovers served no useful purpose.[6] The British public doesn't feel richer when Labour governments nationalize the coal mines and the railways, or poorer when Mrs. Thatcher sells off the state-owned Amersham, Britoil, and British Telecom.

The average voter has as little influence in the operation of a state-owned enterprise as the average stockholder has on the management of a large corporation; consequently, voters have no especial pride of ownership in public enterprises. Just as the driver of a GM car isn't less upset when it breaks down if he owns the automaker's stock, taxpayers aren't more understanding of lost or delayed mail because they own the post office. Citizens concerned about radiation hazards agitate as vigorously against state-owned nuclear power plants in Austria and West Germany as they do against privately owned ones in the U.S. and Sweden.

## Public Investments: Their Money's Worth

When a politician "invests" the public money in a project, it is therefore merely another asset in voters' portfolios, alongside their bank accounts, stocks and bonds, insurance policies, and pension funds. And voters implicitly expect public investments, like all the other assets in their portfolios, to earn real economic returns. Like any other investment manager, the leader is responsible for results. When GM loses money, its stock price falls; if banks offer low interest rates, they lose deposits to money market accounts; similarly, if politicians do not deliver economic value for the public money they invest, they must expect to lose votes.

Politicians are not excused for money-losing investments because they serve some ideological purpose (for example, capturing the "commanding heights" of the economy), just as a private company is not forgiven a poor earnings record by the stock market because of its exemplary community relations. The connection between poor investment and voter backlash may be roundabout and slow (depositors deserted banks offering low interest rates quite gradually too), but the unpleasantnesses will inevitably arrive, in the guise of inflation, recession, or higher taxes. Politicans who believe otherwise are chasing a free-vote mirage.

### Appropriate and Inappropriate Investments

Although from a voter's viewpoint there are many similarities between public and private investments, there are also important differences. The government, in its role of investment manager, enjoys certain advantages. It has access to immense amounts of capital and can undertake larger projects than most private institutions. It is also free to invest in projects that have very long paybacks. But government is also bound by special constraints: it isn't "close" to investment opportunities. It has to make decisions from a distant mountaintop, scanning a much wider range of alternatives than corporate executives or professional money managers who focus their attention on a limited field. Public officials are expected to operate in a fish bowl, with due prudence and respect for equity, so government tends to be slow on its feet. And since the government, unlike the promoter of an oil-drilling venture who puts together a partnership of risk-seeking individuals, represents the interests of the public, it has a particular onus on investing in low-risk projects that create products or services for which there is predictable demand and that involve stable, mature technologies. Bridges, roadways, harbors, and airports are examples of the solid, low-risk investments a government should invest taxpayers' money in. Repairs to public works are particularly attractive (even without the ribbon-cutting ceremonies of new construction) since they provide immediate and certain value.

Vote-seeking politicians should not invest tax money in high technology. The risks are considerable—while less than 20 percent of all private research and development efforts produce marketable products, the success rate is much lower in high-technology industries. The MITI paradigm notwithstanding, government operates from too great a distance to be able to make good investment decisions about what process, product, or company is likely to succeed. It is difficult to imagine how a government could have predicted the technological and business success of Wang, Intel, Digital Equipment, Prime, Tandem, Hewlett-Packard, Polaroid, Honda, or Sharp or the relative decline of Westinghouse or Mitsubishi. How could a government committee have known that bubble memories would flop? How could it effectively arbitrate disputes about the design philosophy of the next generation of 256K RAMs?

It isn't too difficult for politicians to figure out the advantages of a new bridge; in high-technology investments, however, they are entirely in the hands of experts. Huge sums of scarce public money can be wasted by these experts because politicians cannot understand or monitor the progress of their projects. Writes Keith Pavitt: "The large-scale involvement of governments in financing research and development in high technology has led to the creation of large groups of influential and able scientists and engineers. The result of their work is no longer subject to the ultimate sanction of the market, and they themselves create the demand which only they can satisfy."[7]

Professor Lew Kowarski describes how scientists make it impossible for a government to objectively evaluate high-technology projects:

> In a technology like nuclear energy, which has been developed only very recently, the research organizations, the equipment suppliers and electricity producers have a virtual monopoly of visible and recognized competence. These professional groups are strongly devoted and committed to their work; in any controversy they naturally behave like advocates rather than judges. Their commitment is concentrated on what they know well and have worked to achieve; in the face of alternatives, an impartial attitude thereby becomes almost treasonable.[8]

Taxpayers' money is also liable to be lost in high-tech enterprises because the bureaucratic process cannot cope with rapid changes. The deliberate pace of government activity isn't a great handicap in building public works but is entirely incompatible with the speed and flexibility required of high-tech companies. An executive of a nationalized French electronics company asks despairingly: "How can you make rapid industrial decisions required in a very competitive world marketplace when you've got to have 20 meetings for every decision with 40 people representing each branch of the Ministry of Industry and Technology and the Ministry of Finance?"[9]

Nolan Bushnell, the founder of Atari, says: "I guarantee you that no government agency can target the right industry; in fact, I'll almost guarantee they'll target the wrong one. . . . The problem is that these Atari Democrats would never have targeted Atari."[10]

## Monuments over Votes

Although much money was spent in the New Deal simply to increase total public expenditure, several investments did make political sense, in that they were solid, reliable projects, expected to generate economic value. The Public Works Administration, for example, was "operated by Harold Ickes, the cigar waving and curmudgeonly Secretary of the Interior, who was determined to make every dollar produce an honest dollar's worth of government building. He refused, he said, "to hire grown men to chase tumbleweeds on windy days." In six years Ickes spent $6 billion and created, among other things, New York's Triborough Bridge, the Grand Coulee Dam on the Columbia River, the Chicago sewage system, and the port facilities of Brownville, Texas.[11]

The Tennessee Valley Authority (TVA) was another popular New Deal investment. Roosevelt proposed the TVA as a seven-state organization in the South to produce cheap electricity, support the development of local manufacturing, and control floods that frequently devastated the Tennessee Valley. By 1940 the TVA was operating twenty-one hydroelectric plants, delivering 3.19 billion kilowatt-hours of energy at about half the national average rate. The TVA played a major role in the economic revival of the South and continues to supply cheap electricity while turning in a tidy profit.

The New Deal example of stodgy investments to produce goods and services of enduring value is, however, an exception. Modern leaders have preferred to invest like statesmen, rather than vote-seeking populists, in projects of high industrial sex appeal. High technology has been to presidents and prime ministers what the Great Pyramid was to King Cheops and the Taj Mahal to the Emperor Shah Jahan. Monuments have won out over votes; posterity over lower taxes. Consider, for example, the peculiar career of Le Général.

As we saw in chapter 6, General de Gaulle won popularity and power by putting the average Frenchman's interest ahead of nostalgia for colonial glory. Once that was accomplished, however, de Gaulle decided to pursue his vision of France at the expense of the common Frenchman. De Gaulle had a strong vision of what France's place in the world ought to be. As he wrote in his memoirs:

## Public Investments: Their Money's Worth

The emotional side of me tends to imagine France, like the princess in the fairy stories or the Madonna in the frescoes, as dedicated to an exalted and exceptional destiny. Instinctively, I have the feeling that Providence has created her either for complete success or for exemplary misfortunes. If, in spite of this, mediocrity shows in her acts and deeds, it strikes me as an absurd anomaly. . . . France is not really herself unless in the front rank; . . . In short, to my mind, France cannot be France without greatness.[12]

Wrote de Gaulle, only "vast enterprises" were "capable of counterbalancing the ferments of dispersal which are inherent in her people" and were therefore crucial to France achieving her destined "greatness." He therefore determined to fill his country's industrial stable with "national champions"—gigantic enterprises capable of taking all comers. French companies would be world leaders in steel, computers, and the energy industry. France would also have its own nuclear deterrent— the *force de frappe,* and its own space program (started in 1960, its first launch was in 1979).

These projects weren't subject to crass considerations of profits and returns—France's destiny was at stake. Nor was there to be any penny pinching. According to the French National Plan, government investment would increase by 42 percent between 1966 and 1969. That the average Frenchman might not share de Gaulle's enthusiasm for "national champions" with such an appetite for public funds didn't deter *Le Général.* He wasn't going to be a "mere politician"—Frenchmen would have to pay for France's place in the modern world as their ancestors once had to pay for Louis XIV's palaces at Versailles, St. Germain, and Marly. And pay the public did: taxes rose by 40 percent between 1965 and 1968. The inflation rate doubled as the budget deficit, which was Fr 328 million in 1965, jumped to 2.9 billion in 1966 and 15.6 billion in 1968. A wage freeze was imposed as the government attempted to hold down inflation and raise the profits of state-owned companies to generate more cash for investment.

Other circumstances helped increase the burden of de Gaulle's investments on the French working class. The tax system was highly regressive—in 1966 approximately 60 percent of tax revenue was derived from indirect taxes on consumption (compared to 17 percent in the U.S.). France had the highest percentage of its population living below the relative poverty line in the West (16 percent) and the widest disparity between blue-collar and white-collar incomes in Europe.

So the question was not whether the Fifth Plan expenditures and the wage freeze would cause an explosion, it was when. Louis XVI and Marie Antoinette paid for the excesses of Louis XIV's court decades after they were committed. General de Gaulle was not as lucky as the sun king. His dues were paid just three years into the Fifth Plan, in May 1968. Unrest at the Sorbonne among student radicals ignited the workers. Almost the entire industrial work force went on strike. Government officials began round-the-clock negotiations and worked out the Grenelle Agreement with labor leaders, granting extensive concessions on wages and working conditions. The rank and file rejected this agreement and continued the strike.

Eventually this "May Revolution" blew over. De Gaulle rallied the supporters of law and order to his side, dissolved the National Assembly, and defused the strike by negotiating an agreement that gave a 12 percent wage increase. But the era of de Gaulle was over. He retired to the life of a country gentleman less than a year later and died in 1970 in self-imposed obscurity.

General de Gaulle was an extraordinary president who really didn't care about reelection. But his National Plan isn't an unusual sacrifice of voters' funds at the altar of national prestige. Consider the Concorde, whose history spans three French presidents and at least eight British prime ministers. The project started in the early 1960s, when the French and British governments began collaborating on building a commercial supersonic plane that would knock "subsonic aircraft out of the sky" and "end American colonization of the skies."[13]

The project succeeded only in nearly crippling one of the few success stories among France's nationalized companies—Sud-Est, the aircraft manufacturer. In 1946 Georges Hereil was named the head of the company and faced the problem of breaking into a market, 90 percent of which was in the hands of powerful U.S. companies. He found a niche in the Caravelle, a fast, medium-range, twin-engine jet. The Caravelle was the most successful European aircraft of its day—286 were sold to thirty-four airlines. Hereil's successors wanted to follow up the Caravelle with a generation of related models, but instead were forced by their prestige-hungry government to work on the Concorde, a project they were against from the start.

The Concorde proved to be a complete commercial failure because of high fuel costs, low seating capacity, and short range, compared to slower but more efficient subsonic aircraft. It arrived six years behind schedule. Compared to the initial cost estimate of £80 million, by 1980 the U.K. share of the tab alone turned out to be over £5 billion (representing about five years of income-tax payments of the bottom 25 percent of British voters). Since no other airlines would buy the Concorde because of its poor economics, it was foisted on the state-owned British Airways and Air France. As a result, in 1978 British Airways lost $35 million on its five Concordes and Air France lost $25 million on its four planes. These losses also were paid out of the public purse. Taxpayers who were pinched by their bus and train fares thus subsidized the lucky few who zipped across the Atlantic at supersonic speed.

Today both the Socialist French government and the Conservative U.K. government are gambling on electronics and telecommunications. The Thatcher government, which put the Great back into Great Britain in the Falklands war, is looking for a similar triumph in high technology. Harold Wilson's National Enterprise Board continues to flourish, providing capital "for technology ventures that do not appear to attract private capital from the private sector in Britain." The government has reversed its original stand that Inmos, a microchip producer, should stand on its own feet. The Tory Industries Secretary, like his Labour predecessors, expatiates on "the Innovation linked Investment Scheme," "market innovative software products," and "Cadcam awareness" programs.[14]

U.S. presidents have been less prone to the de Gaulle style

of statesmanship because of congressional oversight. The U.S. narrowly missed its own Concorde fiasco in 1971, when the Senate forced the Nixon administration to give up its supersonic transport program. President Nixon reacted angrily: "Today's action by the Senate in disapproving funds for continued development on the supersonic transport prototype is both distressing and disappointing. It represents a severe blow . . . to the United States' continued leadership position in the aerospace industries."[15] At the time the SST program was axed, nearly $1 billion had been spent on its development.

President Carter did manage to win approval from Congress to invest $88 billion of public funds in the U.S. Synthetic Fuels Corporation to develop new synthetic fuel technologies and projects that private capital didn't find sufficiently attractive. If the corporation met its goals and there were no cost overruns, synthetic fuel would be available at the attractive price of $45 a barrel.

The Reagan administration initially tried to scale back public investment in synthetic fuel. Its choice for the chairman of Synthetic Fuels Corporation, Edward Noble, said after his appointment: "We're not going to spend a dime more than we have to." He wanted "only projects that are not along for a free ride" and said he would cast aside all but "mature technologies."[16] Noble was a veteran of the oil industry and shared its skepticism of synthetic fuel subsidies.

Less than a year later, however, *Business Week* reported that "with the slumping oil market and uncertain technology causing synfuels plants to be abandoned and delayed, industry and government are being forced into a sudden reversal."[17] The Synthetic Fuels Corporation began to encourage applications for subsidies. Mobil Chairman Rawleigh Warner, Jr., wrote privately to his peers in other oil companies: "Although we as an industry have always championed the free market, it is apparent that this problem demands the kind of cooperation that can only come from a massive joint effort with government involvement."[18] Mr. Warner proposed that the industry form a consortium to get synfuels grants. "We applaud what

Mobil is trying to do," Noble responded, and his corporation voted to award up to $10 billion within the next year.[19]

## Populist Alternatives

Clues to what the government should be investing in are to be found in "pork barrel" water projects. Today waterways and dams have become the symbol of politically inspired waste— in order to appease a few influential legislators, administrations spend billions of dollars on projects that generate electricity there is no demand for, irrigate a few hundred farmers' lands, or protect against nonexistent flood threats. It wasn't always so. Projects like the TVA once provided real returns on the public's money at very little risk *and* helped presidents build IOUs with senators and congressmen. Over the years, however, the sensible water projects were completed and new projects could deliver only marginal value. But by then the formula was cast in concrete—"Dams hold votes"—and politicians ceased to look for alternative investments.

Solid valuable investment opportunities do exist! U.S. public works are in an appalling condition of disrepair. As Pat Choate, author of *America in Ruins,* says: "I don't want to sound like the Joe Granville of public works, but the fact is that much of America's infrastructure is on the verge of collapse."[20] Repairing and rebuilding the infrastructure could absorb huge amounts of investment and provide real economic value. Nearly 20 percent of the interstate highway system's roads are now beyond their designed service life and must be rebuilt. And, notes a report from *Business Week,* maintaining current service levels on roads that are not part of the interstate system "will require more funds for rehabilitation and reconstruction during the 1980s—over $500 billion—than all levels of government spent on all public works investments during the 1970s."[21]

Nearly half the bridges in the United States are classified as either obsolete or deficient; it will take nearly $50 billion to mend them. It is estimated that $229 billion will be required to provide necessary sewage and water mains, for half the communities in the U.S. have waste-water systems at full capacity. For repairs to the country's public transport projects—more than two-thirds of the nation's subway track needs upgrading and nearly 15,000 railway cars will come to the end of their design life over the next ten years—$50 billion is said to be needed.

Presidents must take the lead in pushing these infrastructure projects, to further their own political interest. Substituting needed road repairs, bridges, and subway cars for technological toys like the Clinch River breeder reactor or pork-barrel construction projects like the Tennessee Tombigee waterway will allow the administration to give voters real value for their money and retain the clout of patronage over legislators.

Such a switch will clearly require active presidential intervention. Leadership is needed to break old pork-barrel beliefs —no collective body of legislators is going to autonomously recognize that its formulas are outdated. Leadership is also required to glamorize the restoration and repair of the infrastructure: maintenance is often neglected because nobody gets a plaque for repainting a bridge. Several mayors have, however, earned considerable political mileage by restoring their downtowns (for example, Mayor Kevin White with Boston's Faneuil Hall); a president could similarly popularize the rehabilitation of the nation's physical plant.

The process of public investment also needs to be rationalized. Unlike state governments and private corporations, the federal government has no capital budget. For many years the Office of Management and Budget, a White House agency, has been opposed to a budget that contains an inventory of construction and repair needs on the grounds that it would put the government "on the slippery slope of increased spending." In practice, ad-hocism has eroded the power of presidents over federal investments and given it to powerful legislators operating out of back rooms. A capital budget, as Representative Bob Edgar points out, would give the White House "more control, some planning ability,"[22] and allow the President to be a more effective investment manager of the assets of his constituents.


## Public Investment and the National Interest

But what about a nation's long-term economic interest? Can an administration afford to invest exclusively in low-technology infrastructure when the governments of competing econo- mies are pouring money to keep their industries and firms at the cutting edge of the new industrial revolution? The evi- dence says yes: the notion that a government can keep its economy ahead by steering investments toward high-tech- nology sectors may be conceptually attractive, but in practice such intervention has been uninspiring.

France provides the best example of the futility of shooting public resources at moving high-technology targets. De Gaulle's forced investments in state-of-the-art dreams inflated GNP and productivity figures, but two decades and billions of francs later, there is ample evidence that the strategy has failed the test of international competitiveness: IBM has nearly half of the computer market share in France (in second place is CII-Honeywell Bull, a joint venture dependent on the American partner's technology). Consumer electronics com- panies survive in France because of heavy protection from Japanese imports. When France's telephone system was re- cently modernized, the government had to reluctantly turn to L.M. Ericsson, a Swedish company that receives no support from its government, for digital switching technology. In semi- conductors, U.S. companies and technologies rule the roost. The "national champions" have turned out to be lame ducks —the eleven major companies under the Ministry of Industry lost about Fr 15 billion in 1982.

The evidence of the few internationally competitive French

companies suggests that exclusion from government capital subsidies is a source of comparative advantage. Maverick entrepreneur Marcel Bic became a world champion with the ballpoint pen. The managements of Peugeot and Renault chose independence over National Plan funds and carved a respectable niche for their automobiles in the world market. The postwar leaders of the French aerospace industry were small but profitable. According to Milton Hochmuth, "They were forced by the turmoil and small government financial support to exhibit entrepreneurial skills, take calculated risks, and develop aircraft with speed and boldness."[23] Then came the Concorde.

The failures of state investment in high technology are sometimes blamed on poor execution or factors beyond the policymaker's control, such as the "British disease" or the elitism bred by France's exclusive colleges. Look at MITI in Japan, advocates of industrial policy say, which has brought about an economic miracle by picking and investing in winners.

The reality of Japan's success is, however, quite different. True, the concentration of Japan's export success in a few sectors—automobiles, TV and audio equipment, cameras, steel, and formerly textiles and ships—indicates a national focus. But there is little evidence that this is due to a planned scheme of MITI capital allocation. MITI has had little influence on the magnitude or pattern of investment in the automobile industry, for example. Toyota, the General Motors of Japan, has protected its independence by avoiding debt and by financing its investments from internally generated funds. Its success is due to astute manufacturing and product strategies (and some luck), not cheap government money. Nor has the consumer electronics industry been bankrolled by MITI. Electronics companies do not need much capital, and competition in the industry is so tumultuous that MITI could not have played resource allocator even if it had wanted to.

The Japanese consumer goods industry has not succeeded through patiently conceived and carefully executed master strokes but rather by advancing like a disorganized guerrilla force. Japanese companies, for instance, seized the opportunity to make private-label TVs for Sears, Roebuck after Zenith and RCA had refused to do so. Hundreds of companies have risen and fallen in Japan's intensely competitive domestic market; innovations like the dual-screen TV set, LED counters on music systems, built-in automatic flashes in cameras, and additional recording time on videocassette recorders have gained companies a few months' advantage in the marketplace, time soon whittled away by imitators and improvers.

MITI is but a spectator in this disorderly boom. Its blueprint for the 1980s is long on rhetoric and short on specifics. The funds MITI actually invests are modest; for example, it has promised $35 million a year for the much-touted fifth-generation computer project over a ten-year period, compared with IBM's 1981 research budget of $1.6 billion.

Steel is perhaps the one legitimate success story of MITI capital allocation. On their own, private companies might not have found, or have been willing to risk, the funds needed to build modern, high-capacity plants. MITI had a vision for the steel sector and found the money to make Japanese manufacturers the world's lowest-cost producers. But these were not risky high-tech investments. Steel was a commodity with predictable and growing demand fueled by high rates of economic growth. The manufacturing process technology was proven and stable. Since capacity could be parceled out among a manageable number of companies with verifiable competence, planning was easy. And the government could legitimately argue that the size and payback period of needed investments were beyond the financial capabilities of Japanese private companies.

On the other hand, the economic need for capital investments in U.S. infrastructure is urgent. As Pat Choate says, "Three quarters of America's communities can't participate in Reagan's economic growth program" because of the state of disrepair of public works.[24] *Business Week* notes how the deterioration of infrastructure increases the costs that must be borne by American business:

U.S. Steel Corp. is losing $1.2 million per year in employee time and wasted fuel, rerouting trucks around the Thompson Run Bridge, in Duquesne, Pa., which is posted for weight restrictions because it is in such disrepair. Companies wanting to locate in certain parts of downtown Boston must bear the additional cost of a sewage holding tank to avoid overloading the system in peak hours. And companies in Manhattan lose $166 million a year for each additional 5-minute delay on the subways and buses.[25]

# CONCLUSION

# *Changing Course*

IN THE last eight chapters we have seen numerous examples of how politicians have persisted with unpopular economic policies. They have increased spending, adding to a tax burden that most voters find intolerable. They have made the tax structure increasingly regressive, with loopholes, indirect taxes, and deficits. Voters have also paid invisible taxes through import quotas and tariffs. And politicians' spending priorities have not been congruent with their constituents' needs.

These unpopular policies, which have been in place for almost a decade, have not been altered because of the inertia and inflexibility of politicians and political parties. Although public dissatisfaction with existing policies is manifestly great, politicians are so tied to their ideological dogmas and political formulas that they refuse to change course; numerous defeats at the polls have not yet led to the needed reevaluation of traditional beliefs.

Our economic and political institutions are seriously threatened by the unresponsiveness and inflexibility of public officials. Unacceptably high spending and taxes, for example, could lead to the rapid growth of an underground economy, a loss of faith in the legitimacy of democratic institutions, and, in extreme cases like Italy, political violence. These bleak outcomes can be avoided, but not by grass-roots movements, constitutional amendments, or new political parties. Mainstream politicians who are convinced that new, electorally responsive policies are in their political self-interest are the only ones who can make the necessary changes stick.

## The Barriers to Change

Unpopular policies are not being discarded because political institutions and culture are extremely resistant to change. The statesmen and ideologues are conditioned to believe that bending their principles in the face of adversity is a sign of weakness, and vote seekers have been conditioned to cling to the security blanket of traditional political formulas. Mavericks cannot easily overturn conventional beliefs and practices because the establishment has great power to enforce conformity. Tradition is also protected by poor feedback mechanisms —as evidence of failure is often not recognized, there is little incentive to change!

Some public officials value inflexibility as a worthy trait and consider holding the course with unpopular policies a hallmark of leadership. When President Carter started his term in 1976, he had a plan to stimulate the economy with tax cuts and spending programs. According to his Treasury Secretary W. Michael Blumenthal, the plan did not produce the expected results but the administration stuck to it because "Carter and his closest associates believed for too long, even when their statistics were telling a different tale, that their original economic policies had been right. And they clung tenaciously to the mistaken notion that to change course was politically the kiss of death—that it was better to ignore the new numbers and hang tough."[1]

President Reagan showed a similar tenaciousness with his

tax cut and defense spending plans, even after it was amply clear that supply-side economics was not working and high deficits were holding up interest rates. His program, George Church wrote in *Time*, reflects "his basic principles and so it must turn out right. That is the approach he has taken with major acts of his Administration."[2]

The President, Church continued, "has a propensity to seize on one comforting truth and magnify it to the whole truth, blocking out all evidence of continuing trouble." He could be induced to change his mind but only by "a complex and tricky process. The key, by unanimous agreement of all who work for him, is to argue that a new position is as compatible with his fundamental beliefs as the one he is urged to abandon. Then Reagan can justify a switch as mere tactical adjustment rather than a reversal of his conservative philosophy."[3]

Vote seekers aren't much more flexible than the statesmen. Political formulas that have outlived their validity and usefulness survive because they are treated more like the secrets of alchemy than the principles of modern chemistry, which are always being revised. Other professions reward nonconformity and challenges to conventional wisdom—Albert Einstein is a scientific hero for having corrected Isaac Newton's laws of motion. Businessmen make their fortunes by finding opportunities that have been traditionally overlooked or considered impossible—Henry Ford's Model T or Henry Luce's national news magazine, *Time*. Politics, however, frowns upon the newfangled theory or the better mousetrap. To question the political wisdom of higher spending is heresy. True innovations like the New Deal are once-in-a-lifetime happenings, and it is a very rare president who will say, as FDR did, "try it, if it doesn't work, try something else."

Political parties are vigilant keepers of the truth. New blood that might question tradition is discouraged. Advancement through the ranks is slow—aspirants to high office are not taken seriously by party elders and contributors until they have served a long period of apprenticeship and learned to respect established wisdom. A high proportion of Nobel Prizes are awarded for work performed by scientists in their twenties and early thirties (Newton invented calculus and discovered the laws of gravitation before he was twenty-five), and many dynamic businesses are started by entrepreneurs of similar age; but there are virtually no presidents or prime ministers below the age of fifty. Even radical candidates for high offices are middle-aged—Senator Eugene McCarthy was fifty-two when he ran for President in 1968 and George McGovern was fifty when he ran in 1972.

Mavericks and iconoclasts cannot circumvent party hierarchies—an unknown political innovator cannot easily launch a national campaign out of a garage with shoestring financing from venture capitalists as in the semiconductor industry. The few alternative campaigns that have achieved any credibility have been started by stalwarts with an existing network of organizational and financial contacts. John Anderson was fifty-eight and had served ten terms in the House when he ran for President in 1980 as an independent. The founders of the Social Democratic party in the U.K. had worked for decades in the Labour party. These veterans are as steeped in conventional wisdom as all the other politicians and, except for a label or image, don't offer anything new. Anderson proposed no major changes in policy; the only "difference" in his campaign was a rhetorical call for sacrifice. The British public had great difficulty in figuring out what the Social Democrats stood for, other than the fact that they did not belong to the Labour or Conservative parties.

Ambitious, innovative young minds that are capable of taking a fresh look at conventional wisdom know their chances of rapid advancement are low and stay out of politics. Politics is usually a second career to be savored after one has made one's mark in some other field. Ronald Reagan first ran for public office in his midfifties, after a successful career as an actor and public speaker. Jimmy Carter became state senator from Georgia after six years in the navy and nearly ten years of lucrative peanut farming. Gerald Ford ran for the U.S. House of Representatives when he was thirty-six after working in a law firm and the navy. In the U.K., a string of prime ministers from 1964 to 1979 were all from the civil service (Margaret Thatcher is an exception; she entered active politics when she was twenty-five, supported by her businessman husband).

Individuals who take to politics as a second career fit nicely into the traditional culture. Age has tempered their youthful impetuousness and their first careers in insular hierarchies have instilled in them a proper respect for tradition and established routines. They like to think of themselves as practical men (which often means, as Benjamin Disraeli once said, that they practice the errors of their forefathers). If they have a passion for reform it is tempered with caution, with the knowledge that Rome was not built in a day. If the lure of respectability attracts them to public life, they are even less disposed to make waves. Very few of them have the inclination to question the existing truths or the drive to conduct bold experiments.

## Faulty Feedback

Political inertia is reinforced by faulty feedback mechanisms. Politicians are protected from the disturbing knowledge that their policies are unpopular and their formulas are outdated because they are content to passively view reality through the mirrors and lenses of external institutions. Politicians and political parties make few attempts to set up their own channels of communication that deliver accurate, objective, and useful feedback from voters. "For a successful man," says a *Time* report, "Reagan is very passive, with little fire or curiosity. He rarely reaches outside the White House for answers or information."[4] Democratic presidential candidates, says Mayor Koch, "listen only to those who push the hardest and yell the loudest."[5]

Politicians often rely on influence leaders for feedback instead of reaching out directly to their constituents. Democratic presidents have a tradition of trying to gauge labor's point of view by consulting AFL-CIO leaders, without verifying whether these leaders are in step with their membership (in the 1980 election, labor leaders were clearly not) and disregarding the fact that a majority of the U.S. work force is not unionized. Similarly, President Reagan is said to rely on a "kitchen cabinet" of millionaire friends to convey to him views of Main Street.

Politicians also set great store by the opinions of influential newspapers like the *New York Times* and the *Washington Post*, which are actually poor reflectors of public opinion. These newspapers have a very restricted readership: neither can be called national, unless one believes that the union does not extend beyond the eastern seaboard; and even within its bailiwick, New York City, the venerable *Times* is read by less than a third of all households. These households are not a microcosm of the national electorate either in terms of income —the influential papers are read primarily by the upper middle class—or occupation—the *New York Times* readership is heavily skewed toward service industries and the *Washington Post* is practically a federal employee newspaper.

As profit-making enterprises, these newspapers reflect the values and interests of their special market segment. The *Washington Post*, for example, cannot afford to be too fervent an advocate of budget cuts or too vociferous an objecter to regulation and regulators. There is no deceit or conspiracy involved—these papers do not pretend to be the voice of the nation. That role is thrust on them by politicians who have not developed alternative means for hearing the views of a wider cross section of voters. Perhaps the deference to the *Times* and the *Post* is the carryover of a habit that politicians acquire early in their careers, of being sensitive to local newspapers. Regional and small-town papers *are* fairly good barometers of local opinion—their readership is diverse and, like their subscribers, the editors and reporters are down to earth. So although to the sophisticated, the Detroit *News* is provincial and boring, the Michigan politician ignores it at his peril.

Politicians lose touch with the grass roots by making the

national capital the center of their universe. As Senator Baker says, members of Congress are out of touch with the rest of the country, its interests, and its desires. He told his colleagues in Congress:

We will not in our lifetime know what the range of those desires and demands and dissent may be if we stay on the banks of the Potomac twelve months a year.

I still go home almost every weekend for a hurried gazing pass at the people of my state, masquerading in the guise of a man trying to find out what is going on. Who in the world can find out what is going on in the people's minds on a Saturday or Sunday when people would rather not be talking to politicians to begin with?"[6]

Opening and reading mail doesn't provide an accurate gauge of public opinion. Over 70 percent of voters have never written a letter to any public official giving their opinion about something that should be done.[7] When a congressman receives a flood of mail, it is more likely to be an orchestrated event than a spontaneous outpouring of voter sentiment. With the increasing sophistication of interest groups, letters written to politicians in Washington are becoming even less representative.

The isolation of politicians in national capitals has been increased by the growth in the influence of their professional, centralized staff at the expense of party activists dispersed among the grass roots. Although they are better educated and have more time for political analysis than the average party hack, staff people are more insulated from the concerns of real voters. They draw opinions from and communicate principally with their peers whose backgrounds, perceptions, and ideas are far removed from the average voter's. Staff based in Washington, London, or Paris never really get a handle on the concerns of common citizens in Wilkes-Barre, Leeds, or Pau.

As one former Edward Kennedy insider says about the failure of the senator's 1980 campaign: "From the beginning, the staff was dominated by people who went to Harvard College and Law School; who lived in Georgetown, didn't own a car and wouldn't recognize a typical American voter if they ran into one by accident."[8] Similarly, a Social-Democratic deputy from the Ruhr in Germany blames the party's disastrous showing in the region in the 1983 elections on its "half functionaries" in Bonn who tried to make nuclear weapons a campaign theme. The "leftist intellectuals" at party headquarters, he complains, failed to realize that "in Germany no election can be won with arms questions" when "unemployment in some areas is as high as 13.5 percent."[9]

The one trend toward better feedback has been the growing sophistication of opinion polls. As sampling and interviewing techniques have improved, opinion polls have become increasingly accurate, especially in predicting election outcomes. But polls have not contributed to shaping responsive policies; in the absence of a rational framework for analyzing the data they generate, opinion polls only reinforce existing dogmas and biases. For example, several opinion polls show that voters want both lower taxes and higher spending. This is not surprising—perfectly reasonable people who have to pay for their groceries would prefer to get them for nothing too. But for politicians who are predisposed to believe it, such polls "confirm" the conventional belief that voters are irrational.

Sophisticated polling schemes based on free-vote assumptions can lead to illogical strategies. For example, pollsters can determine what can be done to win the support of segments of the electorate like working women, blue-collar men, higher income individuals, blacks, the elderly, and so forth. Unfortunately, the favors done to any one segment have adverse consequences for the rest of the public, which the pollsters do not anticipate or measure. Consequently, the sum of the favors done to all the groups can have more political costs than benefits—an effect that politicians dazzled by all the "technology" of polling are not aware of, until their pollsters inform them that the public has inexplicably turned against its munificent government.

## The Dangers

The inability of politicians to gauge public needs and their unwillingness to change unpopular policies poses a serious danger: there is a basic contradiction between a popular democracy and governments that refuse to change unpopular policies. The contradiction has uneasily survived for a decade, but it may not for another—the institutions of popular democracy might give if unpopular policies don't.

One risk is that the public may stop waiting for its elected representatives to enact legitimate spending and tax cuts and slip into the underground economy instead. There are signs this is already happening. The turnover of the underground economy in the U.S. is estimated to exceed $200 billion. In 1972 the number of individuals who didn't bother to file tax returns was estimated by the General Accounting Office to be 5 million; in 1982 the number was estimated to have risen to over 15 million.[10] In Germany the underground economy is estimated to equal about 10 percent of the country's gross national product, and in Britain and Holland, to equal about 8 percent of GNP.[11]

The underground economy is especially prominent in Italy, where it accounts for perhaps 25 percent of national income.[12] Entire industries run on underground labor—operating legitimately by day and illegally after hours, when employees are paid a tax-free wage. Officially there were 2.3 million unemployed in Italy in 1983, but according to Elio Pagnotta of the state statistical institute, only 300,000 were really jobless; the rest had underground incomes and collected welfare benefits as well. "We cannot crack down on the black economy," Pagnotta says. "Without it we would have five million unemployed, no consumers and a population deprived of most of its income."[13]

Underground activity can keep the wheels of commerce turning, but not very smoothly. Too much entrepreneurial energy is diverted to "managing" tax evasion. Labor is disproportionately attracted to the service sector where the underground economy is concentrated. Economies of scale are lost because it is difficult to operate large establishments illegally —small becomes beautiful. Price stability is disturbed as governments are tempted to print money in lieu of the taxes they cannot collect.

A furtive, underground economy cannot generate an adequate number of fulfilling jobs, and the resulting unemployment creates a dangerously disgruntled underclass. As William Whitelaw, Home Secretary in the first Thatcher government, once told Parliament:

There has been a dramatic rise in unemployment among boys and girls. . . . Let no one have any doubt about the danger that has been created in terms of crime of all sorts, violence and vandalism. . . . If boys and girls do not obtain jobs when they leave school, they feel society has no need for them. If they feel that, they do not see any reason why they should take part in that society and comply with its rules.[14]

Worse, the underground economy undermines even the average middle-class individual's respect for the law. As Graham Turner, a British authority, says:

We have become in the course of the last ten or fifteen years, a nation of fiddlers . . .
You've no difficulty in fiddling in this country because other people actually want to help you. Now fifteen years ago that would have been quite different. People would have said, hey, this is not quite as it should be.[15]

Tax evasion and the violation of economic laws can lead to disregard for all other laws. The public loses faith in the legitimacy of democratic institutions; a sneaking sympathy develops on the one hand for left-wing terrorism against the "corrupt" elements of society and on the other for fascist groups dedicated to restoring "order."

Italy provides an extreme example of what can happen. The administration and politicians are discredited as corruption in high places is known to be rife. The Red Brigade abducts, "knee-caps" or assassinates politicians, businessmen, civil servants, and judges. Until it went too far with the murder of President Aldo Moro, one of the few politicians of recognized integrity, the Brigade enjoyed some sympathy among the public. The Brigade's violence has spurred right-wing terrorism and torture by special police forces set up to fight the terrorists.

Modern Italian democracy is not yet forty years old. It could go the way of an ancient Roman republic described by Machiavelli in the *Discourses:*

And since all governments enjoy some respect at the outset, this democratic government survived for a time, but not for long, especially after the generation which had established it passed on. For anarchy, respectful of neither private citizens, nor public men, soon followed with the result that each person acting as he pleased, every day saw a thousand wrongs committed.[16]

Democracy and law and order are most vulnerable in poorer countries with weaker institutions, like Turkey, Spain, and India. But in the long run, no countries are immune to the dangers. Who could have imagined ten years ago that the citizens of the U.S., the U.K., and Scandinavia would take to cheating on their taxes on the scale that they have?

## Only from Within

If this grim scenario is to be averted, unpopular policies must be changed. This can be accomplished only by mainstream politicians, and not by public-spirited reformers operating outside the normal process. Popular economic policies cannot be sustained by constitutional amendments, referenda, or new political movements.

It is true that there is considerable popular support for constitutional amendments, perhaps because the public has lost faith in its elected representatives. Nearly eight out of ten Americans favor a constitutional amendment to balance the budget.[17] The National Taxpayers Union has initiated a drive to get state legislatures to require Congress to call a national convention to consider such an amendment. As of 1981, over thirty state legislatures had. Similarly, the National Tax Limitation Committee has drafted an amendment to limit federal spending, which has been introduced in both houses of Congress.

This is, alas, less of a solution than a machination, and an ineffective one. Ingenious politicians can always find a way around the amendments. If direct expenditures by the federal government are limited, spending programs can be spun off into quasi-government bodies like the Synthetic Fuels Corporation. Or money can be lent instead of spent—as the Congressional Budget Office reports, federal credit assistance in the form of direct loans and loan guarantees has been growing much more rapidly than federal spending. In 1980 the off-budget, credit component of federal spending was estimated to be $269 billion, making the "total" federal budget 44 percent bigger than it looked on paper. Off-budget financing also circumvents balanced budget amendments: for example, in 1979 the federal government raised about $31 billion in the credit markets to finance its deficit, while off-balance sheet borrowing by federal agencies was $46 billion.

Another ineffective approach to reform is the anti-tax referendum. It has been fallaciously hoped that grass-roots movements like Proposition 13 will reestablish the people's will; following a burst of initial success, public-spirited outsiders like Howard Jarvis have been shown to lack the institutional clout to make their changes stick. After the organizers of Proposition 13 had seen property taxes cut, they had no control over the distribution of the ensuing spending reductions. The establishment politicians who did chose (perhaps deliberately) the least popular cuts—two years after Proposition 13, Mervyn Field's California Poll found that 62 percent of Californians felt that "state and local spending has been cut in the wrong places" while only 16 percent thought that the proper cuts had been made.[18] Tax-cutting crusades therefore lost their luster and in 1980, Californians rejected Proposition 9, to slash income taxes. Today there are tax increases on schedule in several states. The people's tax revolt appears to have failed.

Replacing business-as-usual lawmakers with committed revolutionaries does not appear to be a feasible solution either. Firebrands are often disdainful of institutional processes and often seem more interested in notoriety than change. They also lack credibility because they tend to focus on single issues —taxes, welfare cheats, or the gold standard; they don't understand the importance of economic policies outside their specialty and are often altogether ignorant about the noneconomic issues, such as foreign policy, which the public expects their leaders to be competent in. Consequently, after a spectacular start, these fringe politicians peter out and leave little lasting impact.

The failure-zone spender need not fear another Mogens Glistrup, who made a big splash in Denmark in 1971 when, in a TV appearance, he equated taxpayers with the heroes of the wartime resistance movement. A year later he founded the Progress party, dedicated to promoting deep cuts in taxes and spending. In its 1973 election debut, the party won 16 percent of the total vote and a corresponding share of seats in Parliament. By 1983, however, Mr. Glistrup had been convicted of tax evasion and the remaining Progress party members of Parliament had turned "respectable," endorsing the failure-zone status quo.

There is no way around professional politicians. Unlike a New England town or ancient Athens, a complex twentieth-century economy cannot be run by concerned citizens in their spare time. Full-time professional politicians are as indispensable as professional doctors, engineers, farmers, and businessmen. Nor are single-issue extremists an answer. The solution has got to be from within. Spending will be cut out of the failure zone and budgets balanced only when politicians realize that it is in their constituents', and therefore their own, interests to do so.

It isn't necessary for all politicians to appreciate the need for change—one president and a small group of activists laid the foundations of the Great Society, and a similar coterie of calculating populists could take it apart. But these few populists will have to be shrewd mainstream politicians who, like LBJ, understand and know how to manipulate the political process.

## What It Will Take

A politician who wants to replace failed, conventional policies with new, popular ones will have to discard ideology, be prepared to incur political costs and judiciously lose some votes, manipulate rather than be manipulated by special-interest groups, and communicate honestly and listen intelligently to voters.

### DISCARDING IDEOLOGY

Politicians of the left and right must discard many of their traditional ideologies. Liberals must give up their belief in redistribution through higher spending, in the moral imperative of a generous welfare state, and in renewing the industrial base through public investment in high technology. Conservatives must shed their commitment to tax cuts for the rich, to tight money and recessions (to "wring out inflation"), and to steep increases in defense spending.

Leaders must realize by now that ideological policies are at odds not only with popular needs but in some cases with their own ideological goals. The liberal goal of "sharing the wealth" has not been advanced by forcing spending into the failure zone, because expenditure increases have inevitably been financed by regressive taxation. It is the poor who have been the victims. The conservative goal of restoring the work ethic is not promoted by harsh remedies like forcing down wages and demand, which put millions out of work; and, as Michael Blumenthal puts it, throwing money at national security isn't more efficient than throwing money at social programs.

Renouncing old positions and ideologies does expose a politician to the embarrassment of inconsistency. But it is more in the leader's head than in the public eye. Voters don't punish sensible opportunism that is to their benefit. Americans did not turn against President Roosevelt for reneging on his promise to cut federal spending. Sir Winston Churchill became prime minister of the U.K. after changing parties twice. Reagan often had his feet "cast in concrete" on many issues when he was governor of California. When he broke the cast, as he frequently did, he suffered no loss in public esteem. His late conversion to the cause of a state income tax to balance the budget was quite popular. Reagan's successor, Jerry Brown, was handily reelected governor of California in November 1978 even though he first opposed Proposition 13 and then, after its passage in June, turned around and enthusiastically endorsed the concept in the few months remaining before the election.

Now more than ever the public is interested in a brighter future rather than in ideological consistency. Voters' loyalties to parties and ideologies have weakened considerably. The number of voters who "strongly identify" with either the Democratic or Republican party has been steadily dropping, from 37 percent of the population in 1964 to 23 percent in 1978. Ticket splitting—voting for a congressman or senator from one party and a president from the other—is becoming more common. Between 1960 and 1976 ticket splitting rose from 11 percent of voters to 24 percent.[19] The South no longer automatically votes Democratic and Massachusetts can swing from being the only state to vote for George McGovern in 1972 to helping elect Ronald Reagan in 1980.

Some liberals have begun to reevaluate their traditional beliefs. In 1983 some Democrats issued a "Neoliberal's Manifesto" that said: "We still believe in liberty and justice and a fair chance for all, in mercy for the afflicted and help for the down and out. But we no longer automatically favor unions and big government."[20]

In the wake of the left's drubbing in the 1983 general election in the United Kingdom, Len Murray, the general secretary of the Trades Union Congress, told the TUC's annual conference: "We cannot just say that our policies are fine and it is our members who are all wrong." The world has changed, Murray said. "Since 1945 we have made two fundamental assumptions. The first was that everyone saw full employment as a primary, even a dominant objective. The second was that the welfare state was accepted as a binding force in our society. Now these assumptions have been called into question."[21]

Conservatives are not yet submitting their dogmas to a similar scrutiny, perhaps because they are still basking in the electorate's rejection of the liberals. They fail to appreciate that the principal reason for the left's recent debacles is the public's unhappiness with high spending and taxes and believe instead that voters have given them a blanket endorsement to implement all their pet notions of regressive taxes, tight money, and defense spending.

INCURRING COSTS

Ideological dogmas must be replaced by hard-headed political calculation: politicians must not ignore the political costs of their policies and be prepared to judiciously sacrifice some votes. Governments cannot, for example, expect to reap the political benefit of a real tax cut without incurring some political costs of cutting real spending programs. There are no painless options such as eliminating waste and fraud. Waste and fraud are an integral part of government spending. They are deeply entrenched and expensive and time consuming to reduce. Voters cannot be rescued from failure-zone taxation by attacking waste and fraud, just as a large corporation facing bankruptcy cannot be saved by reducing the pilferage of paper clips instead of shutting down the big-money-losing plants. Leaders who hope to avoid unpleasant spending cuts by greater efficiency and control are usually disappointed. The Reagan administration announced in 1981 that fraud, which it said accounted for up to 10 percent of federal expenditures, would be attacked by highly trained, professional inspectors general. Little has been heard about them since. In 1979 the

Thatcher government appointed Sir Derek Rayner, managing director of Marks and Spencer, to bring private-sector cost controls to public administration. Between 1979 and 1982 Sir Derek's team identified £39 million of once-and-for-all savings, plus £274 in potential savings up to the end of March 1982— a total less than the average weekly loss incurred by the government on the nationalized lame-duck industries.

There *are* votes worth giving up: on balance, it is not worth protecting jobs in declining industries from foreign imports or providing generous benefits to the temporarily unemployed. Politicians cannot keep the electoral heartland without surrendering the vulnerable outposts. Politicians must follow a "mass market" strategy of appealing to the majority interest and avoid chasing after special interest niches.

## MANIPULATING LOBBIES

The majority interest cannot be protected unless politicians learn to manipulate and play off special-interest groups instead of reacting to their lobbying. Politicians should actively harness the self-interest of the steel-using automobile industry to resist tariffs on steel imports and the credit-hungry housing industry to fight bailouts and investment subsidies.

Coalitions of special interests can be and have been successfully harnessed to further popular causes. The Reagan administration received significant support for its 1981 budget cuts from the so-called budget coalition, described by *Newsweek* as "a germinating ad hoc alliance of hundreds of businesses and business associations." The coalition was experienced—it had "tested power together shellacking Big Labor in a series of lobbying wars" and was armed with "high technology and telecommunications capabilities."[22]

Another combination of special interests helped bring about the reform of the California health-care system, described in chapter 6. An alliance of insurance companies, business interests alarmed at the rapid increases in providing health coverage to their employees, and trade unions that feared the rising cost of health-care benefits was jeopardizing their wage increases and their jobs overwhelmed the health-care lobby, which had always had its way in the California legislature.

Seen in this light, the much-feared proliferation of special-interest lobbies is actually a favorable development. In chapter 4 I compared the relationship of a politician to special-interest groups to that between a businessman and his suppliers—competitive but necessary. The analogy can be taken a step further: just as the businessman's bargaining position is stronger if there are many competing suppliers, the politician has more room to maneuver if there are many countervailing lobbies. In the 1960s, for example, politicians could draw upon little outside help to fight pro-spending interest groups. Now the influence of the spending lobbies can be neutralized by drawing upon the strength of the rapidly growing anti-tax groups such as the National Taxpayers Union and the National Tax Limitation Committee.

HONEST COMMUNICATION, INTELLIGENT LISTENING

The general public's backing is even more important than that of special-interest groups. Politicians should build support for their changes by honestly and forthrightly explaining their need. Cutting failure-zone spending has more immediate benefits than costs; but both must be spelled out to voters in order to win their endorsement. The public's ability to weigh choices should not be underestimated. As Machiavelli remarked of the plebeians of Rome: "As to judging things, if they hear two equally skilful public speakers present opposing views, rarely will they fail to choose the better argument or show an incapacity to fathom the views they hear."[23]

FDR built support for the New Deal by taking his case to the public with his fireside chats on the radio. President Reagan generated enthusiasm for spending cuts in 1981 by explaining their need on television. Margaret Thatcher has demonstrated that honesty doesn't hurt. As a Conservative member of Parliament says: "She's getting away with a lot of things by saying pretty blunt and brutal truths. A lot of her statements are what people really think." A Labour MP agrees: "After years of

Callaghan's and Wilson's evasions, she has shown it is not necessary to be tricky to be Prime Minister."[24]

The climate of public opinion is increasingly conducive to
the speaking of home truths. Voters are aware of the realities
—they don't believe in or expect miracle cures. "Most Americans today," reports the Harris poll, "are not swayed by the
traditional political campaign promises. They recognize the
empty promises and unrealistic claims. . . ." Harris found that
86 percent of voters believe that "the trouble with most candidates for President is that they are afraid to tell it like it is."
And 81 percent agree that "the trouble with your getting benefits and handouts from government these days is that you'll
have to pay for them four or five times over in higher taxes."[25]

Voters around the world know there is a problem with excessive spending. As Pat Rabitte, the leader of a large Irish
trade union, says, "You even get people from down in Kerry
with straw in their hair who understand what the current
budget deficit means."[26] In Germany attitudes toward the welfare state have undergone a major change: in 1978, according
to the Infas Opinion Research Institute, nearly 75 percent of
Germans were opposed to any and all cuts in the social net. In
1983 that opinion was in a minority; furthermore, the majority
believed that in the future, social benefits should not be uni-
versally available as they had in the past but accrue only to
those who were really in need.[27]

Politicians must also learn to listen better. A permanent,
one-time fix of unpopular policies is impossible, and politicians
should continuously monitor changing voter needs. Opinion
polls, if tied to an objective political cost-benefit framework of
analysis (instead of the traditional free-vote presumption),
could considerably improve the ability of politicians to understand and respond to the needs of their constituents. In the
long run, new technology could be a great aid to a responsive
democracy. We have long been warned about the Big Brother
dangers of communications technology—how it could be used
to control and manipulate citizens. But the same systems could
increase the importance of public opinion in making policies.

Technology could be used to provide politicians with more accurate and reliable feedback than newspaper editorials. Two-way cable TV systems that are being experimented with could revolutionize retail marketing by allowing marketers to be instantly responsive to customer needs; the same systems could easily be adapted to increasing the efficiency of the political marketplace.

## The Outsider's Role

Although the principal cause of the problem and the primary responsibility for its solution lies with professional politicians, there are influential outsiders who, perhaps unwittingly, have contributed to the mess and can play a role in effecting a change. Many economists, political scientists, and business leaders have reinforced the myth that bad economics is good politics. Scholars and business writers fill magazines and newspapers with pronouncements that spending growth and rising protectionism are inevitable "because of politics." These predictions can become self-fulfilling prophesies because politicians are averse to doing their own objective analyses and often take their cues from what they read in the press or see on television.

Influential outsiders who have helped to build the notion of inevitable conflict between politics and responsible economics can undo some of the harm by attacking the flaws of conventional political wisdom. We do not need more articles pointing out that deficits and excessive welfare spending are bad economics—many public officials already believe that. The message that really needs to be communicated, in order for it to have any effect, is that deficits and uncontrolled welfare spending are also bad politics. Outsiders could have a lasting effect on the way all politicians think about their job. Lord Keynes's observation is as valid today as it was half a century ago:

I am sure that the power of vested interests is vastly exaggerated compared to the gradual encroachment of ideas. Not, indeed immediately, but after a certain interval; for in the field of economic and political philosophy there are not many who are influenced by new theories after they are twenty five or thirty years of age, so that the ideas which civil servants and politicians and even agitators apply to current events are not likely to be the newest. But soon or late, it is ideas, not vested interests, which are dangerous for good or evil.[28]

## Favorable Economic Environment

Changing policies might not quickly lead to greater prosperity, if the economic environment was unfavorable. Fortunately, in spite of the dreary performance of the last several years, there are reasons to believe that the economic climate is right and would respond favorably to a change in public policy. Economic growth can speed our exit from the failure zone—the same taxes are less burdensome when incomes rise; and the environment today contains several elements that are conducive to sustained growth: we are poised on the brink of a technological revolution. With machines that approximate human intelligence, robots with the dexterity of human hands, microprocessors, genetic engineering, and fiber optics, the historical constraints on human productivity will soon be left far behind. There are few material wants that mankind will not be able to satisfy better, cheaper, and faster.

The integration of the New Japans (like Korea, Taiwan, Hong Kong, and Singapore) into the world economy is another positive development, although many regard it as a threat. International trade isn't a zero-sum game with nations that win and lose. The more hands that are joined in voluntary economic exchange, the greater the benefit to all. The growth of the U.S. economy has long been sustained by the addition of new hands—surplus labor from the farms, massive waves of immigration, and most recently the baby boom—which helped increase production as well as increase the size of markets. The rapid economic development of the New Japans represents another such welcome addition to the U.S. and the world economy. The East Asian economies bring to bear an industrious labor pool that will free up resources for the new technologies. And as these economies prosper and grow, new markets are created, especially for mature industries that have saturated Western demand. Although the growth in exports from Taiwan and Korea is most often publicized, it should be remembered that the growth of their imports has been almost as rapid.

Economic prospects have been brightened by the destruction of the energy cartel. OPEC's control over oil prices has been broken. Consumers have responded to high prices by learning to conserve and non-OPEC producers by stepping up exploration. The current glut may eventually disappear and the price of energy, like that of pork bellies and soybeans, will fluctuate. But oil production is now shared among too many countries to allow a cartel to put the brakes on economic growth.

Cartels in the labor markets also have been weakened in the current recession. A few workers in oligopolistic industries like automobiles and steel have long been able to extract contracts that bore little relationship to what other workers of similar skills in the U.S. earned or to wages paid by competing firms abroad. In recent years the power of a few unions to preserve artificially high wages has been reduced by falling demand and international competition. Numerous "givebacks" in contracts have occurred in the U.S. steel, automobile, rubber, and transportation industries. In the U.K. also, reports *Businessweek*, "strike calls are being ignored and pay settlements tempered because workers have a better understanding of their companies' financial positions and prospects." Amalgamated Union of Engineering Workers president Simon Duffy says that "bargaining has been transformed, been freed. People bargain on the ability of companies to pay now."[29]

## Protecting Democracy: Vox Populi

Philosophers and scholars from Plato to Daniel Bell have expressed misgivings about a system of government where all
power ultimately rests with an unsophisticated and often shortsighted citizenry. But whatever its absolute inherent drawbacks,
compared to other alternatives that have been tried, democratic
government has produced superior economic and political results. Democracies have unquestionably the best record on
protecting human liberty and rights. Voters in free elections
have, surprisingly, risen above popular prejudice: when Jews
were despised, Disraeli was prime minister of Britain. Where
women are discriminated against, Margaret Thatcher, Indira
Gandhi, and Sirimavo Bandaranaike of Sri Lanka have been
elected to the most powerful offices in the land.

Economically too, democratic government has best nur-
tured the freedoms of trade and exchange that have brought
great prosperity to the common man. Dictatorships that have
preserved a semblance of market freedom can be counted on
the fingers of one hand. Poverty has been inseparable from
totalitarianism; economic growth has gone hand in hand with
evolution toward democracy. Spain and Portugal, which were
ruled by dictatorships for two decades after World War II, are
the poorest countries in Western Europe. Democratic West
Germany started from the same rubble as communist East
Germany after the war but is now an order of magnitude
ahead in its economic development.

Although the public has become disenchanted with specific
politicians and policies, it still strongly believes in the value of
democratic government and elections. Nearly nine voters in
ten reject the proposition that "so many other people vote in
national elections that it doesn't matter much to me whether
I vote or not."[30] (Although nearly half of all voters don't actually vote, because of the paucity of attractive choices.) A similar
proportion also disagrees with the statement that "a good
many local elections aren't important enough to bother

with."[31] Nor has the public rejected government. An 81 to 12 percent majority believes that the federal government "can be well run."[32]

Democracy, with free elections and universal suffrage, is a relatively new and unique experiment in the long history of human civilization. Full enfranchisement of the adult population has been achieved only in the twentieth century: women got the vote in the U.S. in 1920, in Sweden in 1921, in the U.K. in 1928, and in France and Italy only after World War II. Blacks were effectively enfranchised in the southern states only in the sixties.

This relatively new and so far extremely successful form of government needs to be carefully looked after. Traditionally, protecting democracy has meant voter registration drives and educating citizens in their rights and duties. Emphasis has also been placed on reforming institutions and processes: replacing brokered conventions with open primaries, shortening the election season, setting limits on campaign expenditures, and redefining relationships between the presidency and Congress.

The major threat to democracy today, however, isn't posed by institutional imperfections. It arises from inflexible attitudes and preconceptions about what the public should have, wants, or will tolerate—a mindset we have seen exists in all democratic countries with a wide variety of institutional arrangements. The needed reforms are not of the rules of the game but of the prejudices and beliefs of the players. Politicians must realize that their job is to ask priorities of their constituents and not presume to set them. And we as concerned citizens must stop hankering for enlightened statesmanship but instead press our leaders to be more responsive to the popular will.

Some principles of popular politics will endure—like the proverbial free lunch, there will never be free votes. The politics of other specific policies (such as the taxation of corporate profits) may change (if, for example, the ownership of stock becomes more widespread), and the reader may already find my analysis of certain issues questionable. But the critical point is that for a popular democracy to flourish, the needs and desires of the common citizen must be paramount. The voter isn't responsible for bad public policy any more than a customer is responsible for a badly run business. It is for politicians and government to rededicate themselves to the people.

# NOTES

## Introduction

1. Milton and Rose Friedman, *Free to Choose* (New York: Avon Books, 1981), 281.
2. "The Wind Is with Reaganomics," *Fortune*, 26 December 1983, 47.
3. "Thatcher Bends Free Market Policy," *Wall Street Journal* 7 January 1983, European edition, 21.
4. "Non-political Presidents," *Current Opinion* 4 (June 1976), 60.
5. "Approval of Carter Foreign Policy Declines in Poll to 20%," *New York Times*, 25 June 1980, A20.
6. Warren E. Miller, Arthur M. Miller, and Edward J. Schneider, *American National Election Studies Data Sourcebook* (Cambridge, Mass.: Harvard University Press, 1980), table 4.7.
7. Ibid., table 4.15.
8. Ibid., table 4.31.
9. Adam Smith, *Wealth of Nations* (London: Methuen & Co., 1904), vol. 1, p. 16.
10. "How Reagan Decides," *Time*, 13 December 1982, 18.
11. "Carter Sounds Fall Themes," *New York Times*, 30 May 1980, B6.
12. "Hollings Hacks Away at His Rivals," *New York Times*, 8 June 1983, A16.
13. John Ardagh, *France in the 1980's* (Middlesex: Penguin, 1982), 638.
14. "Candidates, Detergent," *New York Times*, 10 June 1983, A18.
15. Herbert E. Alexander, "Can a Candidate Buy His Way into Office?" *TV Guide*, 7 June 1980, 38.
16. Miller, Miller, and Schneider, *American National Election Studies Data Sourcebook*, table 4.13.
17. "Economic Concerns Most Urgent," *Current Opinion*, June 1976, 61.
18. "Laborites Narrow Fight for Party Chief," *New York Times*, 5 November 1980, 3.

## Chapter 1

1. Richard M. Nixon, "Message to the Nation on the Extension of Surtax," *New York Times*, 27 March 1968, 20.
2. Gerald R. Ford, "Economic Address to a Joint Session of Congress," *New York Times*, 9 October 1974, 1.
3. "Carter's Attack on Inflation," *Newsweek*, 24 March 1980, 24.
4. "Reagan on the Key Issues," *Newsweek*, 31 March 1980, 26.
5. "The Debate Goes On," *International Herald Tribune*, 28 September 1982, 3.

6. "The Economic Debate," *Newsweek*, 2 March 1981, 33.

7. "Reagan Rolls Out the Pork Barrel," *International Herald Tribune*, 28 September 1982, 2. (Reprinted from the *Washington Post*.)

8. Ibid.

9. Ibid.

10. "The Democrats Fight the Tide," *Newsweek*, 23 March 1981, 23.

11. Ibid.

12. "President Reagan's State of the Union Message on Economic Recovery," *New York Times*, 19 February 1981, B8.

13. "The Unbalanced Budget," *Newsweek*, 4 February 1980, 59.

14. Milton Friedman, "Carter's Anti-Inflation Plan," *Newsweek*, 24 March 1980, 33.

15. "Carter's Attack on Inflation," *Newsweek*, 24 March 1980, 24.

16. "Goldwater Still Defies Rules," *Wall Street Journal*, 24 September 1964, 4.

17. A. M. Simons, "Packingtown as a Residential Section," in *Current Economic Problems*, by Walton H. Hamilton (Chicago: University of Chicago Press, 1925), 870–871.

18. Richard T. Ely, *Problems of Today* (New York: Thomas Y. Crowell & Co., 1888), 173.

19. Ibid., 170.

20. Ibid., 236.

21. *Presidential Messages, Addresses and State Papers*, ed. Julius W. Muller (New York: The Review of Reviews Co., 1917), 8.

22. Charles P. Kindleberger, *The World in Depression, 1929–1939* (Berkeley: University of California Press, 1973), chap. 8.

23. James Tobin, *The Economists of the New Frontier*, ed. B. Hughel Wilkins and Charles B. Friday (New York: Random House, 1963), 44.

24. "Study in Black and Red," *Wall Street Journal*, 3 July 1936, 7.

25. "The Great Game of Politics," reprinted in the *Wall Street Journal*, 3 August 1936, 2.

26. Ibid.

27. "New Deal's Spending Policies Seem Major Election Issue in Midwest," *Wall Street Journal*, 5 August 1936, 1.

28. "Revision, No Reduction Is the Outlook If GOP Candidate Wins," *Wall Street Journal*, 8 October 1948, 1.

29. "Review and Outlook, Social Responsibility," *Wall Street Journal*, 30 December 1948, 4.

30. Tobin, *Economists of the New Frontier*, 44.

31. Paul Samuelson, *Economics* (New York: McGraw-Hill, 1980), 195.

32. "A Party Goes to San Francisco," *Time*, 2 May 1983, 23.

33. "Bush Begins a Series of Televised Campaign Programs," *New York Times*, 18 October 1980, 9.

34. "The Economists Debate," *Newsweek*, 2 March 1981, 34.

35. "RNR's Own New Deal—Sizing Up One Program," *Newsweek*, 2 March 1981, 26.

36. Ibid., 24.

37. Ibid., 23.

38. "How Reagan Decides," *Time*, 13 December 1982, 17.

39. "Supply-Siders," *Boston Globe*, 25 July 1982, 80.

40. "Put Up or Shut Up," *The Economist*, 16 October 1982, 18.

41. Niccolo Machiavelli, *The Prince* (New York: Bantam Books, 1981), 75.

42. "Stern Doctor, Stern Remedy," *New York Times*, 10 June 1983, A1.

43. "1982: Margaret Thatcher's Year," *Financial Times*, 31 December 1982, 10.

44. "What Jenkins Should Do Now," London *Times*, 29 May 1983, 17.

45. *New Statesman*, 17 June 1983, 7.

46. "Bonn Fears Anti-war Protests Thwart Efforts to Counter Moscow Propaganda," *Wall Street Journal*, 4 April 1983, 20.

# Notes

47. "For Palme Some Thorns on the Roses," *New York Times*, 21 September 1982, A3.

48. Machiavelli, *The Prince*, 74.

49. "Carter's Failure to Reach His Fiscal Goals Fuels Campaigns of Political Opponents," *Wall Street Journal*, 29 January 1980, 5.

## Chapter 2

1. William Greider, "The Education of David Stockman," *Atlantic Monthly*, December 1981, 51.

2. "What David Stockman Said," *Washington Post*, 22 November 1981, 64.

3. "Supply Siders vs. Monetarists," *Business Week*, 24 August 1981, 82.

4. "From Nuggets to Dross: The False Gleam," *Business Week*, 8 February 1982, 17.

5. "Reagan Is Sticking to His Economic Guns," *Business Week*, 23 November 1981, 104.

6. Ibid.

7. "From Nuggets to Dross," *Business Week*.

8. "The Built-in Deficit," *Business Week*, 16 August 1982, 92.

9. George H. Gallup, *The Gallup Poll, 1935–1971* (New York: Random House, 1972).

10. Benjamin I. Page, *Who Gets What From Government?* (Berkeley: University of California Press, 1983), 49.

11. Quoted in ibid., 36.

12. Lester Thurow, *The Zero Sum Society* (New York: Penguin Books, 1981), 169.

13. Everett Carl Ladd, "Americans' Hate Affair With Deficits," *Fortune*, 14 June 1982, 77.

14. Ibid., 78.

15. Edwin R. A. Seligman, *The Income Tax* (New York: Macmillan, 1911), 77.

16. Ibid., 210.

17. Koussuth Kent Kennan, *Income Taxation, Methods and Results in Various Countries* (Milwaukee, Wisc.: Burdwick and Allen, 1910), 77.

18. Ibid., 288.

19. Page, *Who Gets What From Government?* 25.

20. Quoted in ibid., 26.

21. Thurow, *The Zero Sum Society*, 170–171.

22. Page, *Who Gets What From Government?* 47.

23. Ibid., 45.

24. "What Ronald Reagan Can Learn from Jimmy Carter," *Business Week*, 26 October 1981, 17.

25. "President Reagan's State of the Union Message on Economic Recovery," *New York Times*, 19 February 1981, B8.

26. "No Big Breaks for Small Business in the Tax Cuts," *Business Week*, 24 August 1981, 100.

27. "Has Reagan Hurt the Poor?" *Fortune*, 24 January 1983, 78.

28. "How One Family Gained From New Tax Policies," *New York Times*, 16 April 1983, 7.

29. Greider, "The Education of David Stockman," *Atlantic Monthly*, 4, 6.

30. "House Democrats Win a Test Vote on Alternative to Reagan Budget," *International Herald Tribune*, 24 March 1983, 3.

31. Walter W. Heller, "President Reagan Is a Keynesian Now," *Wall Street Journal*, 23 March 1983, 30.

32. Ray Connolly, "Washington Commentary," *Electronics*, 24 February 1982, 58.

33. Sir Geoffrey Howe, Budget Speech in the House of Commons, reported in the *Financial Times*, 13 June 1979, 18.

34. Ibid.

35. Ibid.

36. "Industry Pleased, but Farmers Irked," *Financial Times*, 13 June 1979, 23.
37. Ibid.
38. James Callaghan, Speech in the House of Commons, reported in the *Financial Times*, 13 June 1979, 20.
39. "The Pips Won't Squeak," *The Economist*, 7 November 1981, 88.
40. "The Fed: A $3.7 Billion Mistake," *New York Times*, 28 October 1979, F19.
41. "Pay Up, Big Spenders," *Time*, 18 July 1983, 44.
42. "Ideological Safari: Democrats in Congress Hunt for Policy Ideas," *Wall Street Journal*, 1 April 1982, 20.
43. "Britain's Tax Expenditures," *The Economist*, 27 January 1979, 60.
44. "Perspectives on U.S. Military Spending," *International Herald Tribune*, 22 February 1983, 6.
45. "A Loss of Faith in the Progressive Tax," *Business Week*, 6 September 1982, 15.
46. "Cut Tax Spending Too," *The Economist*, 4 August 1979, 47.
47. W. Michael Blumenthal, "What Ronald Reagan Can Learn," *Business Week*, 26 October 1981, 17.
48. "Midterm Elections, 1982," *International Herald Tribune*, 5 November 1982, 4.
49. "Voters, Trust in Reagan Diminishing, Poll Shows," *Financial Times*, 15 March 1983, 6.
50. "If You Own Real Estate, You're on the Hit List," *Boston Globe*, 3 April 1983, A35.
51. "Subsidy for House Buyers," *The Economist*, 19 February 1983, 20.
52. "Reagan Aides Support a Health Benefits Tax," *International Herald Tribune*, 6 December 1982, 3.
53. Amar Bhide, "Beyond Keynes: Demand Side Economics," *Harvard Business Review*, July–August 1983, 104.
54. Quoted in Adam Meyerson, "The Spirit of Enterprise," *Commentary*, July 1981, 18.
55. "The Built-In Deficit," *Business Week*, 16 August 1982, 86.
56. "Surge at the Center," *New York Times*, 2 June 1983, A23.
57. "Tax Cut's Effect on Work Hours Limited," *Financial Times*, 24 March 1980, 4.

## Chapter 3

1. "President Reagan's State of the Union Message on Economic Recovery," *New York Times*, 19 February 1981, B8.
2. "The Failure of Monetarism," *Business Week*, 4 April 1983, 64.
3. "A Talk with Paul Volcker," *New York Times Sunday Magazine*, 19 September 1982, 70.
4. "Reagan's Interest Rate Dilemma," *Business Week*, 14 September 1981, 29.
5. "Supply Siders vs. Monetarists," *Business Week*, 29 August 1981, 78.
6. "Inflation Fight Costly," *Boston Globe*, 23 October 1983, A51.
7. "The Supply Siders Ride High Again," *Business Week*, 8 February 1982, 117.
8. "The Risks of a Reagan Stalemate," *Business Week*, 8 February 1982, 28.
9. Sidney Blumenthal, "Economic Navigator for the Right," *Boston Globe Magazine*, 3 April 1983, 44.
10. "Rates Could Zap the GOP in '82," *Business Week*, 14 September 1981, 127.
11. "Another Job for Her Boys," *London Sunday Times*, 2 January 1983, 9.
12. "The Bank Advises, But . . ." *Financial Times*, 6 May 1982, 24.
13. "A Talk with Paul Volcker," *New York Times Magazine*, 68.
14. Sidney Blumenthal, "Economic Navigator for the Right," *Boston Globe Magazine*, 25.
15. Edward R. Tufte, *Political Control of the Economy* (Princeton, N.J.: Princeton University Press, 1980).

# Notes

16. "Rates Could Zap the GOP in '82," *Business Week*, 14 September 1981, 127.
17. "A Talk with Paul Volcker," *New York Times Magazine*, 72.
18. Ibid.
19. James Duesenberry, unpublished manuscript.
20. Sidney Blumenthal, "Economic Navigator for the Right," *Boston Globe Magazine*, 44.
21. "No Interest in Little Guy," *Boston Globe*, 29 October 1981, 45.
22. "Volcker Testimony to Congress," *Financial Times*, 17 February 1983, 4.
23. "Goodhart Was Right," *New York Times*, 3 January 1982, p. 1, sec. 3.
24. "Fed's Interest Rate Dilemma," *New York Times*, 15 June 1982, D1.
25. "Singapore," *International Herald Tribune*, 10 October 1982, 115.
26. George G. C. Parker, "Now Management Will Make or Break the Bank," *Harvard Business Review*, November/December 1981, 143.

# Chapter 4

1. "Bashing Japan Isn't the Answer," *New York Times*, 29 October 1982, A26.
2. "Examining Reagan's Record on Free Trade," *Wall Street Journal*, 10 May 1982, 30.
3. "Now Textiles Want Quotas Too," *Business Week*, 24 August 1981, 125.
4. "Exit Kennedy, Enter a Thoughtful Mondale," *International Herald Tribune*, 6 December 1982, 4.
5. "Examining Reagan's Record," *Wall Street Journal*.
6. Ibid.
7. "Walker Milks the British Consumer Yet Again," *The Economist*, 12 February 1983, 61.
8. "Import or Die," *The Economist*, 13 November 1982, 13.
9. "New Barriers?" *Wall Street Journal*, 17 March 1983, 29.
10. "Labour Party Election Manifesto," in the *Financial Times*, 7 April 1979, 5.
11. "Import or Die," *The Economist*, 19 February 1983, 11.
12. George H. Gallup, *The Gallup Poll: 1935–1971* (New York: Random House, 1972), 2264.
13. Robert S. Erickson and Norman Luttbeg, *American Public Opinion: Its Origin, Content and Impact* (New York: John Wiley & Sons, 1980), 3.
14. Ibid.
15. Gallup, *The Gallup Poll*, 2308.
16. "Faith in Free Trade Has Not Waned," *Business Week*, 30 May 1983, 16.
17. Republican Party, National Committee, *Republican Campaign Text Book* (Philadelphia: Republican Party National Committee, 1902), 358, 359.
18. Grover Cleveland, "Third Annual Message to Congress, December 6, 1887," in *Presidential Messages, Addresses and State Papers*, ed. Julius W. Muller (New York: The Review of Reviews Co., 1917), 2715.
19. Robert Z. Lawrence, "Before Industrial Policy," *New York Times*, 30 November 1983, A31.
20. "Unions Necessary, But Leadership Unpopular," *Current Opinion*, March 1977, 26.
21. Steven Stark, "Labor's Kiss of Death," *New York Times*, 22 May 1983, A21.
22. "Poll Says a Labor Endorsement May Have Negative Influence," *New York Times*, 12 June 1983, C32.
23. "Faith in Free Trade Has Not Waned," *Business Week*, 16.
24. Amitai Etzioni, "Some Protectionism," *New York Times*, 29 May 1983, E15.
25. "China's Apparel Sales to Japan Are Booming," *Wall Street Journal*, 25 October 1982, Asian edition, 4.
26. "Japan–U.S. Trade Imbalance," *Japan Times*, 22 November 1983, 12.
27. "April Fool Anniversary," *Wall Street Journal*, 1 April 1982, 26.

## Chapter 5

1. "Tight Money, Loose Deficits, High Interest Rates, Low Politics," *The Economist*, 6 February 1982, 23.

2. "Bad Tidings for the Jobless," *Time*, 13 December 1982, 54.

3. "The Crisis that Growth Alone Will Not Solve," *Financial Times*, 7 January 1983, 13.

4. "Serving Up Jobs: Side Dish of Pork," *Boston Globe*, 3 April 1983, A19–A20.

5. "Playing Politics with Jobs," *Newsweek*, 14 February 1983, International edition, 38.

6. "Serving Up Jobs," *Boston Globe*, A19.

7. "Labour Steps Up Jobs Battle," *Financial Times*, 12 April 1979, 12.

8. "Put Up or Shut Up," *The Economist*, October 1982, 18.

9. "Crusading PM Stresses Jobs," *Financial Times*, 10 April 1979, 9.

10. Advertisement in the *Wall Street Journal*, 21 February 1984.

11. Advertisement in the *Wall Street Journal*, 14 March 1980, 14.

12. *London Times* (Sunday), 23 March 1980, 55.

13. Ibid., 59.

14. Kenneth D. Walters and R. Joseph Monsen, "Nationalization Trends in European Industry," *McKinsey Quarterly*, Spring 1983, 57.

15. "Third World Seeks Easing of Pact on Patents," *International Herald Tribune*, 6 October 1982, 9.

16. "Living Down Scandals," *Financial Times*, 9 April 1979, 22.

17. See, for example, Gale Merseth, "Regulation and Income Redistribution: The Massachusetts Experience" (unpublished D.B.A. thesis, Harvard Business School, 1979).

18. David L. Birch, *The Job Generation Process* (Cambridge, Mass.: M.I.T. Program on Neighborhood and Regional Change, 1979), 4.

19. Ibid., 20.

20. "Proof of Capitalism's Creative Destruction," *Business Week*, 14 December 1981, 16.

21. Walter Kane, "How Not to Help Small Business," *Electronic Business*, April 1982, 23.

22. "U.S. Bailouts: Caution Urged," *New York Times*, 1 June 1983, D2.

23. Quoted in "Proof of Capitalism's Creative Destruction," *Business Week*, 14 December 1981, 16.

## Chapter 6

1. "President's News Conference on Foreign and Domestic Matters," *New York Times*, 18 May 1983, A2.

2. "Reagan Blames Federal Role for Mediocre Schools," *New York Times*, 1 May 1983, A29.

3. National Commission on Excellence in Education, *A Nation at Risk: The Imperative for Educational Reform* (Washington, D.C.: U.S. Department of Education, 1983), 33.

4. "President's News Conference on Foreign and Domestic Matters," *New York Times*, 18 May 1983, A20.

5. "Reagan Blames Federal Role for Mediocre Schools," *New York Times*.

6. "President Ronald Reagan's State of the Union Message on Economic Reality," *New York Times*, 19 February 1981, B8.

7. "Labour Party Manifesto," *Financial Times*, 7 April 1979, 5.

8. "Labour Raise Health Fears," *London Times* (Sunday), 29 May 1983, 2.

# Notes

9. Milton and Rose Friedman, *Free to Choose* (New York: Avon Books, 1980), 167.

10. Philip E. Converse, et al., *American Social Attitudes Data Sourcebook; 1947–1978* (Cambridge, Mass.: Harvard University Press, 1980), table 8.11.

11. "Public's Top Spending Priorities," *Current Opinion*, March 1976, 25.

12. National Commission on Excellence in Education, *A Nation at Risk*, 16.

13. "A Symbol of Change in Mississippi," *Boston Sunday Globe*, 3 April 1983, A20.

14. Ibid.

15. Ibid.

16. "The Spiraling Cost of Health," *Business Week*, 8 February 1982, 69.

17. Ibid.

18. Samuel Davis, "How Hospitals Are Penalized for Efficiency," *New York Times*, 1 December 1979, A20.

19. "The Spiraling Cost of Health," *Business Week*, 59.

20. Ibid., 60.

21. Converse, et al., *American Social Attitudes Data Sourcebook*, table 8.26.

22. Quoted in Milton and Rose Friedman, *Free to Choose*, 172.

23. "America's Bill for Education Likely to Reach $230 Billion," *New York Times*, 28 August 1983, 36.

24. National Commission on Excellence in Education, *A Nation at Risk*, 5.

25. "The Spiraling Cost of Health," *Business Week*, 69.

26. William F. Powers, "Research Indicates Smokers, Drinkers Up Hospital Costs," *Harvard Crimson*, 1 May 1980, 1.

27. "Washington's Metro Is the Solid-Gold Cadillac of Mass Transit," *Fortune*, 3 December 1979, 110.

28. "America's Bill for Education Likely to Reach $230 Billion," *New York Times*.

29. "President's News Conference on Foreign and Domestic Matters," *New York Times*, 18 May 1983, 20.

30. John Ardagh, *France in the 1980s* (Middlesex: Penguin), 494.

31. Ibid.

32. "In France, Quality vs. Egalite," *Time*, 13 June 1983, 47.

33. Milton and Rose Friedman, *Free to Choose*, 221.

34. "Poor Prescription," *Forbes*, 30 August 1982, 40.

35. Goh Keng Swee, *The Practice of Economic Growth* (Singapore: Federal Publications, 1977), 179.

36. Ibid.

37. Ibid., 180.

38. Milton and Rose Friedman, *Free to Choose*, 100.

39. Ibid., 165.

40. "Labour Party Manifesto," *Financial Times*.

41. Quoted in Milton and Rose Friedman, *Free to Choose*, 92.

42. "Computers Pose a Peril for Poor, Lautenberg Says," *New York Times*, 8 June 1983, A1.

43. "Computers May Widen Gap in School Quality Between Rich and Poor," *Wall Street Journal*, 26 May 1983, 1.

44. "Education Emerges as a Major Issue in Campaign," *New York Times*, 9 June 1983, B11.

45. National Commission on Excellence in Education, *A Nation at Risk*, 6–7.

46. "Reluctance to Sue Attributed to Japanese Is Part Myth, Partly Due to Legal System," *Wall Street Journal*, 14 April 1983, 32.

47. Paul Starr, "Medicine Has Overdrawn Its Credit in American Society," *US News & World Report*, 12 September 1983, 78.

48. "Defense Spending," *The Gallup Report*, January 1983, 12.

49. "Toward '84 and Away From Reagan," *New York Times*, 11 April 1983, A16.

50. Sidney E. Rolfe and James L. Burtle, *The Great Wheel* (New York: McGraw-Hill, 1975), 91.

## Chapter 7

1. Milton and Rose Friedman, *Free to Choose*, (New York: Avon Books, 1980), 93.
2. "A Turning Point for the 'New Realism,'" *Business Week*, 6 June 1983, 48.
3. Elizabeth Allison, "Income Maintenance Programs: The U.S. Experience" (ICCH 4-378-210) (Boston, Mass.: distributed by HBS Case Services, Soldiers Field, 02163), 5.
4. Ibid.
5. "The Welfare State in Crisis," *Newsweek*, 25 July 1983, 9.
6. George H. Gallup, *The Gallup Poll, 1935–1971* (New York: Random House, 1972), 2003-4.
7. Merle Miller, *Lyndon: An Oral Biography* (New York: Ballantine Books, 1981), 497.
8. Ibid., 498.
9. Ibid., 535.
10. Philip E. Converse, et al., *American Social Attitudes Data Sourcebook* (Cambridge, Mass.: Harvard University Press, 1980), 387.
11. "Ireland Buckles Down," *Wall Street Journal*, 19 March 1983, European edition, 1.
12. "The Welfare Boom," *Wall Street Journal*, 19 February 1981, 26.
13. "Making the Poor Poorer," *International Herald Tribune*, 18 February 1983, 4.
14. "The Withering of Europe's Welfare States," *The Economist*, 16 October 1982, 65–66.
15. "The Welfare State in Crisis," *Newsweek*, 14.
16. "Mixed Reaction to the Welfare Problem," *Current Opinion*, July 1976, 65–66.
17. "Proposals for Paring Taxes and Spending," *New York Times*, 18 October 1980, A9.
18. Ibid.
19. Sidney Verba and Kay Lehman Schlozman, *Injury to Insult: Unemployment, Class and Political Response* (Cambridge, Mass.: Harvard University Press, 1979), chap. 7.
20. "In the U.S. the Jobless Seem Skeptical About Protesting at the Polls," *International Herald Tribune*, 9–10 October 1982, 3.
21. Ibid.
22. Ibid.
23. "Mixed Reaction to Welfare Problem," *Current Opinion*.
24. Niccolo Machiavelli, *The Prince* (New York: Bantam Books, 1981), 57.
25. Benjamin I. Page, *Who Gets What From Government?* (Berkeley: University of California Press, 1983), 64.
26. Martin S. Feldstein, "Unemployment Insurance: Time for Reform," *Harvard Business Review*, March/April 1975, 55.
27. Milton and Rose Friedman, *Free to Choose*, 99.
28. Herbert Stein, "A Narrow View of the Poverty Problem," *Fortune*, 25 January 1982, 112.
29. "Reagan Halted Growth in Noncash Aid Programs," *New York Times*, 23 September 1983, B10.
30. Milton and Rose Friedman, *Free to Choose*, 99.
31. "Cold Comfort in Cleveland," *The Economist*, 6 February 1982, 24.
32. George H. Gallup, *The Gallup Poll: 1935–1971* (New York: Random House, 1972), 9–10.
33. Ibid., 192.
34. "The Father of U.S. Social Security," *International Herald Tribune*, 25 January 1983, 11.
35. "House Approves a Plan for Rescue of Social Security," *New York Times*, 10 March 1983, A1.
36. Ibid.

37. Peter F. Drucker, "(Really) Saving Social Security Is Thinkable," *Wall Street Journal,* 11 August 1983, 30.
38. Feldstein, "Unemployment Insurance," *Harvard Business Review,* 56.
39. "The Budget: The Chancellor's Speech," *Financial Times,* 27 March 1980, 15.
40. Amar Bhide and Bruce R. Scott, "The Irish Republic," Case study available from Harvard Business School, 1979.
41. Jon Nordheimer, "Belt Tightening in Europe Squeezes the Welfare State," *New York Times,* 8 December 1983, A2.
42. "Knocking Off Early," *International Herald Tribune,* 26 January 1983, 3.

## Chapter 8

1. "Pitfalls in France's Vast R&D Plan," *Business Week,* 23 November 1981, 99.
2. David Marsh, "Why the State Takeover Is Turning Sour," *Financial Times,* 17 March 1983, editorial page.
3. Kenneth D. Walters and R. Joseph Monsen, "Nationalization Trends in European Industry," *McKinsey Quarterly,* Spring 1983, 58.
4. "Callaghan Stresses Jobs," *Financial Times,* 10 April 1979, 1.
5. "The Right Remedy for R&D Lag," *Fortune,* 25 January 1982, 62.
6. Marsh, "Why the State Takeover Is Turning Sour," *Financial Times.*
7. Keith Pavitt, "Governmental Support for Industrial Research and Development in France," *Minerva,* Autumn 1976, 353.
8. Quoted in ibid., 352.
9. "A Tale of 219 Cities," *Time,* 21 February 1983, International edition, 21.
10. "Notable and Quotable," *Wall Street Journal,* 15 September 1983, 31.
11. "F.D.R.'s Disputed Legacy," *Time,* 1 February 1982, 25.
12. Charles de Gaulle, *The Complete War Memoirs,* vol. 1, trans. Richard Howard (New York: Simon and Schuster, 1960), 3.
13. John Costello and Terry Hughes, *The Concorde Conspiracy* (New York: Scribner's Sons, 1976), 41.
14. Samuel Brittan, "Economic Viewpoint," *Financial Times,* 17 March 1983, 21.
15. "Senate Bars Funds for SST," *New York Times,* 25 March 1971, A1.
16. "A Free Market Bias at Synfuels," *Business Week,* 2 November 1981, 50.
17. "A Swift About Face on Aid to Synfuels," *Business Week,* 9 August 1982, 26.
18. Ibid.
19. Ibid.
20. "Infrastructure: A Nationwide Need to Build and Repair," *Business Week,* 26 October 1981, 142.
21. Ibid.
22. "Studies Focus on Decay in U.S. Physical Facilities," *New York Times,* 9 May 1983, A13.
23. Quoted in Amar Bhide, "Beyond Keynes: Demand Side Economics," *Harvard Business Review,* July/August 1983, 102.
24. "Infrastructure," *Business Week.*
25. Ibid.

## Conclusion

1. W. Michael Blumenthal, "What Ronald Reagan Can Learn," *Business Week,* 26 October 1981, 17.
2. George Church, "How Reagan Decides," *Time,* 13 December 1982, 12.
3. Ibid.
4. Ibid.

5. "Candidates Hear 'Extremists' Only, Koch Says," *Boston Globe,* 20 August 1983, 16.

6. "Congress Out of Touch with U.S., Baker Contends," *New York Times,* 16 June 1983, A19.

7. Warren E. Miller, Arthur M. Miller, and Edward J. Schneider, *American National Election Studies Data Sourcebook* (Cambridge, Mass.: Harvard University Press, 1980), table 5.6.

8. Personal Communication.

9. "Blue-Collar Ruhr Valley Moves to the Right," *International Herald Tribune,* 26 March 1983, 2.

10. "Who's Afraid of the I.R.S.?" *New York Times,* 15 April 1983, A27.

11. "Europe's 'Black Economy,'" *Business Week,* 25 June 1983, 12.

12. Ibid.

13. "The Welfare State in Crisis," *Newsweek,* 25 July 1983, 13.

14. Roy Hattersley, "Britain's Bobby: The Best Answer to Crime," *Wall Street Journal,* 18 March 1983, European edition, 8.

15. Quoted in Milton and Rose Friedman, *Free to Choose* (New York: Avon Books, 1980), 277–278.

16. Niccolo Machiavelli, *The Prince* (New York: Bantam Books, 1981), 93.

17. "Most Favor Law to Require Balanced Budget," *Current Opinion,* May 1976, 46.

18. "Bush Begins a Series of Televised Campaign Programs," *New York Times,* 18 October 1980, 9.

19. Miller, Miller, and Schneider, *American National Election Studies Data Sourcebook,* table 6.67.

20. Quoted in "Reaching for Reality," Mobil advertisement in *The Economist,* 3 December 1983, 20.

21. "Reeling Towards Reality," *Wall Street Journal,* 15 September 1983, 30.

22. "The Budget Bumps Ahead," *Newsweek,* 30 March 1981, 23.

23. Machiavelli, *The Prince,* 110.

24. "British Prime Minister Stays Strong Politically Despite Nation's Ills," *Wall Street Journal,* 2 May 1980, 1.

25. "Old Political Appeals Not Working," *Current Opinion,* June 1976, 58.

26. "Ireland Buckles Down to Austerity Program with Hardly a Grumble," *Wall Street Journal,* 18 March 1983, European edition, 1.

27. "How Long Can Germany Rest on Its Laurels," *Institutional Investor,* June 1983, International edition, 106.

28. John Maynard Keynes, *The General Theory of Employment Interest and Money* (London: Macmillan, 1936), 383.

29. "Is it too late?" *Business Week,* 6 June 1983, 51.

30. Miller, Miller, and Schneider, *American National Election Studies Data Sourcebook,* table 4.21.

31. Ibid., table 4.24.

32. "More Fear Big Government," *Current Opinion,* June 1976, 62.

# INDEX

Act to Promote Workers' Participation in Capital Formation (Germany, 1961), 98
Adenauer, Konrad, 7
AFL-CIO, 108, 109, 208
Agricultural interests, 109
Aid to Families with Dependent Children (AFDC), 164, 166, 169
Air France, 195
Airline industry, 156
Algeria, 162
Allison, Elizabeth, 166
Amalgamated Union of Engineering Workers, 224
American Business Conference, 65
American Electronics Association, 133
*America in Ruins* (Choate), 197
American Home Products, 11
American Medical Association, 145
*American National Election Studies Data Sourcebook*, 6
Amersham, 188
Anderson, John, 5–6, 206
Antipoverty programs, 173–76
Apple computers, 7, 79, 114
Atari, 191
Auckland, Lord, 60n
Austria, 72; public investment in, 188
Automobile industry, 79, 80; interest rates and, 95; trade policies and, 101, 103–6, 111, 115

B-1 bombers, 161
Bailouts, 126–27, 129–32, 136
Baker, Howard, 35, 209
Baker, James, 87
*Baltimore Sun*, 27
Bane, Frank, 178–79
Bandaranaike, Sirimavo, 225

Bank of America, 33
Bank of England, 88, 96
Barre, Raymond, 41
Bayh, Birch, 5
Belgium, 5
Bell, Daniel, 225
Bell, T. H., 139
Bic, Marcel, 200
Birch, David, 130–31, 133
Bismarck, Otto von, 167
Blue-collar workers, 80
Blumenthal, Michael, 204
Boeing, 34
Brazil, trade with, 101
Bristol Myers, 11
British Aircraft Corporation, 186
British Airways, 195
British Leyland, 4, 127, 131, 135, 186
British Rail, 127
British Shipbuilders, 127
British Steel Corporation, 4, 126
British Telecom, 188
Britoil, 188
Brookings Institution, 106
Brown, Jerry, 33, 156, 217
Bundesbank, 88
Burns, Arthur, 89
Bush, George, 37
Bushnell, Nolan, 191
*Business Week*, 105, 196, 197, 201–2, 224
Byrd, Robert, 87

Caillaux, J., 61
Canada, 21, 41–42; monetary policy in, 96
California Poll, 214
Callaghan, James, 71, 76, 124, 125, 129, 186, 221

# Index

# Index

Marie Antoinette, 194
Marks and Spencer, 219
Mass transit, 148
Mathew, Terry, 136
Matra (company), 185
Medicaid, 34, 140, 156
Medicare, 142, 154
Meese, Edwin, 69, 87
Meiji restoration, 114
Methven, John, 71
Mexico, trade with, 101, 116
Michel, Robert, 123–24
Military industrial complex, 161
M.I.T., 130
Mitel, 136
Mitsubishi, 190
Mitterand, François, 8, 141–43, 72, 73, 110, 128, 129, 185, 188
Mobil Oil, 196
Mondale, Walter, 101, 102, 111
Monetarism, 38–39
Monetary policy, 84–99; political aspects of, 88–89; small deposits and, 93–95, 98–99
Money market funds, 94–97
Monsen, Joseph R., 127
Moore, Francis, 148
Moro, Aldo, 213
Mount Sinai Hospital, 145
Multifiber Agreement (MFA), 101
Murray, Len, 217–18
MX missiles, 161

Napoleon, 116
Napoleonic wars, 60, 62
National Association of Manufacturers, 65
National Coal Board (U.K.), 4, 127
National Commission on Excellence in Education, 139, 143, 148, 158–59
National Defense Education Act, 158
National Enterprise Board (U.K.), 186, 195
National Health Service (U.K.), 142, 152, 154, 155
National Insurance Act (U.K., 1911), 167
National Republican Senatorial Committee, 160
National Research Development Corporation (NRDC), 125
National Science Foundation, 186
National Small Business Administration, 68
National Tax Limitation Committee, 214, 220
National Taxpayers Union, 213, 220
Nationalization, 126, 127, 188; of high-technology companies, 185, 186
Nelson, Gaylord, 5

New Deal, 17, 21, 24–25, 27–30, 44, 119, 176, 191, 205, 220
New Technological Opportunities program, 186–87
*New York Times*, 5, 74, 171, 208
*Newsweek*, 219
Newton, Isaac, 205, 206
Nippon Electric Company (NEC), 115
Nissan Motors, 80, 111
Nixon, Richard, 3, 14, 54, 60, 74, 112, 126, 169, 186–87, 196; monetary policy of, 89; spending policies of, 18, 30
Nobel Prizes, 205–6
Noble, Edward, 196, 197
Nordheimer, Jon, 182
Norway, 35

OECD, 123
Office of Management and Budget (OMB), 20, 37, 53, 165, 198
Okner (author), 56
Old Age Pensions Act (U.K., 1908), 167
Olsen, Ken, 80
O'Neill, Tip, 102, 179
OPEC, 116, 117, 224
Open University, 140
Opinion polls, 210; *see also* Gallup polls; Harris polls
Osborne, Adam, 136

Packard, David, 80
Page, Benjamin, 55–56, 64, 66
Palme, Olaf, 31, 42–43, 72, 73
Passbook savings, 93–95, 98–99
Pavitt, Keith, 190
Pechman, Joseph, 56, 64, 65
Penn Central Railroad, 89, 126
People's Action Party (Singapore), 153
Pepper, Claude, 180
Peugot, 200
Phillips (company), 136
Plato, 225
Polaroid, 190
*Political Control of the Economy* (Tufte), 89
Pressler, Larry, 87
Prime (company), 190
*Prince, The* (Machiavelli), 174
Proctor & Gamble, 10, 11
Progress party (Denmark), 215
Progressive taxes, 51–52, 54–57; attacked by right, 67–71; economics and, 79–83; history of, 59–62; restoration of, 77–78

# Index